AVENBURY

and the ruined church of St Mary

PHYLLIS WILLIAMS

Published by
The Bromyard and District Local History Society
Bromyard, Herefordshire, HR7 4DL

ISBN 0 9502068 8 1

Set in Times and printed in Great Britain by
Orphans Press, Leominster, Herefordshire

Front Cover Illustration:
Avenbury Church Herefordshire *c*1840-1850.
Watercolour initialled R S H, belonging to Mr and Mrs Peter Stokes.
Back Cover Illustration:
Avenbury Church ruined tower arch, 1999. *Howard Painter*

‘We know very little about Christianity in western Britain in the first two post-Roman centuries, but what we do know clearly demonstrates that there was a thriving church there, complete with bishops and monastic communities. It was a church which was ‘structurally entirely consistent with that of Roman Britain’ and which is likely to have been its direct descendant, if one which had acquired some new blood on the way’.

‘Taken individually these pieces of information are not much to look at, but the whole they make is rather greater than the sum of their parts. We can base on them a consistent, if largely circumstantial case for there having been an active, well-organised British church in the West Midlands when the Anglo-Saxons arrived there, and for its having persisted, moreover, to the time when Anglo-Saxon dioceses were eventually created there.’

Ed. John Blair and Richard Sharpe, *Pastoral Care Before the Parish* (1992), 17, 19

Other titles available from
Bromyard and District Local History Society

Bromyard The Day Before Yesterday, A Book of Photographs (1979)
Whitbourne: A Bishop's Manor by P. Williams (1979)
Herefordshire Under Arms by C. Hopkinson (1985)
Bromyard: Minster, Manor and Town by P. Williams (1987)
A Pocketful of Hops, Hop Growing in the Bromyard Area (1988)
Bromyard Round and About by D. Waller (1991)
Two Churches: Two Communities, St Peters, Bromyard and St James's, Stanford Bishop by E. Pearson (1993)
A History of Bredenbury and its Landed Estate by Jennifer Weale (1997)

AVENBURY
and the ruined church of St Mary

CONTENTS *page*

MAPS

TABLES

GRAPHS

Map 1

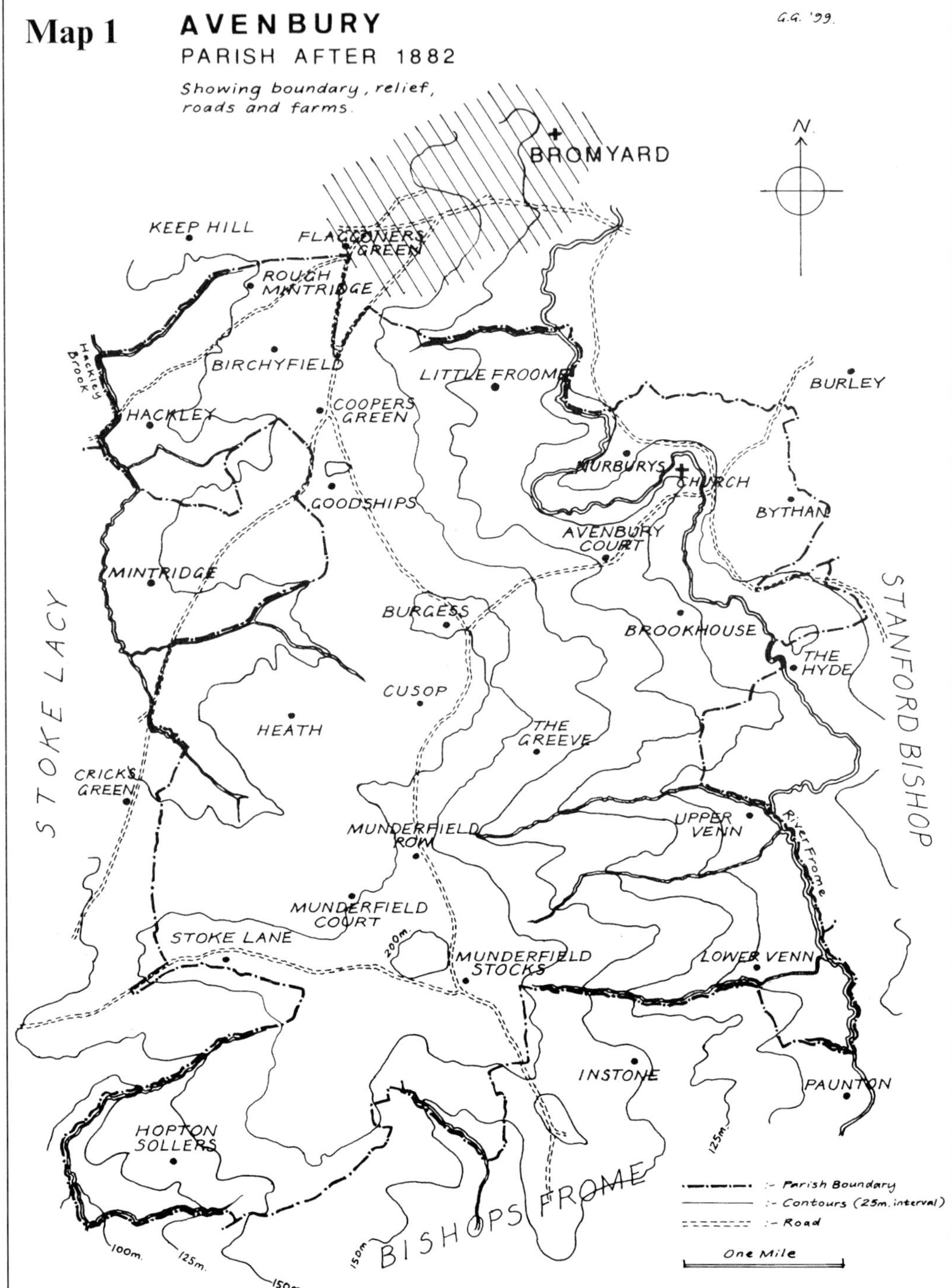
AVENBURY
PARISH AFTER 1882
Showing boundary, relief, roads and farms.
G.G. '99.
N.
BROMYARD
KEEP HILL
FLACCONERS GREEN
ROUGH MINTRIDGE
Hackley Brook
BIRCHYFIELD
LITTLE FROOME
BURLEY
HACKLEY
COOPERS GREEN
NURBURYS
CHURCH
BYTHAM
GOODSHIPS
AVENBURY COURT
MINTRIDGE
STANFORD BISHOP
BURGESS
BROOKHOUSE
THE HYDE
STOKE LACY
CUSOP
HEATH
THE GREEVE
CRICKS GREEN
UPPER VENN
MUNDERFIELD ROW
River Frome
MUNDERFIELD COURT
STOKE LANE
200m.
MUNDERFIELD STOCKS
LOWER VENN
INSTONE
PAUNTON
HOPTON SOLLERS
125m.
BISHOPS FROME
100m.
125m.
150m.
150m.
:- Parish Boundary
:- Contours (25m. interval)
:- Road
One Mile

Preface

Avenbury is the sixth in the series of parish histories published, 1970-2000, by the Bromyard and District Local History Society, and the third to be written by Phyllis Williams. Much of the interest of the series lies in the differences in character which are emerging from these studies.

With some 3,233 acres Avenbury was the largest of the parishes in the ancient hundred of Plegelgate. Bromyard, with its townships of Winslow, Linton and Norton, is in a different category for it is the rump of the 9th century *parochia* of the minster church which originally served the spiritual needs of the whole area. Both topographic and documentary evidence indicate that within the district Avenbury was second only to Bromyard. In the 9th century it belonged to the bishop and cathedral church of Worcester.

Notes made by the great 17th-century antiquary, William Dugdale, on a lost Worcester charter of bishop Waerferth (873-915) relating to Avenbury, can be seen in the Bodleian Library. Waerferth was both the friend and collaborator of Alfred the Great. He translated the *Dialogues of Pope Gregory the Great* into Anglo-Saxon for the king, and the copy which Alfred presented to Worcester cathedral is also in the Bodleian (Hatton MS 20). It was in the first years of his episcopate that eastern Mercia was incorporated into the Viking territory of the Danelaw. Waerferth's grant of Avenbury may well have been made to help meet Viking demands for tribute.

The topographic interest lies in the fact that Avenbury was bisected by the vast Bromyard parish, some 8,600 acres. 307 acres, made up of five detached parts, lay to the north in the upper Frome valley. The Noakes occupied both sides of the valley with Sawbury Hill adjacent, to the west. Further north were the smaller areas of the Stake, Ovendine and Wiggall, with the Bredenbury/Rowden roadway, Harp Lane forming their northern boundary. Only in the 1880s, by an order under the Divided Parishes Act, were they amalgamated with the civil parish of Bredenbury.

The remaining 2,926 acres lay to the south of Bromyard. The Frome valley formed, for the most part, the eastern boundary as far south as Paunton Cross whilst the western boundary left most of the plateau, which rises to 650 feet at Munderfield Stocks, within the parish. Almost all the major farms, which evolved from the chief Domesday manors (page 83) Little Frome, Avenbury Court, Brookhouse, Upper Venn and Lower Venn lie at the foot of its scarp slope.

The heart of the parish must, originally, have lain between the Court and St Mary's church, less than half a mile away to the northeast. Geographically both were very much off centre. In 1291 Avenbury was taxed at £12 compared with £8 for Thornbury and £6 for Whitbourne and Wolferlow. So geography does not fully explain the most puzzling aspect of Avenbury's history. How then was it that Avenbury, the largest and wealthiest parish of the district, was the only one to lose its church? This is of particular significance given Avenbury's position as second only to Bromyard. Domesday book shows that, the minster apart, of all the manors within the hundred, Avenbury alone had its own church where, as at Bromyard, there were two priests.. The explanation may lie in part with the appropriation of the church by Dore Abbey in the early 14th century. With Harescombe and Duntisbourne Rouse and their chapels it was the gift of Sir John le Rous, sheriff of the county 1332-4 and one of its representatives at six parliaments, 1330-43. A judgment given, in the vicar's favour by the bishops court in 1519, certainly suggests that Dore had given him a raw deal. At the dissolution in 1536 the great tithes and much of the glebe which the abbey had previously enjoyed were sold by the crown to a layman and the balance of power swung firmly against the vicar.

Impoverishment of the living is however but part of the answer. The parish church became isolated in consequence of a shift in the population centre from the valley bottom to Munderfield and its vicinity on the plateau above. Phyllis Williams points to the possible site of a deserted medieval village by the Court. The factors leading to its desertion are not easily explained. The Bromyard district was as seriously affected by the Black Death as any part of the county. In 1349 'Sir Thomas', the vicar of Avenbury, was carried off by the plague, as were his colleagues at Tedstone Delamere, Stanford Bishop, High Edwyn, Stoke Bliss and Wolferlow. At Collington the plague had 'so much reduced the people and impoverished the land' that Ralph de Yeddefen successfully petitioned the bishop to unite the parishes of Great and Little Collington. Such was the dearth of clergy that within a year Philip le Smyth, Sir Thomas' successor at Avenbury, had resigned – whether for inadequacy or the attraction of a richer living we shall never know. Certainly the Black Death led to drastic changes in the rural economy, with rising prices, the consequent collapse of demesne and the growth of leaseholds and yeoman farming. By 1517 Little Cowarne was 'perilously close to becoming a deserted medieval village' and 'contraction has left its mark' at Edwyn Ralph and Tedstone Delamere. This was not the case at Avenbury.

In the 1664 Hearth Tax returns Whitbourne (99), Linton township (90) and Norton township (76) all had more than Avenbury's 54 houses. However if the degree of poverty, as expressed by exemption from hearth tax, is analysed a different picture emerges. At Avenbury it was 39%, Whitbourne 55%, Linton 59% and Norton 63%. Lack of resources is certainly no answer to the decline and eventual ruin of the parish church.

The 19th century witnessed the restoration and reconstruction of Herefordshire's parish churches on a quite unprecedented scale. Locally new churches were built at Tedstone Delamere (1856-7), where Sir Giles Gilbert Scott's building was funded by the former vicar and local landowners, at Tedstone Wafre and Edvin Loach (1873), principally at the charge of Edmund Higginson and William Barneby. At Collington (1856) the church was built on a new site nearer the centre of the parish whilst at Bredenbury W H Barneby was responsible for moving the church from the grounds of the Court to a new site near the school in 1874. There was extensive rebuilding and reconstruction at Bishops Frome (1861), Stoke Lacy and Wolferlow (1863), Thornbury (1865) and Little Cowarne (1870). In each case the architect was Frederick Kempson, the son of the Rev William Brooke

Kempson, rector of Stoke Lacy and principal landowner in that parish in the 1850s. In total he was responsible for work at seventeen Herefordshire churches between 1847 and 1880. Subsequently Kempson was able to raise his sights and designed Hereford Public Library and Museum (1872-4), Hereford County College (1881), Kington Market Hall (1885) and Hereford Convent of the Poor Clares (1887). At Avenbury the Kempsons owned Birchyfield from about 1842 and had lived there for many years. They became major landowners in the district, the estate rose from 66 acres in 1840 to 412 in 1871, yet Kempson took no part in the restoration of St Mary's; supervision was left to the Hereford architect, G C Haddon, who built 'the very terrible' Baptist church in Ross. The only landowner to actively support the work on St Mary's was E B Luxmore.

Neglect by resident or non-resident landowners was not the principal reason for the demise of St Mary's. Rather it was the rise of Munderfield Row. This began prior to the passage of the Bromyard Turnpike Act of 1751 but Map 11 shows how, with no available common land in the parish, the properties were able to cling to either side of the road. The turnpike generated trade for the Holly Bush and New House inns and a few artisans but the majority of its residents were farm workers. Here the Board School, built seven years after Forster's 1870 Education Act to accommodate 50 children, had in 1903 to be enlarged for a further 20. The parish church was restored by the efforts of the Rev R Polwhele (1867-78) and Rev John Wilson (1878-97). It was Polwhele's predecessor, the Rev John Archer, who made the fateful decision to build a Mission Hall and Parish Hall at Munderfield in the early 1860s. In appearance it was similar to the Primitive Methodist Chapel built on Bringsty Common in 1861 (see pl 169) in Phyllis Williams' *Bromyard: Minster, Manor and Town.*

As name and appearance suggest, this was an attempt both to take his ministry closer to the majority of his flock and to provide a more acceptable form of service. Nonconformity was well established in Bromyard. At Fromes Hill on the outskirts of Bishops Frome parish the Congregationalists founded a chapel in 1864. The established church replied by building St Matthew's as a chapel of ease; again Kempson was architect. A Wesleyan Methodist chapel followed, in 1886.

The last of the parish priests to serve the people and church of Avenbury over its life of more than a millenium was John Archer's son, the Rev Archer-Shepherd (1897-1931). Only with his death in 1931 could the diocesan authorities take the action which must have been anticipated for some time. The demise of this, one of Herefordshire's most ancient parishes, is graphically described by Phyllis Williams. The ecclesiastical parish was divided between Bromyard and Stoke Lacy. Only Stoke Lacy's octogenarian rector, Rev George Morgan, fought the battle to maintain services where, in his words, 'the bulk of the people live', at Munderfield Row. The church was allowed to fall into ruins. Fortunately for posterity officers of the Royal Commission on Historical Monuments inspected St Mary's two years later and it is to them that we are indebted for the detailed description and the photographs which appear in this book.

Joe Hillaby, Hollybush,
January 2000

Acknowledgements

It is with great satisfaction that I have completed this history of the parish of Avenbury and the Church of St Mary. For now that the parish has no place of worship, no school, no village hall, post office or shop it is important to record its local history while people can still remember an active community.

Avenbury and the Ruined Church of St Mary has taken several years to research and without the help of many friends and colleagues could never have been produced. I am very grateful to the Bromyard and District Local History Society who have funded and supported the publication. Thank you to the Society's publication committee and to the study and research group for their influence, criticism and support over many years. Jennifer Weale initially began studying Avenbury and she generously handed me her notes and the benefit of her research in order to concentrate on her book *A History of Bredenbury and its Landed Estate* which the Society published in 1997.

Midway through writing it became apparent that my text needed to be transferred from my old, comfortable and reliable Amstrad to a word processor compatible with that of Orphans Press. This was achieved with the help of my daughter Kate Percy, her husband Richard Percy and my son Ben Williams. In the later stages the text has been edited by Jennifer Weale, Jean Hopkinson, Allan Wyatt, Stephen Guest, Kate Percy and Matthew Christmas. Thank you for not adding too many extra commas!

Bruce Coplestone-Crow has for many years generously provided members of the Bromyard and District Local History Society with information on the Norman and medieval history of Herefordshire, on which he is an authority, and without his help the early history of Avenbury would not have been so integrated. Allan Wyatt was also instrumental here with his ability to translate Latin documents principally the charters of St Guthlac's Priory. Marnie Caine on her visits to the Public Record Office kindly copied various Avenbury documents.

Sue Hubbard and her staff at the Herefordshire Record Office have again proved incredibly helpful and patient. Jim and Muriel Tonkin of Wigmore deserve a great vote of thanks. Together they have looked at houses in Avenbury and the Bromyard area and given the Society the benefit of their knowledge and expertise. Muriel also found and photocopied suitable Avenbury wills in the Herefordshire Record Office which led to the chapter 'A Fleeting Glimpse'.

Howard Painter of Tenbury, another member of the Bromyard History Society, kindly offered to take photographs of the parish. This offer I seized with alacrity, little realising at the time how fortunate I was. Howard is descended from the 18th-century Cooke family of Munderfield Court and over generations his ancestors have farmed most of the larger properties in the parish. He, with Gwen his wife, visited every corner of Avenbury and his wonderful photographs grace many of the following pages.

The Royal Commission on Historical Monuments of England have a fine collection of photographs at the National Monuments Record Centre in Swindon and provided copies relating to Avenbury with permission to reproduce them in this book. Chris Musson has undertaken a Millennium Air Survey of Herefordshire, which has been organised by Ruth Richardson for the Woolhope Naturalists Field Club. Chris has taken several brilliant aerial photographs of Avenbury Church which he and the Woolhope Club have generously given permission to include in the book.

Other photographs and information have been provided by Avenbury families near and far. I am most grateful to Geoff Gillard of New Zealand, Margaret Rickard of Australia and her cousin John Page of Bromyard, D F Hadley, Janet Jones, Mandy Palmer, Ciss Bloomfield, Audrey Price, the late Ethel Paske, Norma Linton, Marian Grundy, Peter Corbett, Stan Thomas, Janet Parker, Farmer Parker, Vera Hodges and her family, Sue Stephenson, Rebecca Skipp and Martin Hewitt for their help. Dick and Daphne Davies, Jennifer Weale and Marnie Caine combed through the photographs and illustrations in the Bromyard and District Local History Society archives and they were able to provide drawings by the late Charles Grant together with a variety of Avenbury photographs. Peter and Jean Stokes very kindly gave permission to reproduce the mid-19th-century watercolour paintings of Avenbury Church which were photographed by Richard Percy.

Geoff Gwatkin of Ross-on-Wye has brilliantly and patiently drawn the maps which illustrate the text much better than words can achieve.

I am indebted to Joe Hillaby for the advice and unfailing help he has provided with this history of Avenbury and for his masterly preface. Joe has guided members of the Bromyard Local History Society with their researches and publications since its inception in 1966.

Thank you to the management and staff at Orphans Press, Leominster for their co-operation and expertise, with a special mention for Trevor Williams for his arrangement of the text and photographs.

Finally, a thank you to the farmers and residents of Avenbury, who have most kindly and generously given both myself and others access to their land, houses, buildings, documents, memories and knowledge. Without this co-operation parish histories could never be written.

This aerial photograph shows the road from the Burgess to the Avenbury Lane passing Avenbury Court, the Old Vicarage and the site of the ruined church within a meander of the river Frome.

Introduction

'The evidence must first be collected.'
John Morris, *The Age of Arthur* (1973), xi

Avenbury is a large parish in the north-east uplands of Herefordshire and covers some 3,000 acres. In addition to the manor of Avenbury, it includes what were the Norman manors of Hopton Sollers, Little Froome, Venn and, until the end of the 19th century, the parish also included the manors, and formerly royal estates, of Noakes and Sawbury Hill. At one time Bredenbury, too, appears to have been served by priests from Avenbury Church. Avenbury extends from Bromyard on its northern boundary southwards to Bishop's Frome with the parishes of Linton and Stanford Bishop on the eastern side. These were all manors belonging to the bishops of Hereford. The parish of Stoke Lacy bounds Avenbury on the west. With the river Frome flowing through the parish, Avenbury forms part of the beautiful and fertile Frome valley and on either side farm land rises to above 500 feet (154 metres).

Manorial, estate and parish boundaries in this region are frequently marked by features such as water courses, ridges and long-living trees. These boundaries are often ancient and may date from pre-Roman times. Ecclesiastical units later utilised long established and accepted divisions between territories. Hidden beneath the ground lie the remains of countless early settlements and buildings; the fabric of the now ruined church dates back some 900 years. The farms and houses that we can see today were mostly built during the last 500 years.

The rural parish of Avenbury stretches to the outskirts of the 12th-century market town of Bromyard and this proximity must have affected the fortunes of Avenbury over the centuries. The regular markets and annual fairs provided an outlet for livestock, corn and produce and an opportunity to purchase other goods and commodities with the proceeds. The Whit Monday Mop was said to be the greatest Bromyard fair in the whole year, while at the May Mop workers could change jobs by offering themselves to new employers for the next 12 months. The town also offered a greater variety of occupations to country folk who may have wished to practice a craft or trade which was not available in the rural community.

Long before the town of Bromyard was established, there was the meeting place for the folk of the territory at the north-west corner of Avenbury parish on the high flat ground between Cooper's Green and Flaggoner's Green where the roads from Hereford, Ledbury, Leominster and Pencombe converge. Gatherings of people at this point from a seven mile radius several times a year would again offer the inhabitants of Avenbury great opportunities for marketing and could be the origin for the name of the Goodships, earlier *Goodcheps* 'good market'. Has the wheel turned full circle? For since 1997 the annual Bromyard Gala, which also attracts thousands of people, has been held in this vicinity at Birchyfield.

Unfortunately few manorial records for Avenbury have survived and early documents relating to the parish are sparse. The adjacent manors of the bishops of Hereford provide considerable material for what life was like on local estates and it is unlikely that the farming history of Avenbury was very different. Bishops and other important people must have travelled regularly through this parish, visiting their properties and on ecclesiastical and other business in this part of the country.

The church of Avenbury has an important early claim to fame for it was in 1086 one of only nine superior churches in Herefordshire.[1] These were Hereford Cathedral and St Guthlac's Priory in Hereford, the Saxon minster churches of Bromyard, Ledbury and Leominster; Avenbury, Fownhope, Stoke Edith and Llanwarne were included because they had either two or more priests or a large endowment of land. Why Avenbury had two priests at the end of the Saxon period we do not know. It is interesting to note that the glebe or church land of Avenbury principally formed a block which stretched to the eastern boundary of the parish at Burley where it met and almost intermingled with the lands of the three portioners of Bromyard Church (see Map 7). The considerable endowment of property to the church of Bromyard was divided into three prebends or portions, hence the name portioners who were entitled to the profits of a prebend during their term of office. What the relationship was between the minster or mother church of Bromyard and the church of Avenbury we may never know. At one time in the Saxon period, according to a charter dated between 873-915, Avenbury was in the hands of the church of Worcester.[2]

After the Norman Conquest of 1066, Avenbury parish comprised several manors or estates, of which the manor of Avenbury was the largest and most important. Here was the superior and important church with its two priests, the glebe allocated to support the church ministry, a manor house and a community of villagers. The other manors or estates would have had their own settlements and farming systems, but would have looked to Avenbury Church for worship and the celebration of their life events of baptism, marriage and burial which were from the 16th century recorded in the parish registers. The surviving registers date from 1661 and can be seen in Herefordshire Record Office. Parochial care and responsibility devolved on the whole parish and was organised by the vestry which met in the church under the chairmanship of the vicar.

The lords of Avenbury would have regarded the church as their personal property, and for the benefit of successive lords' souls it was granted in late Saxon times to the priory of St Guthlac in Hereford, and then in the 13th century to Dore Abbey in the south-west of the county. At the Dissolution of the Monasteries, it was in 1536 purchased by John Harford of Upleadon, Bosbury, Herefordshire and by John Farley. Thenceforth the church of Avenbury was in the hands of lay impropriators and this caused great problems in the parish which lasted until the 20th century when the last vicar to serve the parish acquired the benefice which he later transferred to the bishop of Hereford.

The church of Avenbury lies in the east of a large parish and it would appear from earthworks in the field to the west of the churchyard that there was at one time settlement and houses here. A writer in the *Bromyard News and Record* of 13th August 1908 thought that the ancient church stood between the present church and the wicketgate to the Vicarage, whilst the last vicar thought a monastery had stood here in earlier times. Neither suggestion is likely as this was not church land and there is no record of the church being moved nor of a monastery in Avenbury. More likely this is a deserted village site. The tithe map of 1840 shows cottages by the road and there is a great deal of stone here, and some sherds of 14th-century glazed pottery were found on a visit made by the Bromyard and District Local History Society in 1973. The animal pound was close by and the village probably extended between the ecclesiastical precinct and the lord's manor house now called Avenbury Court. We do not know when the village was finally deserted, but an archaeological exploration could doubtless solve that problem. Possibly the Black Death was partially responsible for in that series of plagues, the greatest being in 1349-50, it is thought that one third to one half of the population of this country perished. The shift from the village site near the church to Munderfield Row, which may already have developed as a linear community, was a natural development for here on the main road from Bromyard to Bishop's Frome and Ledbury there was opportunity for craftsmen, innkeepers and tradespeople to pick up more than local business.

Before the church was closed and abandoned in the 1930s, there was in the chancel a rare and notable 13th-century effigy incised on a stone slab and usually referred to as the Avenbury Knight. The monument probably represents either Walter of Avenbury or his son Osbert, who was the last of that family to reside here and it can now be seen in the north aisle of Bromyard Church. Many more members of local families have been buried and recorded here in their parish church which is now an isolated ruin. How could it happen that a well loved church could now have almost disappeared from view? The untidy and vandalised state of the churchyard causes distress not only within the parish, but also to visitors looking for the final resting place of their forebears.

Within the 20th century parochial care included not only the parish church but also a school, mission room and village hall. Today Avenbury has no church, school, mission room or village hall and its focus of settlement is still Munderfield Row, a line of houses which stretches along the road which leads from Bromyard to Ledbury.

The church provides the linchpin around which the history of Avenbury revolves. Part I of this book deals with Avenbury Church and the Domesday Manors from Saxon times to about 1600 principally using national records. Part II covers the period after 1600 when local records become abundant and available, recording the names of local families and their activities in the parish. In the following pages we shall try to unravel some of the history of the parish during the intervening centuries and meet the ancestors of some present day Herefordshire families.

PART I

EARLY DAYS

Chapter 1

Past Times and Plegelgate Hundred

> 'In technological terms - Mesolithic, Neolithic, Bronze Age, Iron Age - are used here as a loose framework on which to hang 8,000 years of prehistory. It is widely recognised that they are as meaningless as referring to the late twentieth century as the 'computer age' or the 'car age' but as they have gained such wide acceptance they are useful labels.'
>
> Robert Bewley, *Prehistoric Settlements* (1994), 31

Avenbury is situated in the Bromyard District of the north-east uplands of Herefordshire, and until Anglo-Saxon times at least, the history of Avenbury can not be seen in closer focus than as part of the history of this district. Discoveries of flint and stone artefacts, many dating back to the Palaeolithic Era or Old Stone Age, circa 12000BC show that people have lived and settled in this part of the country for many thousands of years. In addition to many individual finds, there are two large and valuable local collections, both produced over decades of diligent searching by two keen-eyed farming people. Deborah Waller amassed a considerable amount of flint artefacts and chippings which she found mainly in the vicinity of Keephill, just outside Avenbury's north-western boundary, and on other farms in the area. Ivan Turner's rich collection from all periods was amassed from Netherwood land some 4 miles further north in the parishes of Thornbury and Stoke Bliss.[1]

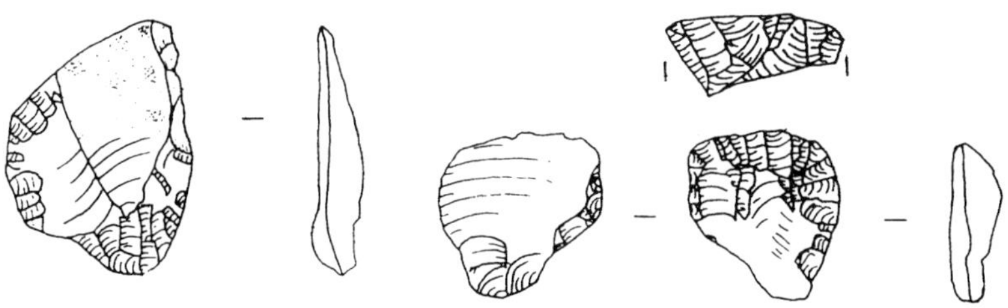

Two flint end and side scrapers found at Keephill by Deborah Waller.

All Drawn by Philippa Bradley

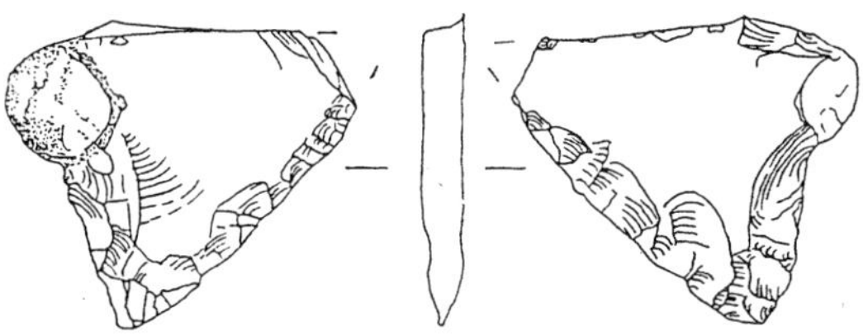

Chisel arrow head found at Keephill by Deborah Waller.

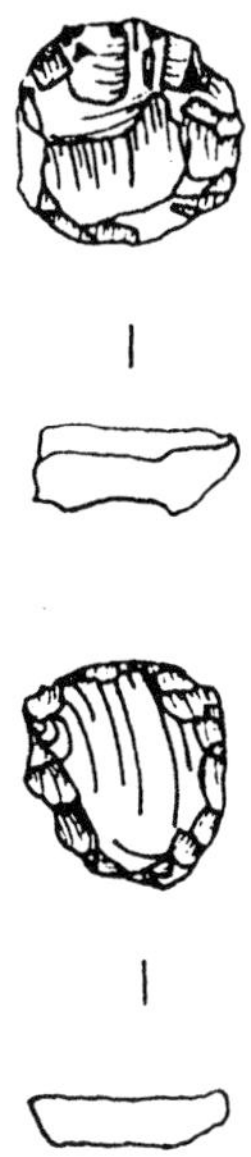

Two flint thumbnail scrapers found at Keephill by Deborah Waller.

The earliest people would have been hunter-gatherers and fisherfolk, and they in time would have become nomadic pasturalists who augmented the available natural resources with their herds of domesticated animals. Eventually - it was around 5000BC in England - the growing of cultivated crops led to the establishment of permanent settlements and farming communities. The exploitation of metals began with copper and bronze and then the working of iron. With the Iron Age came the hill forts so plentiful in Herefordshire. The earthworks

Wall Hills Iron Age hill fort Thornbury 1994. *Jensen Jones*

comprised one or more rings of massive banks probably 20 feet high, surmounted by a wooden stockade, surrounded by a deep ditch and approached through carefully planned entrances and huge wooden gates. An Iron Age hill fort at - Whitbourne, some four miles to the north-east of Avenbury, enclosed over 25 acres, and the Wall Hills earthwork at Thornbury, five miles to the north-west, covers a similar area. There is a smaller but well preserved hill fort at Risbury some 6 miles to the west towards Leominster. These fortified Iron Age villages or towns would have served as focal points for surrounding farmsteads and hamlets. Tradition and place-names indicate that there may have been an Iron Age settlement at Burley 'the wood or clearing by the fortified place' on the eastern boundary of Avenbury and another on the high ground to the north of Bredenbury. The accounts of Roman historians and the findings of archaeology suggest that such fortifications as these were in active use, and in some cases hotly defended, when the Romans invaded.

Before the Roman invasion Britain was divided into large tribal kingdoms, each with its own rulers and administration. Within these areas there were smaller units with their own folk and chiefs. The Iron Age Britons, who had a rich culture of learning and art, had their own language and, although they understood writing, preferred to commit knowledge to memory, giving rise to great poems and story telling.[2] They were successful farmers and were exporting wheat, wool, tin, hunting dogs and other commodities to the continent before the birth of Christ. What is now Herefordshire appears to have been the western territory of the tribe called the *Dobunni,* while further west the tribe of the *Silures* occupied the Welsh border lands. It has been suggested that Herefordshire was in fact a buffer state between these two dominant peoples.[3]

The Roman army reached the Bromyard/Avenbury area around 70AD and within a short time established a marching fort on the High Lane at Tedstone Wafre and another at Upper Sapey, both on high land and alongside what appear to have been prehistoric routeways. Romano-British artefacts and pottery have been unearthed at several places in the district, and at Batchley Farm in Grendon Bishop there appears to have been a pottery kiln of this period. The Romans occupied Britain for nearly 400 years and the Empire was officially Christian for the last century of their occupation. Even before the final Roman withdrawal in 410AD, warriors and settlers of the Germanic tribes on the Continent were coming to Britain; after 410AD these predominantly pagan people called Angles, Saxons and Jutes after their tribal homelands emigrated to this country in increasing numbers. With no overall Roman control the British tribes and kingdoms were now governed by petty kings and princes who were progressively overcome and replaced by Anglo-Saxon rulers who, like the British before them, formed alliances and absorbed smaller territories. Despite the influx of pagan settlers whose beliefs gained strong following in the east of the country, west of the river Severn, Celtic Christianity continued and possibly flourished.

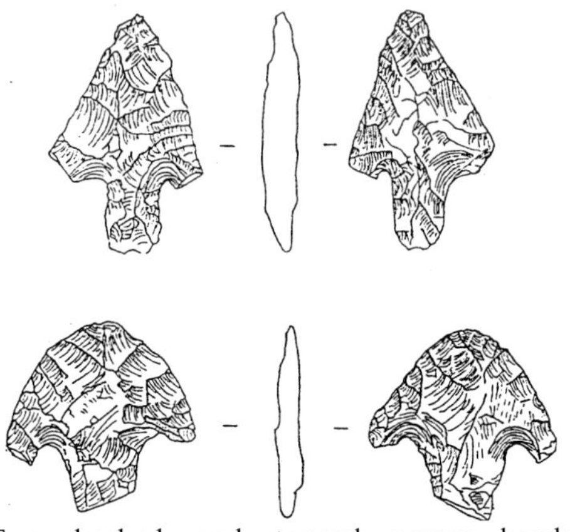

Two barbed and tanged arrow heads (possibly Neolithic) found at Keephill by Deborah Waller. *Drawn by Philippa Bradley*

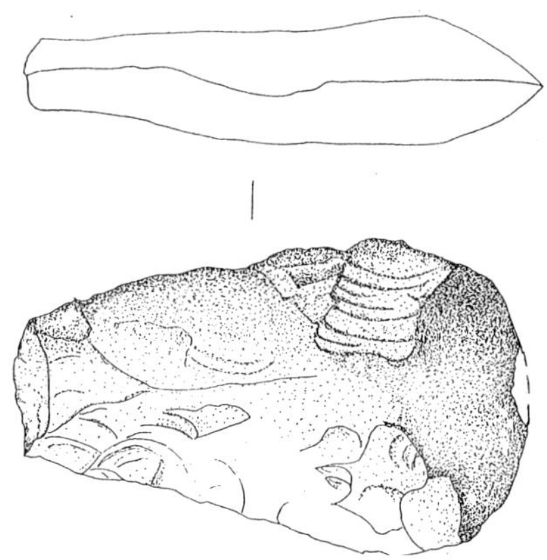

Neolithic stone axe found at Keephill by Deborah Waller.
Drawn by Philippa Bradley

The Kingdom of The Magonsaete

The people of Herefordshire in Saxon times were probably the descendants of the British population who saw the arrival of the Romans four to five centuries earlier, and they were farming much as their predecessors had before them. What did certainly change were the place and district names. Herefordshire was now known as the land of the Western *Hecani.* The word may derive from the name of the people, the *Hwicce,* who occupied land east of the Severn in Worcestershire and Gloucestershire. Later the Western *Hecani* territory became known as the *Magonsaete* and the kingdom stretched from the river Severn in the north to the river Wye in the south, and is today virtually the same as the diocese of Hereford. It was a sub-kingdom of the great midland province of Mercia which appears to have been centred on the Tamworth-Lichfield area and which takes its name from the Old English word *mierce* meaning 'the borders' or 'dwellers on the march', that is the borders with the Welsh Britons.[4]

The first known ruler of the *Magonsaete was* Merewalh 'Illustrious Welshman', a son or son-in-law of the great Mercian King Penda (*c*626-654). Merewalh was converted to Christianity in 660 and he founded and endowed churches including that at Leominster. His was a devout family, for he and his second wife Eofe had three daughters all of whom were revered as saints: St. Mildburg who became Abbess of Wenlock, St. Mildthryth who became Abbess of Minster in Kent and St. Mildgyth who became a nun at Eastrey also in Kent; their only son Merefin died in childhood. Merewalh abdicated as king of the *Magonsaete* in about 680, retired to a monastery and was buried at Repton *c*685. Merchelm and Mildfrith, the two sons of his first marriage, succeeded to his kingdom. Eofe his queen became Abbess of Thanet where she was also known as Domneva; it is thought that Domneva is the result of combining *domina* meaning abbess with her personal name of Eofe.[5] Around 690 one of Merewalh's sons, either Merchelm who died in that year, or Mildfrith who succeeded him to the kingdom, established the cathedral at Hereford to serve the kingdom of the *Magonsaete.* It is thought that the estates at Bromyard Minster were gifted to the bishopric by Mildfrith. Bromyard and Avenbury were on the eastern border of the land of the *Magonsaete.* Here also the developing dioceses of Hereford and Worcester met. Religious communities of both territories were endeavouring to gain influence and property at this boundary.

Early Minster Churches

Both the cathedral at Hereford and the church at Leominster were built and endowed by royal patronage, and there must have been other religious centres and churches in the area. The Celtic Church practised a form of Christianity which had been introduced to this country early in the Christian era and relied on monk-missionaries to spread the gospel and to minister to the people. The monks frequently lived in communities, sometimes with their families, where several dwellings could be contained in an enclosure. This movement was strong in the

St. Peter's Church Bromyard, formerly a Saxon Minster.
Bromyard Local History Society Collection

north of the country as well as to the west of the Severn. The church of Rome was brought to Britain by Augustine in 597 and after the Synod of Whitby in 664, it took over and adapted the customs and practices of the British Celtic Church.[6] With the adoption of Roman ways, large minster churches were established where priests could live and be trained to serve the local population. Many of these early minsters were founded at focal points already administrative, judicial and marketing centres. It is likely that shortly after the bishopric was formed, grants of land were made, not only for the building and support of the cathedral, but also for the missionary work that would be needed and that a positive and strategic decision was made for the siting of minster churches. They offered to the people of the area facilities for baptism and burial and a central place to celebrate the great Christian festivals. Mothering Day was originally the day on which parishioners attended their mother church to celebrate their baptism. Certainly before 840, and possibly soon after the founding of the cathedral of Hereford, a minster church had been established at Bromyard; this was proved by the chance discovery during the last century of a charter of 840. This records the gift by the bishop of Hereford of four hides of land which was later to revert to 'the minster which is called Bromyard (*Bromgearde*)' and also provides that 'whosoever has the land shall give each year to Bromyard 15 measures of unclouded ale , that is a full butt, and a hive full of honey or its value in mead ...and one plough beast, together with a hundred loaves and one sheep with one pig...'.[7]

With the passage of time lesser churches were built within the area served by Bromyard Minster. They were to become parish churches and were usually founded by owners of estates, close to their own manor house and to serve their families, retainers and villagers. A document of 1574 describing Bromyard Church explained that there were stalls in the choir not only for the officials of the minster but also for fifteen other priests of 'xv inferior churches thereabout who come continually once a year upon Witsun Monday to help say service in the Collegiate Church confessing the same to be the Mother Church, the Dean or first prebendary there then calling the said parishes by their names.' Any parish not represented by its priest was then fined 6s 8d.[8] At this time the vicar of Bromyard was still entitled to the burial fees of seven neighbouring churches and not only from the parish of Bromyard but also those of Stanford Bishop, Grendon Bishop, Wacton, Grendon Warren, Collington, Tedstone Delamere and Brockhampton. On Easter Day 'of antient right due and accustomed to bee paid to the vicar of Bromyard' the incumbents of the following churches paid: Stoke Lacy 6d, Tedstone Delamere 2s 6d, Upper Sapey 6d, Collington 6d, Edwyn Ralph 6d, Stoke Bliss 3s 4d, Wolferlow 2s and out of the lands of the Hide in Stanford Bishop 4d.[9] This list of 12 churches does not include Avenbury, Bredenbury, Little Cowarne, Tedstone Wafre, Thornbury and Whitbourne which were also in the district served by Bromyard. The absence of Avenbury so close to Bromyard may be related to two other interesting historical facts regarding Avenbury Church to which we shall very shortly come.

Plegelgate Hundred

Churches ministered to the inhabitants and were supported by the produce of their parish; parish boundaries frequently follow the line of early secular land units. The boundary of the diocese of Herefordshire equates with that of the kingdom of the *Magonsaete*. Within the diocese and kingdom, the land was divided into administrative units and it would appear that early minster churches such as Bromyard were established in their heartland to serve such territories. Bromyard was at the centre of an Anglo-Saxon division of land known as a hundred, that is 100 hides of land, each hide being a taxable unit which varied in size in different parts of the country partly reflecting land productivity and use. It is believed in many places, including the Bromyard area, to represent some 120 to 160 acres. There is a document called The Tribal Hidage dating, it is now thought, to the reign of Penda (*c*626-654) which records the number of hides in the kingdom of Mercia as 30,000 and in the kingdom of the *Magonsaete* 7,000.[10]

Avenbury was in Plegelgate Hundred and close to its heart, which was Bromyard. Bromyard stands on raised ground partly encircled by the river Frome and at the foot of Bromyard Downs which rises to over 245 metres (800 feet) and is one

Map 2

THE
MANORS OF PLEGELGATE HUNDRED
From the Tithe Maps c.1838–42

of the highest points in this north-eastern part of Herefordshire. Plegelgate means either 'the gap of a man called Plega' or 'the gap where the deer play'. Meetings of the people of the hundred were compulsory for every male over 14 and held monthly in the open air at a notable and easily reached spot, the name of the meeting place usually being the name of the hundred. Flaggoner's Green, which in an old title deed was referred to as Plegelgate Green, is a favourable site for the meeting place as it lies on high ground above 154 metres (500 feet), where several important roads converge and parishes meet.[11] With every male over 14 years of age expected to attend the monthly meetings, there could have been some 500 men present, for there were at the least 320 families recorded in Plegelgate Hundred in 1086 and in many of these households there would have been two or even more adult men. When the whole household attended for fair days and feast days the number could have risen to well over a 1,000. This may explain the name of the Goodships Farm which appears to derive from Goodchaps or 'good market'.

A hundred such as Plegelgate would have been an integral estate serving a folk group and providing the greater part of their needs. Within this hundred there

Map 3

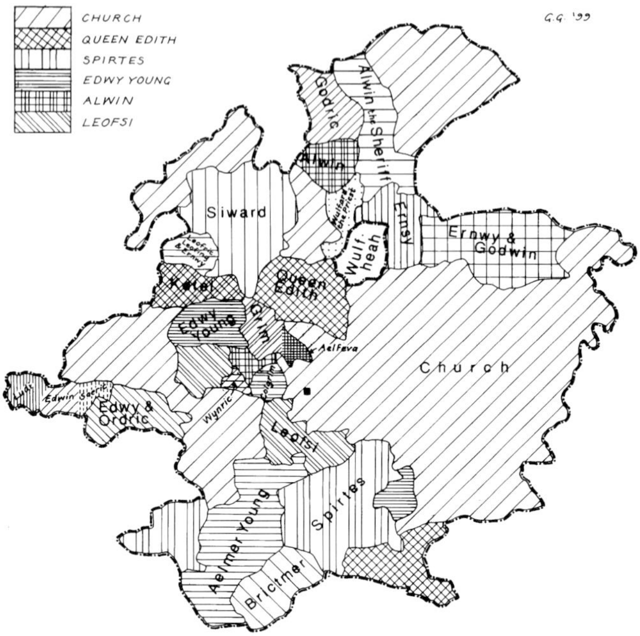

LANDOWNERS : PLEGELGATE HUNDRED – 1066

Map 4

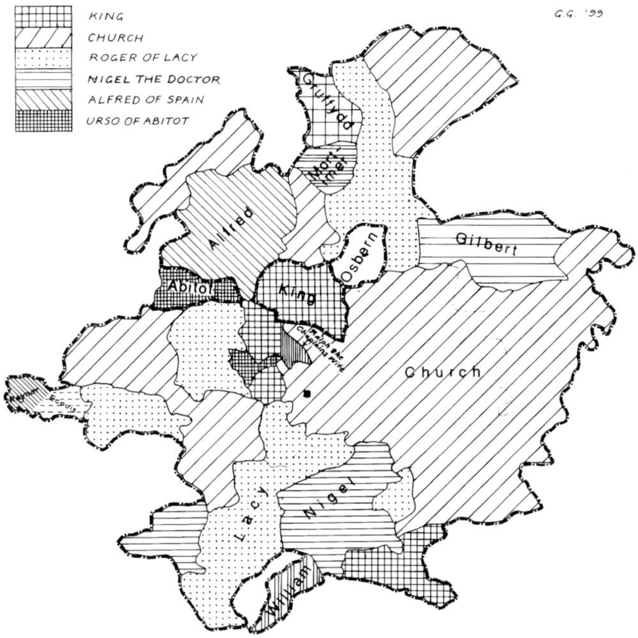

LANDOWNERS : PLEGELGATE HUNDRED – 1086

TABLE 1 LANDHOLDERS AND HIDES 1066 and 1086

PLEGELGATE HUNDRED

1066			1086
Bishop, church & Canons of Hereford	37	Bromyard 30, part of Bishop's Frome 4, Collington Magna 3	as in 1066
Aelmer Young	10	Stoke Lacy & Mintridge	Roger Lacy
Spirtes	9	Avenbury 6	Nigel the Doctor
		Little Cowarne 3	Nigel the Doctor
Siward	6	Thornbury	Alfred of Spain
Alwin the Sheriff	6	Wolferlow	Roger Lacy
Edwy Young, father of Alwin	4½	The Hide 1 (Stanford Bishop)	Roger Lacy
		Butterley 3½ (Wacton)	Roger Lacy
Queen Edith	4	Stanford Regis	The King
Edwy and Ordric	4	Grendon Warren	Roger Lacy
Alwin	3¼	Underley 2	Ralph of Mortimer
		Wicton 1¼	Urso of Abetot
Leofsi	3	Little Froome 1	Roger Lacy
		Keephill 1	Roger Lacy
		Bredenbury 1	Roger Lacy
Wulfard the Priest	2	Collington Parva	Roger Lacy
Ernwy and Godwin	2	Tedstone Delamere	Gilbert son of Thorold
Brictmer	1¼	Hopton Sollers	William son of Norman
Colgrim	1	Noakes	Charbonnel from the King
Grim	1	Rowden	The King
Godric	1	Stoke Bliss	Gruffydd of Maredudd
Ernsy	1	Tedstone Wafre	Roger Lacy
Ketel	1	Butterley	Urso of Abetot
Leofric, Leofing & Ernwy	1	Wooding	Alfred of Spain
Wynric	2½v	Sawbury	Roger Lacy
Aelfeva	½	Rowden	Ralph the chaplain's wife
Saeric	½	Marston Stannett	Roger Lacy
Ludi	½	Marston Stannett	Raynor Carpenter
Edwin	½	Marston	Wm. of Ecouis
Alnoth	½	Hanley	Roger Lacy

Total 101 hides + ½ virgate

In Worcestershire			
Wulfheah	1	Edvin Loach	Osbern
Manor of Leominster			
Queen Edith	3	Edwin Ralph	The King

TABLE 2

POSSIBLE FAMILIES IN PLEGELGATE HUNDRED 1086

Manor & (hides)	Lords	Villagers	Smallholders	Slaves	Others	Families
Avenbury (6)	1	22	1	4	2	30
Bishop's Frome (4)	-	5	1	3	-	9
(Stanford Bishop ? but not The Court Farm)						
Bredenbury (1)	1	4	-	5	-	10
Bromyard (30)	1+5	42	9	6	3	66
Collington						
Magna (3)	1	2	4	-	-	7
Parva (2)	1	1	-	2	-	4
Little Cowarne (3)	1	1	4	7	-	13
Little Froome (1)	1	3	-	2	-	6
Grendon						
Bishop	1	-	-	-	-	1
Warren (4)	2	-	-	-	-	2
Hanley (½)	1	1	-	-	-	2
Hopton Sollers (1¼)	1	3	2	4	-	10
Keep Hill (1)	1	1	-	3	1	6
Marston (½)	1	-	-	2	-	3
Marston Stannett (1)	2	-	1	2	-	5
Noakes (1)	1	2	-	-	-	3
Rowden (1½)	2	1	-	-	1	4
Sawbury (½+)	1	-	-	-	-	1
Stanford (1) (Bishop Court?)	1	-	1	-	2	4
Stanford Regis (4)	1	5	4	4	8	22
Stoke Bliss (1)	1	6	-	3	-	10
Stoke Lacy (10)	1	22	-	11	-	34
Tedstone						
Delamere (2)	1	7	-	6	-	14
Wafre (1)	1	4	1	7	-	13
Thornbury (6)	1	4	4	6	-	15
Wooding (1)	1	2	-	-	-	3
Wacton with Butterley (4½)	2	4	12	5	4	27
Wicton (1¼)	1	-	-	-	-	1
Wolferlow (6)	1	6	-	3	-	10
Underley (2)	1	1	-	-	-	2

Total Hides 101 + ½ virgate Possible total families 337
Lords of Manors or their tenants of the demesne farm 38

Villages	149	Smallholders	44
Slaves	85	Others	21 which include:

3 priests, a chaplain, 14 ploughmen, a pigman, and a cowman.

are such place or farm names as: Poswick, '*Possa's* dairy farm'; Hardwick, 'the farm of the herd'; Hinksmoor, 'the moor of the horses'; Huntlands, 'the land of the huntsmen'; Linton, 'where flax grows'. These were specialist agricultural places. The large estate would have been divided into small settlements and manageable mixed farming units where the basic corn and other crops were grown and livestock reared. For ease of communication the radius of such an integral estate is unlikely to have been more than about five miles, which would enable the inhabitants to travel for meetings, jurisdiction, the payment of taxes, religious festivities and marketing within the daylight hours. The boundaries and function of the territory were probably in existence during Roman times and possibly earlier back into the Iron or even the Bronze Age.

Avenbury's Special Position

The estates of Avenbury extend almost to Flaggoner's Green and this proximity to the hundredal meeting place may have influenced its fortunes in earlier times. However we have to try and account for what seems to have been the separation and the significance of Avenbury in Church terms at some period before the Norman Conquest. In the first place another remarkable piece of evidence has been preserved from another Saxon charter dating from some time between 873 and 915.[12] In this Bishop Waerfrith of Worcester granted Avenbury to an unknown recipient. If the church at Worcester gave Avenbury, it must first have owned it, but how, when and why? Our second piece of evidence comes from the *Domesday Book* which was drawn up in 1086 for the Norman Conqueror, King William. From it we can discover the identity of the owners and many tenants, the size of manors, the numbers working on estates and other information. Churches were not generally recorded in Plegelgate Hundred in the *Domesday Book* although by this date many would have been built. The 'special status' of two churches is noted by the entry of two priests and a chaplain at Bromyard and two priests at Avenbury.[13] In both cases this indicates a religious community rather than a parish incumbent. Bromyard, we know, was a minster church with a college of priests, but why was Avenbury, so near at hand, of 'special status'?

Perhaps at one time Avenbury was a part of Bromyard Minster for as Map 7 shows the glebe lands of Avenbury were, as late as 1840, contiguous at Burley with those of the Portioners of Bromyard. The glebe terrier description for Avenbury in 1589 was 'One acre of arable land lying in Burley Field between the land of William Collye on one side and the lands belonging to the third portion of the church of Bromyard on the other side'. Alternatively in the early years of the establishment of minster churches the dioceses of Hereford and Worcester were in competition at the boundaries of their territory. We know from the charter of 873-915 that Avenbury was then in the hands of the church of Worcester, when Bishop Waerfrith granted Avenbury to an unknown recipient. Did Avenbury retain some importance after belonging to the church of Worcester, to then be granted a privileged position in the Hereford Diocese?

Chapter 2

Military and Manorial Tenure

'*Monument:* In chancel - flat slab with incised figure of man in banded mail armour with long surcoat, hands sheathing sword, head on cushion, shield hanging from shoulder, legs crossed, mid-13th century.'

Royal Commission on Historical Monuments England Herefordshire Vol. II - East, 7. Description of incised figure in Avenbury Church

The manorial estates had Anglo-Saxon names by 1066, which must have replaced British descriptive place-names. In some cases the name of the manor commemorated the names of lords or leaders, for instance Edwin Ralph and Edvin Loach were named from one Gedda who settled on this fen or marshy land; after the estate was divided, one land-holder was named Ralph and the other de Loges. Winslow was 'Wine's burial mound', Tedstone 'Teoda's thornbush', Avenbury possibly 'Agena's fortified place'. Collington was 'the estate connected with Cola' and was later separated into the bishop's manor of Collington Magna and Wulfard's manor of Collington Parva. Other place names were descriptive: Whitbourne 'at the white brook', Bredenbury 'fortified place made of boards', and Thornbury 'fortified place protected by a thorn-hedge'. What was the significance of the name of Bromyard 'broom (bush) enclosure' or 'enclosure by the broom bushes'? This is the only example of the name in this country. It could have been describing the enclosure around the early church and accompanying buildings.[1]

Map 5

The *c*1270 incised figure of a knight, probably a member of the Avenbury family. When this photograph was taken in 1931 the 7 foot long stone lay in the chancel of Avenbury Church. Today it lies in St. Peter's Church Bromyard.
Royal Commission on the Historical Monuments of England

THE AVENBURY KNIGHT

Archaeologia on Miscellaneous Tracts relating to Antiquity (London 1845), 267

Other changes were taking place as the old Anglo-Saxon hundreds were being reorganised to form larger units. Plegelgate was united with the adjacent Thornlow Hundred and with the manor of Much Cowarne from Radlow Hundred. The new district was called Broxash, with a meeting place at Little Cowarne. The remainder of Radlow merged with Wygmunstree Hundred to form a larger Radlow district.[2] With the establishment of the boroughs of Bromyard and Ledbury in the early 12th century, the importance of the hundred courts diminished. Nevertheless they continued to be called and meetings of Broxash hundred were certainly sometimes held in Bromyard.

'1515. Bromyard Borough. At a Hundred Lawday holden there on Tuesday the feast of SS. Philip and James, 7 Henry VIII., Robert Pyt acknowledged that he held of the lord three quarters of one burgage of free land lying in the new street within the borough aforesaid'.[3]

Military Tenure

In Saxon and Norman times all land was regarded as belonging to the ruler, who could grant property and estates to the church, nobles and followers, who became lords of their holdings in return for their allegiance and services. Tenants of the crown were known as 'tenants in chief' and they in turn could make grants of their land to sub-tenants as long as the principal service due to the crown was fulfilled. The main royal need was for military support known as knight service and a tenant with this type of holding was said to hold a knight's fee. In return for his estate he (or she) was bound to provide a knight to serve in the army for 40 days annually; if the service was needed for more than 40 days payment could then be claimed. Many local estates were held for a fraction of a knight's fee, possibly because the original grant of land, which was usually said to have been five hides, had been divided between heirs. This service could be replaced by a money payment known as scutage, but in time as a regular army was established and paid for out of taxes the system died out. Nevertheless estates held by knight service were usually the largest and most important in the district and frequently bore the title of manor or court.

The other important service by which land was held in the Bromyard district was by sergeanty, this entailed a personal service to the ruler. Paunton Court and Instone Court, parts of the manor of Stanford Regis (now in the parish of Bishop's Frome), Noakes and Sawbury Hill (now in the parish of Bredenbury) were all at one time royal manors and the subsequent sub-tenants owed such service as escorting the king's treasure to London, providing a hunting dog and so forth.

It is possible to trace the medieval tenants of these holdings from returns that were made for the crown and these include: *Domesday Book, Close Rolls, The Red Book of the Exchequer, Inquisitions Post Mortem*, and *Bishop's Registers*. Knight's service was served under the banner of military leaders, which were known as honours.

Manorial Tenure

Locally in late Saxon and Norman times, the lord and the manor were paramount. There was a pyramid of land-holding with the crown at the apex. By a process of sub-infeudation the greater lords let portions of their lands to local lords, who then owed service (usually military) at the castles of their honour, that is their overlord. The manors of Avenbury and Fenne (Upper and Lower Venn) were held of the honour of Kington and the manor of Hopton Sollers of the honour of Kilpeck; Sawbury was held of the honour of Bishop's Castle. In 1280 Walter, lord of Avenbury, held one hide of land at Bredenbury, for which he owed military service at the bishop's court in Bromyard; in 1304 it was John of Salisbirie who owed service for the land at Bredenbury. Avenbury was held for one knight's fee which required 40 days annual attendance, Fenne owed a half knight's fee and therefore 20 days service, Hopton Sollers a fifth and Sawbury a sixteenth of a fee. These last probably represented fragmentation by inheritance or purchase of the original grant. Noakes was held directly from the king and owed a personal duty called sergeanty, these duties varied, but in the case of Noakes meant finding a horse to escort the king's treasure from Hereford to London. Stanford Regis was also held by personal service to the crown and one responsibility for that manor was to provide a hunting dog when called upon.

Within the manor there was also an apex and a base. The lord was deemed the head and the feudal service and rents of his tenants enabled him to fulfil his military obligations and pay any dues and taxes expected from the land. Tenants could hold their property by military tenure, by freehold or by copy of court roll according to the customs of the manor. Each manor, however small, was economically independent with its own agricultural system, while larger manors such as Avenbury contained more than one estate each with its own village or hamlet and fields.

Domesday Book, the name meaning 'Day of Judgement Book', revealed the taxable value of his new kingdom to the Norman King William. The evidence was based on sworn statements from nobles, administrators and officials together with those of local priests, reeves, farmers and other parties. Lords of manors also had surveys and rolls drawn up to show the value of their own estates. Unfortunately no manorial records have been found for Avenbury and its associated manors. Manorial records for the neighbouring bishop's manors of Bromyard, Bishop's Frome, Stanford Bishop and Whitbourne have survived and extend back to *c*1280 and they present an illuminating picture of land-holding by manorial tenants over the centuries. Present day farms can be recognised by the names of their occupiers and the rents, services, status and size of the holdings can be traced. There is no reason to suppose that the history of the Avenbury farms is any different. These manorial records show that on the bishop's manors, the lord, the church and the farmers had individual strips in common open fields; the farmers owed the lord a rent of money, produce or agricultural services. For instance *c*1280 it was recorded that the farmers of five virgates (four virgates equalled one hide of land) at Stanford Bishop had to mow for the lord one day and weed for one day or give in money 20d. The farmers of 15 virgates at Bishop's Frome not only owed work on the lord bishop's demesne farm there, they also had to work each year in the vineyard at Ledbury (another manor belonging to the bishop of Hereford) 'by ancient custom' for which they were not paid.

Gradually all manorial rents were paid in money and the strips were amalgamated by exchange and purchase until most farms and holding were within a ring-fence. However as maps and documents show, church lands which belonged to an institution and not to private owners retained the original dispersed pattern for much longer. The tenants of bishops' manors continued to have their rents and farms recorded in court rolls until this century, whereas Avenbury, where the importance of the lord disappeared centuries ago, appears to have no surviving manorial records.[4]

The Parish

The manor and parish were not necessarily the same and the parish of Avenbury included the Domesday manor of Avenbury with the smaller manors of Fenne, Hopton Sollers, Little Froome, Noakes and Sawbury.

Why did these less substantial manors choose to share their religious life and parochial welfare with Avenbury? Certainly they were unlikely to have the resources to build and fund a church of their own. They could, however, have allied themselves with the church of Bromyard or in the case of Hopton Sollers to the church of Stoke Lacy. The reason probably lies with the inclinations, unions and relationships of their Saxon and Norman lords. They may have preferred some independence from the influence of the bishop of Hereford within whose manor the minster and parish of Bromyard was situated. Bredenbury, with its own church, was at one time a chapelry attached to the church of Avenbury. An assessment made in 1292 for Pope Nicholas IV valued Avenbury at £12 together with the chapelry at Bredenbury. However by 1385 Bredenbury had become an independent rectory, although a payment of 2s from the chapel of Bredenbury was still paid to the vicar of Avenbury in the 16th century.[5]

The manor house was the focus of the manor but the church was the heart of the much larger parish which covered 3,178 acres in 1840 and was probably the same in 1086. As the importance of the manor diminished, the parish church, through the vestry, took on many of its functions and duties. At Avenbury Church the parishioners met to worship and to record their life events of baptism, marriage and death; here also they administered the business of the parochial community and it was the produce of the land that provided the income needed for this obligation. Families appeared and disappeared; some surnames survived for centuries, others for less than a lifetime. It was the farms and the local industries which were dependent on agricultural produce which persisted as the economic base for the inhabitants. The parish had to be more than self sufficient for resources were drained away by many factors such as:

- church tithe which was a tenth of the profit of most crops and livestock, including timber and bees, and in the case of Avenbury was from about 1320 granted to impropriators outside the parish
- other ecclesiastical dues
- national taxes imposed by the Crown
- county rates to support the needs and expenses of justice and administration
- rents and services due to absentee landlords.

The Farms

The lord's demesne was usually the largest farm on the manor (and in the case of small manors may have been the only farm); even today these important farms may still retain the suffix of manor or court. The village farms were assessed in virgates or yardlands, of which there were four to the hide; a survey of *c*1580 for Whitbourne reported :

'And it is noted, the customary lands the jury did estimate after the rate of 4 perch brode and 40 perches long to be an acre of ground, (every perch containing 16½ feet according to the statute). And guess the same by view as rightly as they could.....Further the said jury do say that by the custom of the country, 60 acres of land is a yardland, 30 acres a half yardland, and 15 acres is a nooke of land.' The clerk went on to explain the discrepancy 'According to the rate as we have estimated the custom lands (which is as near as we could unto the statute measure) 2 acres as we have estimated is three acres of the old measure; and after that rate it seems that 40 acres as we have estimated is a yardland and commonly. But 60 acres is here accompted for a yardland. There for I think their measure at the time of the Red Book was not so great as the statute measure now'.

The Red Book of the Bishops of Hereford dates from *c*1275 and the measurement used was the old Herefordshire acre which was two thirds of the statute acre.[6]

Within the parish of Avenbury were the Domesday manors of 1086:

AVENBURY - six hides (which pay tax). In lordship (that is the demesne farm) there was arable for three ploughs, which is taken to mean sufficient plough land for three plough teams to work in a year; there were four slaves who worked on the lord's own farm. There were 22 village farmers, two priests and a smallholder who between them had enough arable land for 12 ploughs. There was also a mill which paid no tax and may not have been working. Taxable value of the whole manor was 100s.

LITTLE FROOME - one hide paying tax with one plough on the lord's farm and three village farmers with one plough. There were two slaves and a mill worth 32d; this manor had been worth 20s in 1066 but by 1086 was only worth 15s.

HOPTON SOLLERS - one hide and one virgate which paid tax, there was one plough on the demesne with three villagers and two smallholders possessing land for three ploughs; there were four slaves and the manor was worth 30s as it had been in 1066.

NOAKES - one hide paying tax, half a plough on the demesne with two villagers with one plough; this manor too had been worth more in 1066 at 30s, and had then dropped to 20s but the situation was improving and Noakes was in 1086 worth 24s.

SAWBURY was a small two and a half virgate manor with land for one plough and it had paid no tax in 1066 or again in 1086. 'It was and is waste'.[7]

It is the history, as we know it, of these lands and their occupants, that we now hope to unravel.

Chapter 3

The Church of St Mary, Early Years

'What Ruins of Religious Houses, Churches, Chapels and Chantries? By whom and when demolished? What Wakes and Processions; and on what Days? What remarkable Crosses? Who Patron of the Living, now and anciently? Whether it be a Rectory, Vicarage, Donative, or Sine-Cure? If a Vicarage, to whom are the rectorial Tythes appropriated or impropriated, now or formerly?'

HRO *'Letter from R Walwyn to Dr Roberts at Ross'* (1749)

The now ruined church of Avenbury stands in an enchanted and unusual setting within a loop of the river Frome as it flows down the valley between Bromyard and Bishop's Frome (see Map 6). Church sites in a river meander are usually ancient and can date from the earliest days of Christianity in this country and were particularly favoured by monastic communities. The curvilinear churchyard possibly indicates that when Avenbury Church was founded here it followed

The river Frome as it flows through the glebe just east of the church. The bridge is on the road to Avenbury Court. *Howard Painter*

the customs of Celtic Christianity. The earliest spelling of Avenbury, *Agnanbyrig,* could mean 'Agene's fortified place' and is found in an Anglo-Saxon charter *c*873-915 when Avenbury was in the hands of the church of Worcester. Why and for what period of time Avenbury, which lies so close to the great minster of Bromyard, was granted to Worcester we may never know. In the 7th and 8th centuries a great deal of land was granted to the church by the newly converted rulers of the English kingdoms. Bromyard was granted to the bishop of Hereford at about this period and it is known that Ecgwine who was bishop of Worcester *c*699 acquired considerable estates for the church of Worcester in the early 8th century. By the charter of 873-915 Bishop Waerfrith of Worcester was granting Avenbury to a person who remains unknown, since unfortunately the charter is now lost. [1]

Before 1066, Avenbury was in the hands of Spirtes the Priest, a wealthy churchman at the court of Edward the Confessor, who had served the Saxon royal family for some 25 years. Spirtes possessed land in Herefordshire at Little Cowarne, Little Thinghill and Sutton St. Nicholas, and he had extensive estates in other counties. He was a canon of St Martin's, Dover and of Brimfield, Shropshire, and his brother Earnwi was a secular reeve of Worcester Cathedral. For some reason Spirtes was banished from Court in 1065. After the Norman Conquest many of his estates were granted to Nigel, William the Conqueror's doctor. In the *Domesday Survey* of 1086 the manor of Avenbury was in the hands of Nigel the Doctor, and two priests with land were recorded amongst the inhabitants. At this time Bromyard, a manor five times the size of Avenbury, and with the minster or mother church which served the hundred of Plegelgate, was recorded with just two landholding priests and a landholding chaplain.[2] Avenbury and Bromyard were, in 1086, the only manors in the hundred of Plegelgate where priests were recorded. This surely means that Avenbury like Bromyard was an early and important Christian foundation.

The two priests at Avenbury certainly indicate a special status church here and probably a monastic community. This was a large parish and, after Bromyard, was one of the most populous in the hundred (see Table 2). It included several other manors that were recorded separately in the *Domesday Survey*, namely Hopton Sollers, Noakes, Sawbury, Little Froome and apparently for a time Bredenbury. The manor of Avenbury not only covered the central estate from which it took its name but also comprised the large estates of Hackley, Munderfield and the Venn on the periphery (see Maps 1&10).

We do not know when Avenbury passed out of the hands of the church of Worcester but later Avenbury Church was granted to St Guthlac's Priory. This initially stood in the grounds of Hereford Castle on the bank of the Wye, on Castle Green. St Guthlac (672-714) was the saint in whose honour Crowland Abbey, Lincolnshire was founded in 716; it is not certain when the Priory in Hereford was established but it was well endowed with Herefordshire lands and churches which included Avenbury and Little Cowarne.[3] A castle bailey was hardly an ideal site for a religious house, especially in times of war, and around

1140 Roger de Port, who was sheriff of Hereford and constable of the castle there and who was also overlord of the manor of Avenbury, expropriated the church of St Guthlac and its possessions.

The Priory was refounded in 1143 beyond the castle and city walls where the bus station now stands near the County Hospital. Osbert the lord of Avenbury then granted or regranted 'the church of Avenbury with all its appurtenances as a free and perpetual gift-of-alms to God and to the Church of the Apostles Peter and Paul and of St Guthlac at Hereford and to the monks who are serving God in that place'. Some 50 years later the Priory agreed to pay a silver mark annually to Osbert for so long as Hugh of Mappenoure served as vicar of the church of Avenbury and in return Osbert was to pay the community at Hereford two shillings a year during Hugh's lifetime. At about the same time, in return for a fixed rent, St Guthlac's made over to Osbert and his heirs for ever, any rights they held in the advowson of the church at Avenbury (i.e. their right of presentation to the benefice).[4]

The Avenbury Family and The Church

Spirtes the Priest and Nigel the Doctor, may have visited their manor and church of Avenbury, but they are unlikely to have resided here for more than a night or two, if at all. The manor could have been managed by a bailiff or rented out to a sub-tenant. It is quite possible that the family who were subsequent lords of this manor and bore the name of Avenbury had been there in Saxon times. By 1166 Walter of Avenbury was lord, and the ruins of the church today incorporate walls that were erected even earlier.[5] Avenbury is one of the few churches in the

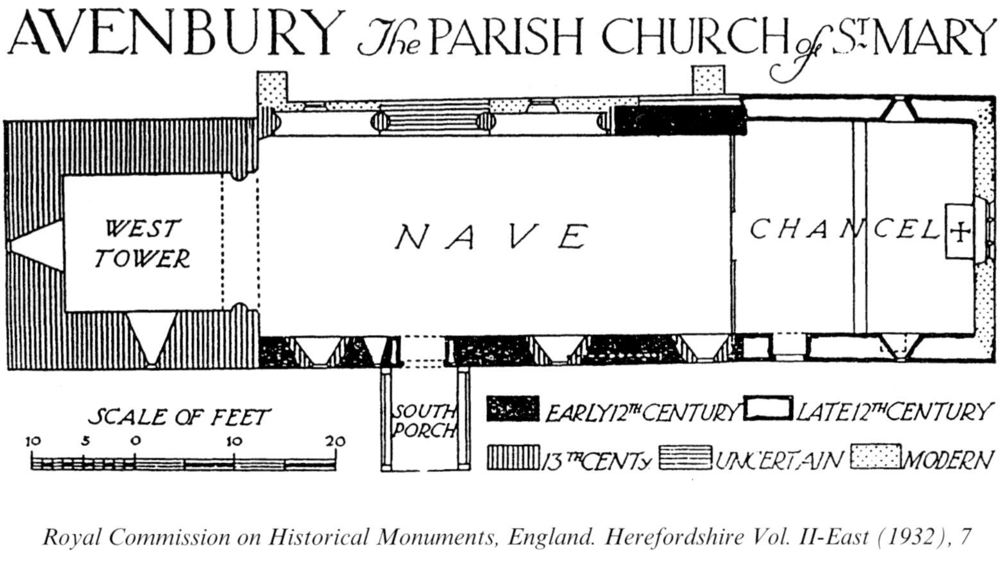

Royal Commission on Historical Monuments, England. Herefordshire Vol. II-East (1932), 7

Avenbury Church 1897.

area with building work that dates from about 1100. Tedstone Delamere appears to have a Saxon north doorway, whilst Bromyard Church incorporates re-used carvings and stones of pre-Conquest date and the small now ruined church at Edvin Loach dates from the 11th century. The great period of church re-building of 1050-1150 came to the rest of Bromyard District nearer to 1160.

The nave at Avenbury was built or rebuilt about 1100 or shortly after, but the chancel was rebuilt and possibly enlarged in the late 12th century. This may indicate that the chancel was in sufficient repair or possibly particularly venerated at the time of the earlier building work. The west tower was erected soon after 1200. Osbert of Avenbury was lord here in 1210 and could have inaugurated that work. His son, another Walter of Avenbury, held the manor around 1230-40 and came to an agreement with Jocelyn the prior of St Guthlac's and the community there that the silver mark which his father Osbert had agreed to pay as fixed rent to the Priory would in future be derived from his fulling mill at Avenbury and four acres of adjacent land then let to Walter Crumpe. To ensure that the full sum of one mark was paid, Walter made a further gift of two acres of his own demesne in Avenbury to the Priory.[6] Walter was probably responsible for building the north arcade and aisle about 1250; this addition could indicate a rise in the population of the parish or it may have been a desire to improve the church and facilities for worship.

By 1250 the fabric of the church was less than 200 years old and, recently extended with a tower and north aisle, it would have been a handsome sight. When the church was still standing there was in the chancel a flat slab with the incised figure of a knight in banded mail armour and a long surcoat. The hands sheathed a sword and the head rested on a cushion, the man's legs were crossed and a shield hung from his shoulder. This monument dates from the mid- to late 13th century and surely represents either Walter or his son, another Osbert, who was the last of that family in Avenbury. The slab, which is of a rare type, can now be seen in Bromyard Church.[7] (Table 3 on page 38 Chapter 4 identifies the several Walters and Osberts in this family).

Rous Family of Avenbury

The Avenburys were now to be followed by the Rous family, for Eleanor, Osbert's heiress, married Roger le Rous of Allensmore, and she presented to the living in 1313 and 1314. Her son John le Rous had licence from the king in 1319 to grant the advowson and main income of Avenbury Church, together with a garden in Avenbury, to Dore Abbey which had been founded in 1147. Despite this authority, in September 1320, Adam of Orleton, the bishop of Hereford, commissioned the rector of Whitbourne, Richard de Sydenhale, to enquire into the proposed appropriation before giving it his sanction the following January.[8] John le Rous died around 1334 and his son, another John, died in 1345 leaving his widow Mabel holding the manor of Avenbury in 1346. Their son Thomas died in 1358 and his daughter Juliana, who married first Andrew Herle (who died in 1392) and second Thomas Mylle, carried the manor

The 14th-century south porch of Avenbury in 1931 with the 17th-century door.
Royal Commission on the Historical Monuments of England

of Avenbury into the Mylle family. The Rous family may have encouraged the erection of the timber-framed porch of Avenbury Church which dated from the 14th century and was still standing in 1932.

The Appropriation of Avenbury Church to Dore Abbey

It is said that by the end of the 12th century about a quarter of parish churches in England had been granted to religious houses, while most of the remainder answered directly to bishops.[9] Since the Norman Conquest England had enjoyed mounting prosperity and an increase in population, and church incomes had prospered accordingly. The village church was frequently regarded as belonging to the lord of the manor, for it was built on his land and with his patronage and was consequently seen as a manorial asset. The parishioners probably contributed to the structure, fabric and furnishings and may even have given some of their land for the glebe, for they too belonged to the manor and owed allegiance and service to their lord. For a lay lord and owner of a church to grant the advowson (or patronage) and main revenues to a religious house was an act of christian piety and sacrifice, although it usually represented a loss to the parish.

Avenbury's 14th-century church chest which was 7 feet long.
Royal Commission on the Historical Monuments of England

When this happened, the religious house in effect became the rector, had the privilege of appointing the vicar and usually took the great tithes of the parish, which were the tenth part of the main cereal crops and the hay. In return it had to maintain the chancel, and provide a vicarage and an adequate stipend for the vicar, who usually retained the right to the small tithes on minor produce and livestock. The division between rector and vicar of church collections and other minor receipts would no doubt be a matter of negotiation in a particular case. Without such gifts in perpetuity the monastic houses could hardly have survived financially. Presumably the church of Worcester and then St Guthlac's Priory,

Hereford had enjoyed the income and privileges. When the Avenbury family commuted St Guthlac's right of patronage to a perpetual money rent at the end of the 13th century, Avenbury Church's advowson and revenue were restored into the hands of the lord of the manor who was then free, if he wished, to grant the revenue and the right of appointment of the incumbent of Avenbury to his own favoured community. And this John le Rous duly did to Dore Abbey. Before doing this he may have gained assent in the parish, but in any case the gift was in his name.

From 1321, therefore, R Petyt, who had hitherto been rector, had to resign. In his place the abbot and convent of Dore appointed William Tokye as vicar who was unfortunately disabled by an incurable disease and Thomas le Webbe of Bromyard was appointed to assist him. The bishop then apportioned between the vicar and the abbey the tithes and other possessions of the church of Avenbury, these included the house in which the rectors were accustomed to live with a hall, other buildings and a barn, a garden, orchard and 60 acres of land. There was also a pension of 2s a year from the chapel of Bredenbury which suggests that then or earlier Bredenbury had been served by the rector of Avenbury.[10]

The late 15th-century screen with later additions which separated the chancel and nave of Avenbury Church in 1931.
Royal Commission on the Historical Monuments of England

In 1519 Bishop Bothe gave judgement at Ludlow regarding a dispute between John Longford, the vicar of Avenbury, and the abbot and community of Dore. It would appear that the controversy, which concerned the share of the church assets and income rightfully due, was longstanding and, unable to solve the problem

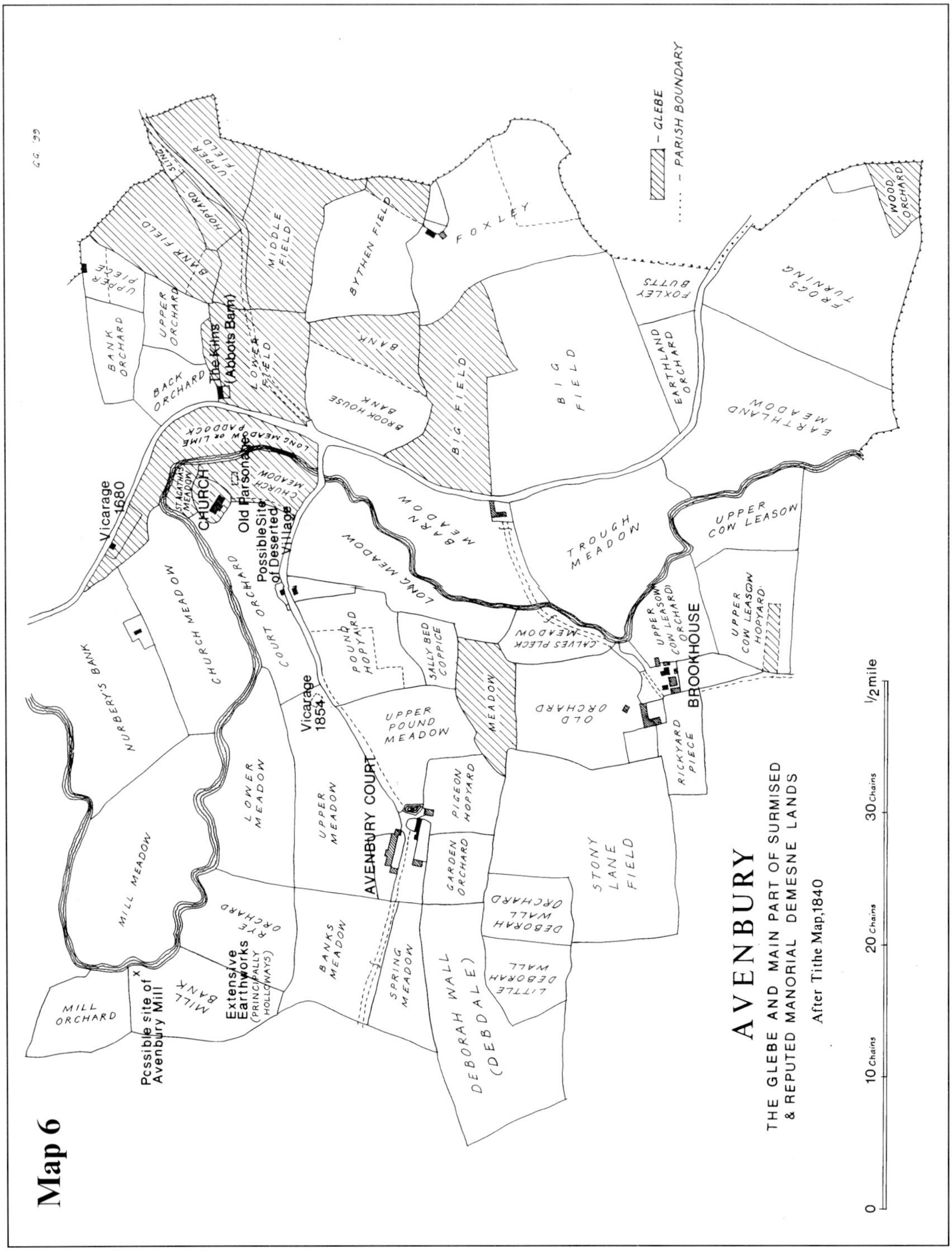
Map 6
AVENBURY
THE GLEBE AND MAIN PART OF SURMISED & REPUTED MANORIAL DEMESNE LANDS
After Tithe Map,1840
- GLEBE
- PARISH BOUNDARY
0
10 Chains
20 Chains
30 Chains
1/2 mile
GG '99
UPPER FIELD
HOPYARD
BANK FIELD
UPPER PIECE
MIDDLE FIELD
BYTHEN FIELD
FOXLEY
WOOD ORCHARD
FROGS TURNING
FOXLEY BUTTS
BANK ORCHARD
UPPER ORCHARD
The Kilns (Abbots Barn)
LOWER FIELD
BANK
BIG FIELD
EARTHLAND ORCHARD
EARTHLAND MEADOW
BACK ORCHARD
BROOK HOUSE BANK
LONG MEADOW or LIME PADDOCK
Vicarage 1680
ST AGATHAS MEADOW
CHURCH
Old Parsonage
CHURCH MEADOW
Possible Site of Deserted Village
BARN MEADOW
TROUGH MEADOW
UPPER COW LEASOW
LONG MEADOW
NURBERY'S BANK
CHURCH MEADOW
COURT ORCHARD
POUND HOPYARD
SALLY BED COPPICE
CALVES PLECK MEADOW
UPPER COW LEASOW ORCHARD
BROOKHOUSE
UPPER COW LEASOW HOPYARD
Vicarage 1854
UPPER POUND MEADOW
MEADOW
OLD ORCHARD
RICKYARD PIECE
MILL MEADOW
LOWER MEADOW
UPPER MEADOW
AVENBURY COURT
PIGEON HOPYARD
GARDEN ORCHARD
STONY LANE FIELD
DEBORAH WALL ORCHARD
RYE ORCHARD
BANKS MEADOW
SPRING MEADOW
LITTLE DEBORAH WALL
DEBORAH WALL (DEBDALE)
MILL ORCHARD
MILL BANK
Extensive Earthworks (PRINCIPALLY HOLLOWAYS)
Possible site of Avenbury Mill

themselves, the two parties agreed to accept the verdict of the bishop at his episcopal court. 'Therefore to bring agreement and freedom from strife to the aforementioned parties and for the sake of peaceful relationships' it was agreed that John Longford was to have his income augmented to £7 6s 8d a year, paid quarterly in the parish church of Avenbury; also the present vicar and his successors shall

> 'have for ever the house in which the vicars have been accustomed to live, together with all the outbuildings belonging to the said house with the exception of the barn and of the principal room with the cellar underneath, with the responsibility for repair and upkeep of the said house and of the said outbuildings'.

The vicar and his successors were also to have the garden next to the house and a meadow called St Agatha's Meadow, together with all the mass pence received on Sundays, after burials, at matrimony and after the recitation of the *bederolle*, which was a list of the church benefactors. The abbot and community were to receive all other offerings, tithes, income and benefits, including whatever offerings were made in the chapel of St Agatha next door to or adjoining the church. Abbey Dore was also from its own resources to provide for every obligation 'ordinary and extraordinary' affecting Avenbury Church. It was also adjudged that if any payment was in arrears the vicar should withhold all the revenues, offerings and tithe due to the abbot and community.[11]

With hindsight, it is clear that for all its wordiness there were two important omissions in the document. No mention was made of the glebe which had belonged to the priests of Avenbury as early as 1086, and no allowance was made for inflation. A dispute regarding these two points was still rumbling on 200 years later in the 18th century.

It must not be thought that religious houses which in this way 'impropriated' church benefices necessarily retained all the property for their own use. Sub-letting, which became common after the Dissolution of the Monasteries, had already begun. Thus Abbey Dore is found to have been renting out part of its interest in the ecclesiastical estate of Avenbury. Edward Myll, the lord of Avenbury, had been paying £5 6s 8d annually for a barn called the Abbot's Barn and all tithes of grain, that is the great tithe of the parish. Not all this money went to the Abbey: 6s 8d was paid to the choristers of Hereford Cathedral, £3 to the vicar of Avenbury and only the balance of £2 went to Abbey Dore. John Myll, Edward's son, had this lease by 1536.[12]

St Agatha's Chapel

The mention of 'the offerings made in the chapel of St Agatha next door or adjoining to the church' is the only known reference to St Agatha's Chapel at Avenbury although a meadow to the north of the churchyard retained the name. It was possibly in or near the north aisle which disappeared and of which only the arcade pillars were retained in the north wall of the church. Agatha was a 3rd-century martyr, whose feast day is on February 5th. Little is known of her life although she appears to have come from Catonia in Sicily and was venerated in very early times.[13] She became the patron saint of bell founders and in some places bread is blessed in church on her feast day. There are few English church dedications to St Agatha and these include Brightwell in Berkshire and Llangmynach in Shropshire, as well as Easby and Gilling in North Yorkshire both of which are connected with St Agatha's Abbey at Easby.[14]

The interior of Avenbury church in 1931 looking north-west and showing the blocked 13th-century arcade.
Royal Commission on the Historical Monuments of England

Chapter 4

The Domesday Manors 1066-1600

Avenbury including Brookhouse, the Venn, Little Froome, Hopton Sollers, Noakes and Sawbury Hill

The name of the place. Who held it, before 1066, and now?
How many hides? How many ploughs, both those in lordship and the men's?
How many villagers, cottagers and slaves, how many free men and Freemen?
How much woodland, meadow and pasture? How many mills and fishponds?
How much has been added or taken away? What the total value was and is?
How much each free man or Freeman had or has? All threefold , before 1066, when King William gave it, and now; and if more can be had than at present?

Inquisitio Eliensis from John Morris, *Herefordshire Domesday* (1983)

The parish of Avenbury covered 3,178 acres in 1840 and there is no reason for thinking the area to have been very different at the end of the Saxon period. However, there is no way that we can today precisely equate hides with acreages. The number of farms based on the number of village farmers and smallholders would appear to have been in 1086:

	farms	smallholdings	other holdings
Avenbury	22	1	Glebe and a mill
Hopton	3	2	
Noakes	2		
Little Froome	3		a mill
Sawbury Hill	waste		

In addition each of these manors had a manor house and home farm or demesne and the slaves recorded at Domesday probably worked on the lord's estate; there were four slaves at Avenbury, four at Hopton Sollers and two at Little Froome. These figures suggest that the number of farms in Avenbury parish in 1086 were: the four large farms of the lords of the manors, plus surely some kind of dwelling at Sawbury, 30 village farms, three smallholdings, the Glebe and two mills. In medieval Wales the average estate of possibly 120 acres which equates with the possible size of the English hide of land, is thought to have supported some 30-40 people which could be five to six families. Avenbury appears to have had a similar density of population.[1]

To what extent these manors and farmers practised common field husbandry is difficult to ascertain. Church terriers of the 16th and 17th centuries firmly indicate glebe lying in different fields in the parish. Certainly Avenbury had at one time common arable fields and probably the meadows and pastures were cut and grazed communally. Three fields north of Avenbury Court were in 1840 called Arnage Fields, a name that derives from *inning* and means 'land taken in and enclosed'. There appears to have been a settlement between the church and the manor house (Avenbury Court) where earthworks can still be seen and some sherds of 14th-century glazed pottery have been found in this field. In Saxon and Norman times some of the present-day farms would have taken the form of small hamlets, and the remains of house platforms have been discerned at the Venn and Munderfield Court.

The Manor, Lords and Demesne of Avenbury

LAND OF NIGEL THE DOCTOR

> 'AVENBURY. Spirtes held it. 6 hides which pay tax. In lordship 3 ploughs, 4 slaves; 22 villagers, 2 priests and 1 smallholder with 12 ploughs. A mill which pays nothing. The value is and was 100s.'[2]

A manor was an estate or land unit held from the king or an overlord, for which the lord of the manor had responsibility and control. The lord had his manor house and home farm known as the demesne, which in Avenbury contained enough arable for three plough teams and could have been one fifth of the manorial arable land. The slaves would have worked on the lord's lands; the 22 - village farmers and two priests together with a smallholder had land for 12 ploughs and averaged half a ploughland each. There was also a manorial mill which paid no tax and later references show that 150 years later this was a fulling mill in the hands of the lord. There is no mill in Avenbury now and the corn grown here may have been milled since Domesday at Little Froome Mill.

Avenbury was described as a six hide manor in 1066, of which Venn comprised two hides, the remaining four hides included the demesne or home farm of the lord, the church lands, the large estate of Munderfield and the remaining village farms. Nigel the Doctor died between 1094-1098 and Avenbury came into the hands of the king, who a few years later granted this and other Herefordshire manors to Adam de Port, whose honour, or principal castle, was at Kington. Adam or his son Roger enfeoffed, that is established, before 1135, a knight at Avenbury, possibly Osbert of Avenbury, and he probably in 1143 granted or regranted the church of Avenbury to the refounded priory of St Guthlac, at Hereford. Walter was the next lord of Avenbury, and he was also lord of the manor of Little Thinghill in Herefordshire which had belonged to Spirtes, then Nigel the Doctor and by 1166 to Adam de Port, and which was like Avenbury associated with St Guthlac's Priory.[3] By 1195, Walter had been replaced by another Osbert, probably his son (the name sometimes appears as Osbern) and he negotiated with the ecclesiastical authorities to regain the advowson and income of the church of Avenbury for as long as Hugo of Mappenoure should be vicar of Avenbury and in return Osbert was to pay St Guthlac's and the monks there 'one mark of silver annually' in the form of rent. Osbert was still alive in 1211-1212 when he returned for one knight's fee of the barony of Kington.[4]

Osbert's son Walter confirmed between 1228-1243 the payment of this rent to the prior and community at Hereford for the advowson; the sum of one mark was to be paid annually from 'my fulling mill at Avenbury and from four adjoining acres of land.....which Walter Crumpe has held from me'. In addition as an unconditional and permanent gift-of-alms, Walter of Avenbury granted to St Guthlac's Priory two acres of his demesne land at Avenbury:

> 'One of these lies in the field which is called La Helde between the land of Adam le Chirchman and the land of William the reeve...the other in truth lies next to my demesne at Chirnewall, and it extends 24 perches in length and 7 perches in width and it has one perch of pasture, and one headland extends as far as the land of William the reeve and another up to the land of Ungo of Frome'.

The wording of the land grant would appear to indicate that the land of Walter the lord of Avenbury lay, certainly in part, in the common fields of the manor intermixed with the lands of the village farmers. Walter also promised:

> 'And in order that the said Prior and Community may have free suit of my men at Avenbury to the aforesaid mill without cause for grievance, truly neither I nor my heirs will construct another mill on the same water in the said manor, nor will we put there any hindrance to the detriment of the aforesaid fulling mill'.

Walter of Avenbury flourished during the mid-13th century and it is surely either Walter or his son Osbert who is commemorated by the incised figure of a knight that at one time lay in the chancel of Avenbury Church and now can be found, somewhat hidden, in the north-west corner of Bromyard Church. Walter witnessed a charter relating to land at Hennerwood in Pencombe in 1236, and in 1243 confirmed his knight's fee of the barony of Kington which by now was in the hands of the earl of Hereford.[5] In 1265 Walter was summoned to defend Hereford against the forces of Simon de Montfort.

Walter had a brother, Giles of Avenbury, who was well-known in ecclesiastical circles at about this time. A sentence was delivered in the Court of Canterbury on 27th January 1271/2 in a suit concerning the deanery of Hereford. Giles of Avenbury, 'Canon of Hereford and Chaplain of the Pope' was contesting John of Aquablanca's claim to be dean of Hereford. The judgement was that John of Aquablanca was to be removed and the deanery restored to Giles of Avenbury, together with 800 marks for the profits due from the deanery and 400 marks for expenses. Apparently Giles was treasurer of Hereford Cathedral in 1262 and dean in 1271.[6]

Maud of Avenbury was another member of the family; she was the second wife of Humphrey de Bohun, earl of Hereford and Essex and overlord of the manor of Avenbury. Humphrey was slain at Boroughbridge in 1321 and Maud died about the same time in Gascony; her remains were later interred near those of her husband at Llanthony Abbey, near Monmouth, by her son John, earl of Hereford.[7]

Walter was followed as lord of Avenbury by yet another Osbert and the last lord of that name; he is recorded between 1276 and 1283 and was in 1278 called upon with Geoffrey d'Abitot of Hindlip, Worcestershire to decide a dispute between the bishop and the earl of Hereford regarding land in Malvern Chase.[8] As was said in Chapter 3, Osbert evidently had no living male heirs to carry on the Avenbury name and the manor was inherited by an heiress, Eleanor, who married Roger le Rous of Allensmore in Herefordshire. Roger died in 1296 and Eleanor had the knight's fee at Avenbury in her own right in 1303 and 1316; and shared the full fee with Payne of Burghill who was lord of Thinghill, which had been another possession of the Avenbury Family.[9] Eleanor also presented Roger le Rous to the living at Avenbury in 1313. R Petyt, the next rector, as we saw in Chapter 3, lost his living when Abbey Dore appropriated Avenbury church in 1321.

John le Rous, the son of Roger and Eleanor, inherited the manor of Avenbury and also succeeded in 1294 to his father's office of sheriff of Hereford, an honour he was to serve again 1332-1334. During 1317-21 John had licence from the king to alienate in mortmain to the abbot and convent of Dore (Dore Abbey, Herefordshire which had been established in 1147) the advowson of Avenbury Church and a garden in Avenbury, and this was confirmed by Bishop

Bromyard Local History Society Collection

Adam of Orleton in 1321.[10] Although earlier the church had been granted to St Guthlac's Priory, that gift appears to have been commuted to a money rent of a mark together with some land belonging to the Avenbury family; hence the advowson was now available for another act of piety by the lord of Avenbury, an act that was encouraged by Humphrey de Bohun, John's overlord, who married Maud of Avenbury.[11]

The manor of Avenbury was in the hands of the le Rous family for several generations, until as with the Avenbury family there was no direct male heir. Consequently the manor passed to the heirs of Juliana le Rous by her second husband Thomas Mylle and the Mylle family of Avenbury became lords of this manor from about 1400 until about 1540.[12]

Avenbury Court with Brookhouse

Avenbury Court is surely the site or close to the site of the early manor house of Avenbury, probably that from which the parish took its name 'Agena's fortified place'. The name Court would indicate that this was where manorial courts were held, but the magnificent site itself would further suggest a fortified place or *bury*. The present house is built on a partly circular mound and the ground drops away on the south, east and north, where there are interesting traces of earthworks; could the pond just below the house be the remains of a moat? Possibly the site was moated on three sides. To the west the ground rises and Avenbury Court stands on a promontory above the river and church. It also stands on the road which leads from the Avenbury Lane to the Munderfield Road and gates below and above the farm ensure a certain amount of privacy and security. The field name of Pigeon Hopyard behind the house indicates that a dovecote or pigeon house stood near here at one time; closer to the church was the village pound where straying animals could be impounded and penned.

The Avenbury, Rous and Mylle families, served as lords of the manor of Avenbury for at least 400 years, and were descended by the female line from the de Avenburys. The same family may have been resident on the manor, as tenants during or since Saxon times. These influential families and their forerunners surely lived near here in a manor house long gone. Later documents refer to Brookhouse as 'the manor, or reputed manor, of Avenbury'; did reputed in this case mean 'passing as being but probably or possibly not being'?[13] Maps 6 and 10 show that the lands of the Court, the church and Brookhouse occupy the Frome Valley between Little Froome at the north and the Hyde and Venn to the south and to the east extend to the parish boundary and Bromyard Church lands. Nurburys 'north of the fortified place' appears to be part of this integrated area. Were these component parts of a small estate, with the site of the Court, the original manor house, and the manorial rights possibly transferred to the owner of Brookhouse at a later date? For some two centuries, Brookhouse has been regarded as the reputed manor of Avenbury and later owners of the property have been recorded as lords of this manor.[14]

Avenbury Court came into the hands of the Berrington family of Much Cowarne in the 16th century. They are also the earliest known owners of Brookhouse; the same family had the manors of Stoke Lacy and Mintridge in Stoke Lacy and were large landowners in the district around 1600.[15] At this time the farmers of Avenbury Court and Brookhouse appear to have been Richard Barnes and William Collye.[16] It may have been when the properties were in the hands of the Berrington family that Brookhouse became the reputed manor of Avenbury and its subsequent owners were then lords of this manor.

TABLE 3

OVERLORDS AND LORDS OF THE MANOR OF AVENBURY

Overlords

Before 873 The Church of Worcester
915 Unknown
1066 Spirtes the Priest
1086 Nigel the Doctor
1100 The Crown
Barony of Kington (later Huntington)
1135 Adam de Port
Roger de Port
*c*1200 Earl of Hereford

Lords of the Manor

1143 Osbert of Avenbury
1166 Walter of Avenbury
1195 Osbert of Avenbury
1210 Osbert of Avenbury
1230 Walter of Avenbury (Giles, his brother, dean of Hereford Cathedral)
1242 Walter of Avenbury
1277 Osbert of Avenbury
1284 Elinor and John le Rous (sheriff of Hereford 1293)
1303 Elinor le Rous
1332 John le Rous (sheriff of Hereford 1332-4)
John le Rous
1346 Mabel le Rous (the widow of John who died 1345)
Thomas le Rous died 1358
John le Rous (died without issue)
Andrew Herle who died 1392 =1 Juliana le Rous (John's sister) =2 Thomas Mylle
1431 Thomas Mylle
1500 Thomas Mylle = Joyce Croft of Croft Castle, Herefordshire
1530 Edward Mylle
1536 John Mylle
Berrington Family of Much Cowarne

The Venn

The Venn is today and has been for many centuries, two major farms; these are probably the remnants of very ancient settlements. Upper Venn and Lower Venn are so named from their position on the river Frome, Upper Venn being up river and nearer Bromyard than Lower Venn, which is downstream. Venn derives from the Anglo-Saxon word *faenn* which means 'fen or marshland', and the area known as the Venn in Avenbury is low lying ground at the south-east tip of the parish, bounded on its eastern side by the River Frome. The name suggests marginal lands but with drainage this is a fertile area, growing ample grass and good grain. Hops do well here and Lower Venn is today the largest hop growing farm in Avenbury.

Venn appears to have been an important independent estate in Saxon times, but because in the late Saxon and early Norman period it was held by the same overlord as the larger manor of Avenbury it was assessed with that manor. Avenbury comprised four hides and the Venn two making the six hide Domesday manor of Avenbury. Spirtes was the last Saxon overlord and it is possible that the tithes of both the Venn and Avenbury were granted to St Guthlac's Priory, on Castle Green, Hereford in his day. After the Conquest Nigel, King William's doctor, acquired this and other manors formerly in the hands of Spirtes. Following Nigel the Doctor's death at the end of the 11th century, Avenbury and Venn came into the king's hands, probably about 1109. These and many other Herefordshire manors were then granted to Adam de Port who founded his headquarters or honour at Kington. Before 1135 either Adam de Port or his son Roger had established a knight at both Avenbury and the Venn. Osbert was the lord of Avenbury by 1143, but the name of the early lord of Venn is not known.

In 1164 Thomas *Delfanc*, his name is thought to be a corruption of de Venn, witnessed together with Walter of Avenbury a charter for Adam de Port, and this Thomas may also be the *Thom' de Fac'* annotated against Avenbury in *c*1160-1170 *'In Agenebiria vi h (hides) Walteri et Thom' de Fac'*.[17] William of Venn had this half knight's fee by 1211-1212 held from the lord of Kington, and another Thomas was holding the estate in 1243, and another William in 1249. William de la Fenne again appears as a witness to a notification of Bishop Cantilupe between 1275 and 1285. Thomas and William were apparently the principal first names of the lords of Venn for a century.[18]

William of Fenn is likely to have been the last male heir in that family and the estate at Venn passed to two heiresses one of whom married an Avenbury and the other a Hakelut. The Hakeluts were an old Herefordshire family with property in Leominster and Eyton. In 1295, Walter Hakelut was renting to Henry of the Rhea, Stanford Regis (now part of Bishop's Frome), an acre of arable ground in Venn. Eight years later Walter Hakelut together with Giles of Avenbury shared the lordship of Venn.[19] The Hakeluts were probably in possession of Lower Venn while the Avenburys held Upper Venn. Walter was followed by Edmund Hakelut and in 1327-8 Isabel le Croupes with her husband Richard sued Edmund Hakelut and William of Orleton for Isabel's dower in 'Venn by Avenbury'. It would appear that Isabel was the mother of Edmund and after the death of her husband had married Richard le Croupes.[20]

Edmund was followed by another Edmund Hakelut who in 1373 had a half knight's fee at Lower Venn (*La Venne Inferiore*) from Humphrey de Bohun, earl of Hereford, who was also the lord of Kington. Venn had passed by 1431 to the Walwyn family of Longworth, perhaps by marriage, and in the 16th century was part of the extensive possessions of the Pichard or Pychard Family of Paunton Court and Avenbury.[21]

DESCENT OF VENN

Overlords

1066 Spirtes the Priest
1086 Nigel the Doctor
*c*1109 the King
*c*1135 de Port Family, of the honour of Kington

Sub-tenants

1143 Lord of Venne
1164 Thomas *Delfanc*
1211-12 William of Venn
1243 Thomas of Venn
1249 William of Venn who left 2 heiresses

	Upper Venn	**Lower Venn**
	one married an Avenbury	one married a Hakelut
1303	Giles of Avenbury	Walter Hakelut
1327	Unknown	Edmund Hakelut
1373	Unknown	Edmund Hakelut

1431 William Walwyn of Longworth
1556 William Pychard of Avenbury?= Margaret Abington of Brockhampton
John and Alice Pychard of Paunton
2 daughters and heiresses

	Upper Venn	**Lower Venn**
	Margery m George de la Dounes (died 1598)	Dorothy = Robert Dounes
1567	Robert Dounes sold ½ the Venn to William Tyffin	
1585	Margaret Pychard	
1663	John Pembridge	Mr Stitch

Dorothy and Margery Pychard were the daughters and coheirs of John and Alice Pychard and married respectively Robert Dounes and George de la Dounes, who may have been brothers. In Bishop's Frome church there is an enchanting painting to the memory of Margery de la Downes 1598, with two kneeling figures facing one another across a prayer-desk. We know that in 1567, Robert Dounes sold half of the Venn in Avenbury to William Tyffin (see above). Nearly three centuries later in the tithe survey, Lower Venn was 172 acres and Upper Venn 180 acres, and this might be evidence that this had been a fairly equal partition of the estate.

Little Froome

'LAND OF ROGER DE LACY

> 'FROME. Hugh holds from him. Leofsi held it; he could go where he would. 1 hide which pays tax. In lordship 1 plough; 3 villagers with 1 plough. 2 slaves; a mill at 32d. Value before 1066, 20s; now 15s.'[22]

Little Froome was a small estate, bounded on the north and east by the manor of Bromyard with the river Frome forming much of its eastern boundary; the manor of Avenbury formed the southern boundary. The manor of Little Froome belonged in 1066 to Leofsi who also held the nearby manors of Keephill and Bredenbury, and he could 'go where he would', that is choose his own over-lord. By 1086 the great Norman landowner Roger de Lacy was the overlord and his tenant, his brother Hugh de Lacy, held Little Froome together with Sawbury Hill, Collington and land in Wolferlow. Little Froome had been worth 20s in 1066 but 20 years later the value had diminished to 15s. The estate comprised one hide of land, with the lord's farm having land for one plough with two slaves, and two village farmers having sufficient land for one plough between them; there was also a mill worth 32d. Little Froome is so close to Bromyard that it is difficult to understand how this small manor could have achieved independence from that great ecclesiastical territory. Perhaps a former lord here was honoured by his ruler or the church for loyalty and service worthy of such a reward.

By 1137 the Lacy family had established a sub-tenant, Ansfrid de Cuillardville, on their manors of Wolferlow and Little Froome.[23] By 1166, - Cuillardville held three knight's fees from Hugh de Lacy, lord of Weobley, one of which was Wolferlow and Little Frome.[24] These two manors continued to be held of the honour of Weobley and were in 1243 held by Roger English, who may have been kin to Gilbert English who held Stanford Regis from Henry II in 1170.[25] In 1303, John de Genevill, Walter Underliche and Robert of Swindon were named together to provide one knight's fee for Wolferlow and Frome value 40s. Robert of Swindon was the next sub-tenant of Wolferlow and Little Froome and he held the manors from Joan, the daughter and heiress of Peter de Genville by an heiress of Walter de Lacy of Weobley. Joan married Roger de Mortimer, earl of March, who was executed in 1330; Joan died in 1356. It was at about this time that Little Froome came into the hands of the Brown family, for when a later Roger de Mortimer, earl of March, died in 1396, it was recorded that one knight's fee at Little Froome had formerly been held by John Brown.[26]

An undated deed, possibly pre-1300, relating to two acres of land upon Bromyard Down, which were being granted by Walter Clement to Roger Paris 'to aquit him from the Jews', was witnessed by Hugh the lord of Little Froome, Hugh the younger, Adam of Horton, Walter of Frome and William the younger of Frome with Elias the clerk.[27]

The Brown family are known to have been lords of this manor and to have resided at Little Froome for many generations. John Brown represented Herefordshire in Parliament in 1326 while William Brown served the same office in 1335, having been bailiff of Bromyard four years earlier. In 1356-7 John and William Brown were witnesses when the bishop of Hereford made a grant of lands at Keephill. Richard Brown was lord here in 1575 and had considerable property in Bromyard at the same time.[28] The Brown family of Little Froome were active at both local and county level and 'Anthony Brown of *Frome Parva*, gent' was recorded in a 17th-century catalogue of 'the nobility and principal gentry of this county'.[29] In many cases they married into other important local families. William Brown married in the 15th century Perin, a daughter and coheir of John Domulton of Brockhampton, and subsequently the Brown family were part owners of Dumbleton (Domulton) Hall in Bromyard. A branch of the family later moved to Hall Court in Bishop's Frome and remained there until this century.

OWNERS AND OCCUPIERS OF LITTLE FROOME MANOR

1066 Leofsi
1086 Roger de Lacy
Hugh (his tenant)
Hugh the Lord of Little Froome

Sub-Tenants of the Lacy family of Weobley
1137 Ansfrid de Cuillardville
1166 Ansfrid de Cuillardville of the honour of Weobley
1243 Robert English
1303 John de Genevill, Walter Underliche, Robert of Swindon
Robert of Swindon
1326 John Brown MP
1331 William Brown, bailiff of Bromyard
1335 William Brown MP
1356 William and John Brown
1387 William and Stephen sons of William Brown
1431 John Brown
*c*1450 William Brown = Perin Domulton
*c*1500 John Brown = Ann Unett
1535 John Brown decd.
John Brown
1575 Richard Brown
1650 Anthony Brown

Hopton Sollers or Upper Hopton

> 'William (son of Norman) also holds Hopton (Sollers), and Richere from him. Brictmer held it; he could go where he would. 1 hide and 1 virgate which pay tax. In lordship 1 plough; 3 villagers and 2 smallholders with 3 ploughs; 4 slaves. Value before 1066, 30s; now as much.'[30]

Hopton means 'settlement in a secluded valley' and the estate is situated at the south-west of Avenbury where the land slopes down towards Stoke Lacy. The prefix Upper distinguishes this Hopton from Lower Hopton further down the valley in Stoke Lacy parish. Brictmer, who held the manor in 1066, may be the same Brictmer who then held Castle Frome, Munsley and Ledicote in Herefordshire. William son of Norman, otherwise known as William Fitz Norman the overlord in 1086, was also lord of Kilpeck in Herefordshire. His son Hugh founded the priory of Kilpeck in 1134 and gave to it the tithe of his demesne lands at Hopton. With the lords of Kilpeck as overlords, Hopton came into the hands of the Sollers family who originated in Solieres near Caen in Normandy. It is possible that Richere, the tenant of 1086, was Richard de Sollers who at that time held Sollers Hope, Herefordshire from Ansfrid de Cormeilles.[31] Today the farm is known locally as Hopton Sollars, not Sollers.

Hopton was enfeoffed, that is held by knight's service, before 1135, and Margery de Sollers had one hide at Hopton Sollers from Hugh of Kilpeck for one fifth of a knight's fee in 1243. In 1310, Thomas de Sollers who appears to have been a descendant of Margery, had a half knight's fee at Hopton Sollers for which he paid 20s to the barony of Kilpeck; by 1346 Juliana de Sollers was responsible for this payment and service. Hopton Sollers then passed to the Whittington or Whytington family by the marriage of Maud Sollers with William Whittington of Pauntley, Gloucestershire, to whom also passed the manor of Sollers Hope. Guy of Whittington held this manor by military service in 1431. He also appeared in a charter relating to Much Cowarne, Herefordshire when Thomas Mylle, then lord of Avenbury was a witness.[32] The Sollers and Whittingtons were followed by a family called Hopton who possessed the manor of Hopton Sollers for many generations 'the former giving their name to the place and the latter taking theirs from it'.[33]

The Dudgen family were at Hopton Sollers during the 16th century and Phillipe Dougyn (whom it is thought was a Dudgen of Hopton Sollers) married Anne Wykes of Moreton Jeffreys during that century. Anne Wykes was a grand-daughter of Richard and Elizabeth Habington of Lower Brockhampton near Bromyard.[34] George Dudgen of Hopton Sollers signed the church terrier in 1589 as one of the guardians of Avenbury Church. His will dated 1609 is in the Herefordshire Record Office and in it he requested to be buried within the chancel of Stoke Lacy Church 'neare unto the place where my father is buried'. He gave to the parish church of Avenbury 3s 4d and a similar sum to the church of Stoke Lacy; in addition he left money and loaves of bread to named poor of the parishes of Avenbury, Stoke Lacy and Bishop's Frome 'to be equally divided between them by the division of our overseers' (this developed into an annual charity). George

Dudgen left a considerable number of legacies to servants and relatives, but the bulk of his estate went to his wife Margaret and their daughter Anne, the wife of William Nicholett.

William Nicholett's family came from Eastham near Tenbury in Worcestershire. A Richard Nicholett of the Hill, Eastham had married *c*1525 Alice Percival Fitzurse of Hall Court, Bishop's Frome and their son William married Ann Rowden of Rowden near Bromyard, so the family had strong local ties. William and Ann's eldest son Richard married Beatrix Baylie of Shropshire. Richard died in 1620 and it was his son William who married Anne Dudgen of Hopton Sollers; they may have lived at Hopton but were both buried at Eastham. John Duncumb claimed that the Nicholett family purchased Hopton in about 1550 but C J Robinson was of the opinion that it was the marriage to George Dudgen's daughter and heiress that brought the Nicholetts to Hopton.[35]

'Here lieth the body of William Nicholets, esq. Late high sheriff of Herefordshire, and Ann his wife, daughter and sole heir of George Dudgin of Hopton Solers, in the county of Hereford, gent. being both deceased. viz: the said William, the 18th day of February, Anno Domini 1643, and the said Anne, the ....(undated, but after 1649). They had issue five sons and three daughters.'[36]

OWNERS AND OCCUPIERS OF HOPTON SOLLERS

1066 Brictmer
1086 William son of Norman, lord of Kilpeck
Richere
Sollers family
1216 Margery Sollers
1303 Thomas de Sollers
1346 Juliana de Sollers
Maud Sollers = William Whytington
1431 Guido (Guy) de Whityngton
William Hopton of Hopton Sollers = Margaret Hevyn
Richard Hopton = Jone Langford
*c*1550 Hopton Family
Phillipe Dougyn = Anne Wykes
d1609 George Dudgen of Hopton Sollers = Margaret
Anne Dudgen = William Nicholett
d after 1649 d1643

Noakes

Noakes was a detached portion of Avenbury parish until 1882 and is now a part of the parish of Bredenbury. In Saxon times Noakes had possibly been - episcopal land, for under the heading of 'LAND OF THE CHURCH OF HEREFORD' the following entry appears in Domesday:

> 'These hides paid tax with Bishop (Walter) before 1066:
> in Tedstone 2½ hides, in Sawbury (Hill) ½ hide, in Yarsop 3 virgates of land ,
> and in Noakes 1 hide and 1 virgate.'[37]

These estates could have represented a five hide holding, which is thought to have been originally one knight's fee. By 1086 Noakes was evidently held from the crown by Charbonnel or Carbonel, an ancestor possibly of the Shropshire family who gave their name to Ashford Carbonel.

LAND OF CHARBONNEL

> 'Charbonnel holds Noakes from the king. Colgrim held it; he could go where he would. 1 hide which pays tax. ½ plough. 2 villagers with 1 plough. The value was 30s; later 20s; now 24s.'[38]

Here we have an estate with a demesne farm belonging to the lord, and two village farms. The name has been spelt in many ways over the centuries and was originally *atten okes* which means 'at the oak trees'. It then became *La Okes* 'the oak trees', which names became respectively Noakes and *Lacre*.[39]

Charbonnel's hide of land at Noakes passed, possibly by marriage, to the de la Hay family of Urishay, near Snodhill, Herefordshire, and W(illiam) de Lac whose name appears against Noakes in 1160-70 is thought to have been William de la Hay[40]. In 1198, Roger of Hay had land at Noakes valued at l0s a year; and the hide at Noakes held by Roger in 1212 was said to have been held since the 'Conquest of England' (that is 1066) for the service of summoning the lord of Richard's Castle to war and for conducting the king's treasure, the royal revenue of the shire, to London at Easter and Michaelmas at the cost of the king. Noakes was held directly from the crown by a personal service called 'grand serjeanty'; for this reason, many early references to the estate have survived. Roger of Hay married Emma the widow of Hugh de *Aqua* (of the Rhea, Stanford Regis now in the parish of Bishop's Frome), but Noakes passed to his younger brother Thomas of Akes who between 1226-8 held land at Noakes valued at 40s a year. After the death of Thomas before 1242-3, Noakes was inherited by his two daughters Agnes and Lucy; although for a time William de Helyun held the hide of land in *Hakes* as their guardian.[41]

Agnes, who had married John(?) of Blaisdon, died in 1295 leaving her son Thomas of Blaisdon her heir to a part of Noakes comprising nine houses, 60 acres of arable land, two acres of meadow, an acre of pasture and one and a half acres of wood. Six free tenants paid a rent of 8s 6½d a year. The estate was the royal reward for 'the service of finding one horse towards conducting the King's treasure from Hereford to London, for which she was to be allowed twelve pence per day in going and nothing on the return'.[42]

The other part belonged at this time to Lawrence d'Abitot and was the inheritance of his wife Lucy. Lawrence and Lucy were both dead by 1303 and Lucy's daughters, Cecily born in 1267 and Sybil born in 1272, were heirs to this portion of the Noakes estate:

'La Okes...a messuage, 30a. arable, la. meadow, 1½a. wood, and 5 free tenants rendering 40s. l0d. yearly, held of the king in chief, by the courtesy of England of the inheritance of Lucy sometime his wife by the grand serjeanty of conducting the king's treasure from the castle of Hereford to London, taking 12d. daily in going and nothing in returning, and he ought to summon the bishop of Hereford to Bromyard when impleaded by the king.'[43]

Richard of Blaisdon, son of Thomas and grandson of Agnes, died in 1337 and left his share of Noakes to his kinsman John of Holford, who was the grandson of Lucy and Lawrence d'Abitot, and the son of Cecily d'Abitot who had married Thomas of Holford. Consequently after about a century of divided ownership, Noakes was reunited in the hands of John of Holford. In 1387 William Brown, surely a member of the family associated with Little Froome, died seised of property in the Okes, Avenbury, which he held from the Crown by the service of grand sergeanty. Did William Brown come to the estate by marriage, inheritance or purchase? We may never know.[44]

Such a full record of the owners of an estate and also the rents, number of tenants, acreage and houses is uncommon in the Bromyard district for that date. It illustrates that from the lord's farm and two villagers in 1086, there were by 1300 at least nine houses and families and probably more. The population of Noakes could then have exceeded 40-50 persons, possibly supported by agriculture, or supplemented by a local industry such as timber which might have developed 'at the oak trees'.

DESCENT OF NOAKES

Saxon Times Bishop of Hereford
1066 Colgrim
1086 Charbonnel
de la Hay family of Urishay, Herefordshire
1160-70 William de la Hay
1198 Roger de la Hay = Emma widow of Hugh de *Aqua*
1226-8 Thomas de la Hay younger brother of Roger

Agnes d1295
= John? of Blaisdon

Thomas of Blaisdon

Richard of Blaisdon d1337

Lucy
=Lawrence d'Abitot

Cecily
=Thomas de Holford

John of Holford

Sybil

John of Holford
1387 William Brown
Brown family of Little Froome

Sawbury Hill

> 'These hides paid tax with Bishop W(alter) before 1066: in Tedstone 2½ hides, in Sawbury (Hill) ½ hide, in Yarsop 3 virgates of land, and in Noaks 1 hide and 1 virgate'.

LAND OF ROGER de LACY.

> SAWBURY (HILL). Hugh holds from him. Wynric held it. 2½ virgates. Land for 1 plough. It was and is waste.[45]

At the time of the Norman Conquest this small but prestigious estate was called Sargeberie which means 'sallow-willow hill'.[46] At some time it may have been a fortified site, for the house stands in a commanding position at above 154 metres (500 feet). Like Noakes, Sawbury Hill was a detached portion of Avenbury parish situated beside the ancient droveway from Wales to the Midlands. This later became the coaching road from London to Aberystwyth and today is the A44. The two and a half virgate property (just over half a hide) had belonged to Wynric at the end of the Saxon period and was his only estate in Herefordshire; Sawbury like Noakes had paid tax with Bishop Walter of Hereford. Twenty years later Sawbury was part of the Herefordshire fief of the great Norman baron Roger de Lacy and was sub-let to his brother Hugh who held other land in the district including Wolferlow, Little Froome and Collington. Sawbury had sufficient land for one plough but paid no tax as it was waste and had been in Wynric's time.

Roger de Lacy lost his lands in 1095 for rebellion, and some of his Herefordshire manors including Sawbury passed to Bernard de Neufmarche, the conqueror of Brecknock. After Bernard's death in 1125 his lands passed by way of his daughter to her husband Miles of Gloucester; between 1137-9 Sawbury was held by knight service.[47] From Miles the lands again went with the female line via his daughter to William de Braoze who died in 1175. Another William de Braoze subsequently exchanged Sawbury and other manors in north-east Herefordshire with manors belonging to the lord of Richard's Castle near Radnor and Kington. After this Sawbury was held of the honour of Richard's Castle. Richard de Curzon in 1243 had the half hide at Sawbury by military service for the 16th part of a knight's fee and John le Moigne of Rowden was his sub-tenant.[48] At the same time the tenant of Noakes had the responsibility for summoning the lord of Richard's Castle to attend the king when it was necessary.

Sawbury apparently remained with the manor of Rowden, which lies about a mile to the north, and they are separated by the intervening estate of Hardwick.

THE DESCENT OF SAWBURY HILL 1066-1600

1066 Bishop Walter
Wynric
1086 Roger de Lacy
Hugh de Lacy his tenant
1095 Bernard de Neufmarche
1125 Miles of Gloucester
William de Braoze
1175 William de Braoze
1243 Richard de Curzon
John le Moigne his sub-tenant
*c*1274 Sir Ralph le Moigne
Sir John le Moigne
Sir Ralph le Moigne
*c*1310 Alice le Moigne = Thomas Townley, esq
*c*1321 John Townley of Rowden
*c*1362 Richard of Rowden
*c*1428 William of Rowden
John of Rowden = Ann, daughter and heir of James Helyon of Bredenbury
James Rowden = Joan Brown of Little Froome, Bromyard
1505-1564 Richard Rowden = Sibyl, daughter of Sir John Baskerville of Combe
The Rowden Estate

A close view from the air of the site of Avenbury Church showing the ruined tower within the churchyard.
Copyright 2000, *Chris Musson and the Woolhope Naturalists Field Club.* (*Photo Ref: MB-0545*)

PART II

AVENBURY PARISH FROM THE TUDOR PERIOD

Chapter 5

The Church of St Mary after the Dissolution of the Monasteries

> 'I give and bequeath unto the said Richard Whitehead and Thomas Corbett the p[ar]sonage howse nowe in my occupacion, the one baye of the p[ar]sonage barne wherein the mustmill nowe standeth and the use of the mustmill. The p[ar]sonage fould the garden belonginge to the said p[ar]sonage howse and the Churchyard there with all the fruite belonging to the saide p[ar]sonage howse for the space of tenne years next after my decease...the saide Richard and Thomas keepinge the Channcell there in rep[ar]acions'
>
> HRO Will of John Corbett of Avenbury 1637

The Dissolution of the Monasteries 1536

When the Crown suppressed or dissolved the monasteries between the years 1536-1540, it acquired not only the monasteries themselves, but also their other possessions including the advowsons, income and property of many churches which had been given them over a long period. The Crown sold off or let most of these to lay people who are known as 'lay impropriators' or sometimes 'lay rectors' who also acquired the obligation to provide for a vicar. Impropriators sometimes let or sub-let all or part of this property to others who were known as lessees. A church's glebe (that is, the land with which it had been originally or progressively endowed within the parish to help provide a living for the priest) was not involved in these changes unless all or part of it had been given to a religious house with the advowson and tithes. Later evidence (below) suggests that this had in fact happened in Avenbury.

As we saw in Chapter 3, in the centuries before the Dissolution, Avenbury Church had been held at various times by the church of Worcester, St Guthlac's Priory and Abbey Dore. In 1536 Abbey Dore was suppressed by the crown and its tithes and income confiscated; at that date the annual income of the abbey was just over £100.[1] The Crown retained the advowson of Avenbury for some 300 years but was soon to sell the property and tithes to John Harford and John Farley (see pages 60, 65). There is no record before the late 16th century of the extent of the parish glebe. Whatever the situation in the earliest days of the church, by the time of the Conquest the church and its lands were evidently regarded as the property of the lord of Avenbury.

Property and Land belonging to the Church 1547-1628

In 1547-48 the chantry certificates for Avenbury disclosed that there were in the parish 100 'houselynge people', that is 100 communicants; there was a lamplight in the church for the upkeep of which two acres of land had been given; there were no plate or jewels here and 'In an ancient MSS ...without date apparently written some Hundred years ago the Church of Avenbury is valued at £12 yearly.'[2]

The houses occupied by the incumbents of Avenbury have been built in at least three different locations over the centuries. The final vicarage which is now called the Old Vicarage stands south-west of the church beside the road that leads from the church to Avenbury Court. This house was built in 1854 on land belonging to the Court and given by John Freeman for the purpose of providing an appropriate home for the Avenbury vicar. The previous vicarage, erected in 1682 and taken down in 1854, stood north of the church in the Avenbury Lane on glebe called Lime Paddock and opposite the Kilns. This house stood for only 172 years. Was the site not suitable? Or was the house not very well constructed? For this seems a short life for such an important parish building. Before this, the Parsonage House stood in the more traditional position adjacent to the churchyard.

Avenbury Chalice, London hallmark 1571. Maker's mark H B possibly H Y Boswell. Cover paten undated and later than Chalice. Now in Hereford Museum. It is thought that the chalice or paten could have been a gift to the parish by the Cooke family of Munderfield Court.
Howard Painter

The Old Parsonage

The original parsonage was probably on the site used by the earliest religious community here and a slight sign of earthworks still remains in Church Meadow adjacent and east of the churchyard (see Map 6). Although very close to the river the site may rarely have flooded. The river bed is very deep, as much as 12 feet, and quickly clears of flood water. A flooded field is remembered but on that occasion a great deal of loose hay had been washed against the road bridge. The bridge would not have been there when the site was chosen and the river would have been crossed by a convenient ford. A footbridge on very substantial stone foundations anchored into the bank still remains for access from the church and St Agatha's Meadow to the Lime Paddock; it was no doubt used by both vicars and parishioners and is today kept in repair for farmers and walkers.

In 1589 a terrier of 'what glebelands and other privileges doth belong to the parsonage and vicarage there' was drawn up by Richard Boyce and George Dogin who were the Avenbury guardians (churchwardens) and by Roger Corbett and

Lady on the footbridge across the river Frome. The way leads to Avenbury Church.
Bromyard Local History Society Collection

Earthworks and site of old parsonage. *Richard Percy*

Richard Comynge who were probably the sidesmen.[3] Belonging to the parsonage was 'one dwelling howse one barne one stable and oxe howse', Walle Meadow of three acres, the Barn Meadow of two acres, two plocks of two acres and one acre of meadow in all eight acres. Belonging to the vicarage, the church officers described 'one dwelling house called the vicaradge house and garden before the door, one orchard and one little meadow containing one acre and adjoining to the churchyard'. The vicar also received £7 6s 8d by composition: and £3 6s 8d given by the parson out of the rectory: and out of the rectory of Bredenbury yearly 2s. A description of 62 acres of land which belonged to the vicarage followed. 'And we do present the vicar to be presented the patron of the Parsonage.' A parsonage was the house of the parson, who could be a rector, vicar or beneficed clergyman; this could mean that the vicar occupied the parsonage. It is difficult three centuries later to say with confidence just where the vicar's dwelling stood. It is quite possible that the vicars lived in part of the parsonage next to the church.

Thirty years later 'a terrier of all the glebe belonging to the vicarage of Avenbury' was drawn up for the parish by Edward Lane dated 28th September 1619, which reads:

> 'One parcel of meadow ground called St. Agatha's meadow being one acre or thereabouts. One orchard adjoining parte, on the other side unto the Parsonage House and Churchyard being one quarter of an acre or thereabouts. A fold called the Vicar's Fold. The Vicar doth challenge 60 acres of arable land more but where it lye knows not neither can he testify.' Signed by their marks Edward Lane, Richard Boyce, Richard Mayfort.

Finally a terrier of 1628 explains:

> 'Whereas the churchwardens of Avenbury are enjoyned to put in a terrier into the registors office for the diocese of Hereford according to the 87 cannon we the minister and churchwardens and others the parishioners of Avenbury whose names are hereunto subscribed doe hereby testify that here belongeth unto the vicarige of Avenbury one parcel of meadow ground commonly called St. Agatha's meadow compassed about with the broke or river running near unto the said church on the west north and east and on the south with the churchyard. One orchard unto the sayd vicarige likewise belonging and appertaining which orchard is bounded on the east with the said broke or river and on the north side with the said meadow, on the west with the sayd churchyard and on the south with a footpath or way about two yardes distant from the parsonage house of Avenbury and which parcel of meadowe and orchard contain one acre of ground or there about and are all the landes which the several vicars and churchwardens to a severall knowledge and remembrance apperteynith or hath been enjoyed but whether there be more land due by the first endowment of the sayd vicarige or that the same be taken away by any latter composition we shortly know not but refferre those whom it in any way concerns unto the sayd endowment and composition if any such there be. And further we testify all the stipend which the vicar or curate now hath owing our memory is seaven poundes six shillings eyght pence yearly payed by equall portions quarterly and two

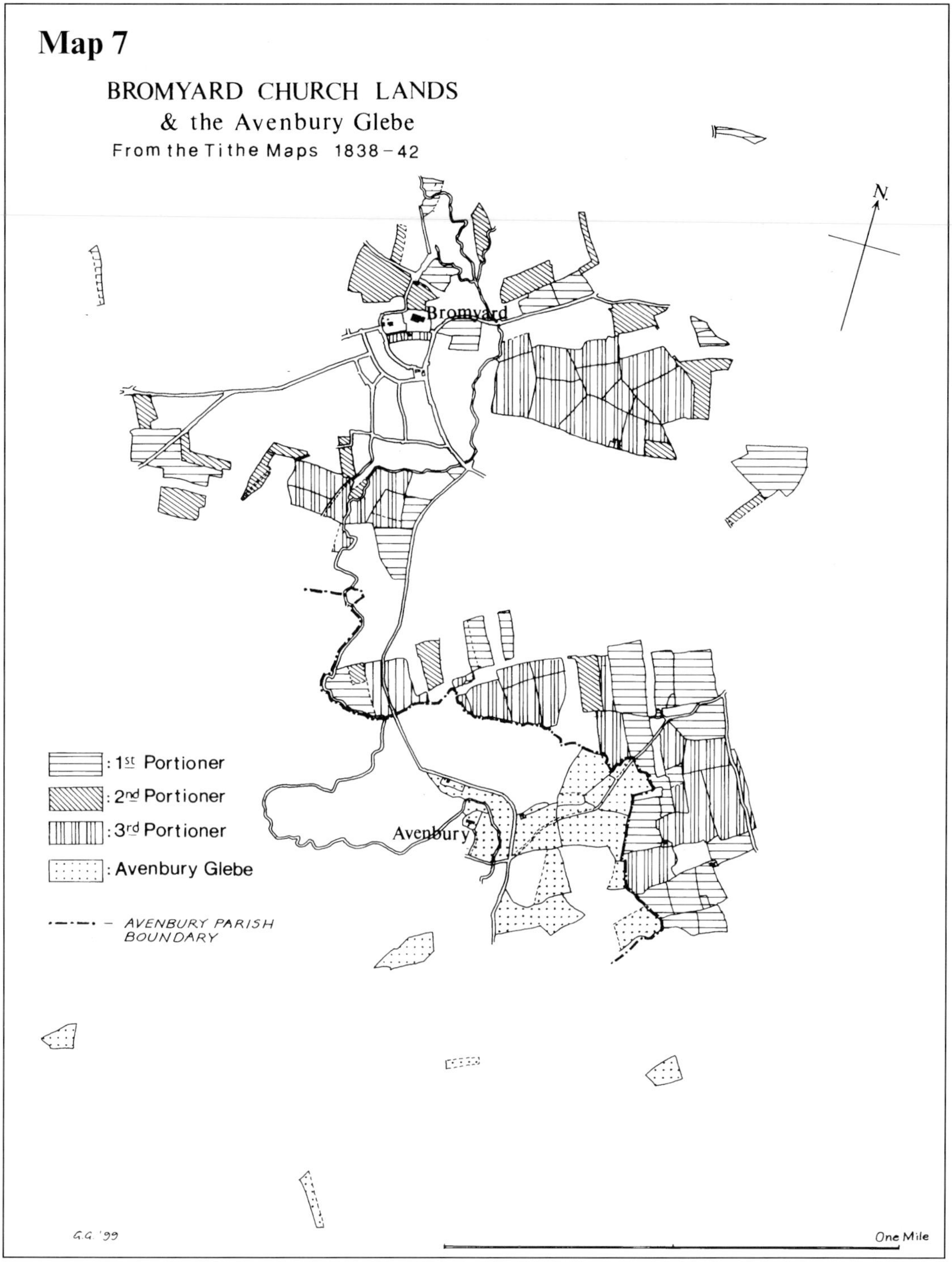
Map 7
BROMYARD CHURCH LANDS
& the Avenbury Glebe
From the Tithe Maps 1838 – 42
N.
Bromyard
Avenbury
: 1st Portioner
: 2nd Portioner
: 3rd Portioner
: Avenbury Glebe
– AVENBURY PARISH BOUNDARY
G.G. '99
One Mile

shillings upon Michaelmas day every yeare besides what shall happen to be due by churchinge marriages and burialls in the sayd parish whose truth of perfect knowledge herein in witness whereof we have put our hands the day and yeare above written

Richard Wilkes curate there
Richard Boyce and Henry Hill guardians
Henry Boyce sideman
John Fould, William Colly, John Handcox, with others.'

These terriers indicate that the parsonage and vicarage were on the same site in the meadow to the east of the churchyard between the church and the river. The house platform can just about be discerned on the ground and there are other earthworks and a fair quantity of stone in the vicinity. Before 1321 the parsonage would have been the house of the rectors of Avenbury in which subsequently the Abbot of Dore retained the use of the principal room and cellar beneath. The - vicarage is recorded as being repaired and extended in 1530 when George Borwych or Berewyche was vicar.

Problems

Of course the vicar and parish knew where the glebe lay. Even today the farmers who farm that land are aware of its earlier history as church land, and part is still called Church or Vicarage Banks. Less than 40 years had elapsed between the 1589 terrier and that of 1628. We are fortunate that the earlier terrier survived and it enables us to see that the tithe schedule of 1840 shows similar fields belonging to the glebe. It seems likely that the land belonging to the two priests in 1086 was a ploughland allocated to the church, a twelfth of the villagers' arable in the manor.[4] The lord himself had only three ploughs on his farm. It is thought that where the church and village farmers were listed together for their plough lands the manor may have been practising a common open field type of farming.[5] Certainly the 1589 terrier describes at several points what appear to be common fields: 'Grove Field', 'Burley Field', 'Tutt Hill' (look-out hill), 'Debdale Field' (deep valley or portion), 'Thorne Batch' (thorny valley with a stream), 'one acre of pasture land lying in A Bach' (wet or watery valley with a stream). 'A Bach' can be found on the tithe map as Abbage near the Venn when it still was part of the glebe.

The reason for the discrepancy was that lay impropriators were now in possession of the tithes and church land, but from which they were supposed to allocate sufficient income to support the vicar. The Puritan Survey of *c*1642 explained that Richard Lechmere was impropriator of Avenbury, then worth £100 a year. Mr Barber the curate served there for an annual salary of £8 'and seldome preacheth, a careless schoole master of the Free Schoole of Bromyard and serveth the one also at Brockhampton and a very dissolute man in life'. [6] Poor Avenbury, perhaps Mr Barber had to teach to earn sufficient to live on and then had little energy left to preach.

About 1648 the vicar, Humphrey Barber, together with some Avenbury parishioners who included John Eckley, Richard Bullock and Henry Boyce were taken to court by Richard Corbett, tenant 'for divers years yet to come' and Thomas Hackett, farmer 'of the rectory & parsonage impropriate of Avenbury', in a case relating to the great and small tithes of the parish. These it was said had been enjoyed since the reign of Henry VIII by the impropriators until Humphrey Barber as vicar there did claim all the small tithes for his use. Judgement was finally given in 1650 by which time Phineas Jackson was vicar. The impropriators were to have both the great and small tithe and the glebe and were to pay the vicar a clear annual sum of £30 and the vicar was also to enjoy St Agatha's Meadow.[7]

This judgement apparently did not stick. The Corbett family had the tithes and glebe for several generations and in 1682 the vicar, Thomas Kettleby, took a suit in the Court of the Exchequer against Richard Corbett. Kettleby claimed that when the rectory came to the crown, Edward VI granted it to John Harford and John Farley but reserved the small tithes and £3 annually for the vicar. He also said that in the original grant to Abbey Dore, the bishop and abbot had ensured a 'competent maintenance' for the vicar together with the rectory house (excepting to the use of the abbot the principal room and cellar beneath), the garden, orchard, 60 acres of land; the tithes of hay and other small tithes were also reserved for the vicar's income and use.[8]

A New Vicarage

For his part Richard Corbett claimed the rectory, all the lands and the small tithe and said that the vicar was only entitled to a yearly stipend of £7 6s 8d and St Agatha's Meadow. The court decided that the vicar should certainly enjoy St Agatha's Meadow and the stipend with any arrears. In addition he was to have the rectory house, garden and orchard. Furthermore the vicar's dwelling was to be rebuilt by Richard Corbett and commissioners were appointed to oversee this and to mark out the site. The new vicarage was built adjacent to the Avenbury Lane, in Lime Paddock which lay north-east of the church and river. The house was duly built at an estimated cost of £60, with another £1 15s spent on fencing; this was conveyed to the vicar and his stipend was raised to £30.

Why was it decided to build another house for the vicar? Either the Corbett Family decided to retain the old parsonage for their own occupation or use, or the building was by now very dilapidated. This old house was probably that in which the Abbot retained two rooms for the use of Dore Abbey by the settlement of 1321. By 1682 the building would have been standing for at least 350 years. Not a great age for a well-built house; many Avenbury farmhouses standing today are of that age or older and will certainly last another century or more. However the old parsonage could have been built well before 1321 and may have been ancient by the end of the 17th century.

An entry in the parish registers, opposite the year 1745 but referring to earlier events, recorded the marriage of John Walker, vicar of Avenbury, with Jane Earsley in January 1699 and continued:

> 'The aforesaid Mr. Walker was buryed in ye chappell of Brockhampton August ye 29 1713, he was Minister of that place 24 years & of Avenbury 23 years, he Recovered ye 30 pounds a year to ye Church by Edn Tryals in ye Exchequer with Mr Richd Corbett ... he was ye only Vicar that can be remembered to live at Avenbury'

and he must have lived in the new vicarage built about 1682.

The Abbot's Barn

The Abbot's Barn was also mentioned in the 1682 suit in the Court of the Exchequer; it was stone built and stood about a quarter of a mile from the church. This would be the barn reserved for the use of the Abbey Dore community in 1519 to house their tithe corn. The parsonage house stood between the church and the river and there may never have been farm buildings here for lack of space. The site of the Kilns close to the road and surrounded by glebe offers much more scope for handling, storing and keeping stock, corn, hay and straw. The 60 acres of glebe alone would require farm buildings and in 1086 this glebe was about 1/12th of the manorial arable; in addition the church was entitled to the tithe or tenth part of all the produce of the parish which was much more extensive than just the manor of Avenbury. The tithe was paid in produce, frequently bulky and requiring storage, not only for the corn and grass crops, but for the tenth part of flax, wool, hemp, apples and orchard fruits, honey and wax from bees, garden produce, the tenth lamb, pig, calf and chicken and so forth. In Bromyard by 1589 a sum of money was paid for each sheep sold, 4d for each foal, and for a pipe of cider 4d; the remainder of the produce however was still paid in kind.[9] No wonder tithe barns were often so large. The Abbot's Barn was built of stone and was apparently rebuilt about 1760 on the same site, presumably by one of the Corbett family who were still the lay impropriators.

The Corbett Family of Avenbury

The Corbett family have been associated with Avenbury since earliest records and their name derives from the Old French word *corb* which means 'raven'; the Avenbury Corbett crest is the raven within a shield. The family understand that they came to England from Normandy with William the Conqueror. Between 1665 and 1765 this was the most prolific family in the parish with some 80 entries in the parish registers. Corbetts served regularly as parish officers with a John serving as churchwarden in 1703, 1717, 1732, 1775 and 1786; a Richard in 1746, 1755 and in 1759 for the Heath Farm. Men named John and Richard Corbett were active overseers of the poor between 1730-1786. Richard Corbett, gent died in 1689, John Corbett, gent in 1703, Edward Corbett, gent in 1728, another Richard Corbett, gent in 1746, and in 1764 Mr Thomas Corbett (sometime Impropriator of Tithes of this parish).

There are several family wills in the Herefordshire Record Office including that of Roger Corbett the elder dated 1602, John Corbett dated 1637 and Richard Corbett dated 1689. Both John and Richard were in possession of the parsonage house and the glebe and tithes of which they disposed in their wills. There is a memorial to Charles Joseph Corbett in the Church of Wareham le Hen in the County of Lincoln which says:

> 'Here lyeth in the Churchyard the body of Charles Joseph Corbett of Imber Court in this Parish Esquire the son of Joseph Corbett of Wareham le Hen in the Co. of Lincoln and grandson of John Corbett of Avenbury in the Co. of Hereford who was born the 29th day of May 1824 and died the 24th day of March 1882 leaving his daughter Elizabeth....'

Crest of the Corbett Family of Avenbury. *Charles Grant*

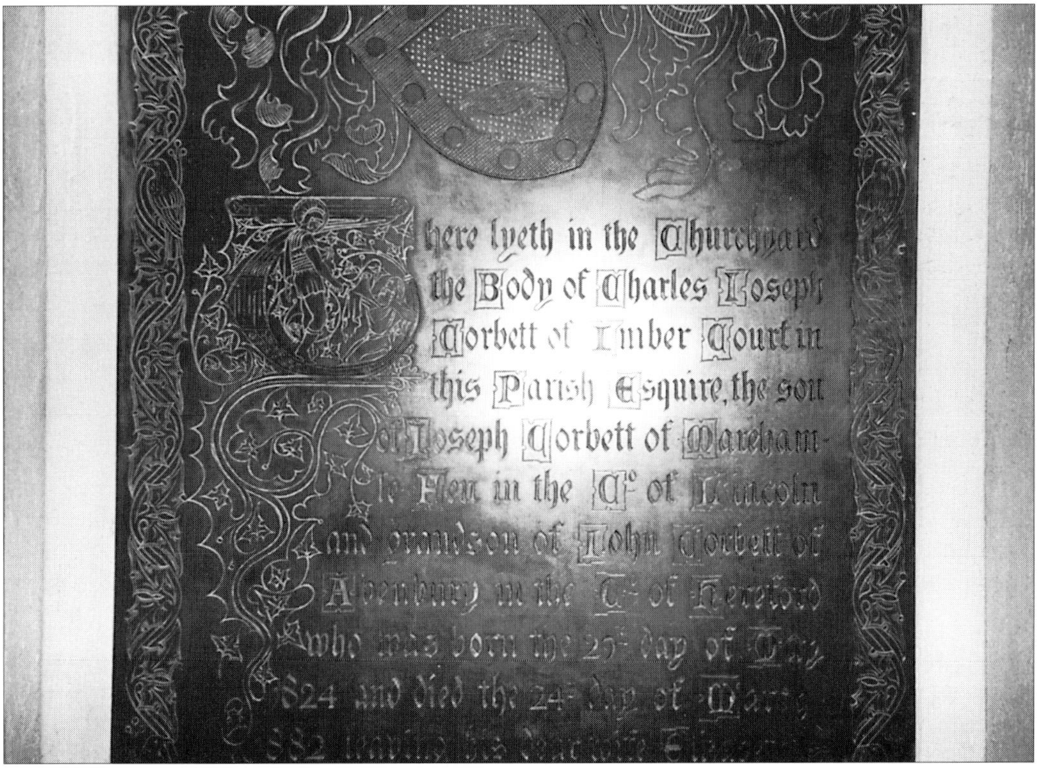

Corbett Memorial. *Peter Corbett*

John Corbett sold the tithes and glebe in 1794 to Ralph Cope Hopton, T Price and Richard Barneby, the last two men being solicitors of Worcester. Later Ralph Hopton's share was sold to a Bromyard solicitor, James Wormington. In 1812 the lay rectory of Avenbury comprised 60 acres of glebe, the great and small tithes and all other ecclesiastical dues from the whole parish, subject to £30 to the vicar annually and £23 17s 4d payment of the land tax.[10]

TABLE 4
IMPROPRIATORS, FARMERS AND LESSEES OF THE RECTORY OF AVENBURY

		Lessees
11th, 12th, 13th centuries	St Guthlac's Priory, Hereford	
1320-1536	Dore Abbey	
1530		Edward Myll
1536		John Myll
	Impropriators & Farmers	
1554	John Harford and John Ffarley	
1605	Thomas Hackett	Richard Corbett
1642	Richard Lechmere	
1648	Thomas Hackett	Richard Corbett
1663	John Hackett	
1686		Richard Corbett
1698		Richard Corbett
1703	Richard Corbett, grandson of Richard Corbett	
1771	Mr Hayles	
1783	Corbett	
1793	John Corbett	
1794	Ralph Cope Hopton, Messrs Price and Barneby (solicitors)	
	James Wormington, Messrs Price and Barneby (solicitors)	
1812	John Barneby, Messrs Price and Barneby (solicitors)	
1840	Edmund Higginson	

The Glebe

By 1840 the glebe and the tithes were in the hands of Edmund Higginson of Saltmarsh Castle, a Barneby by birth who changed his name after inheriting - Saltmarsh from his great-uncle William Higginson. The glebe comprised 59 acres and included the buildings of the Kilns. The vicarage still stood in Lime Paddock and was about 160 years old, the house was taken down 14 years later in 1854.

The vicar, the Rev William Haddy, was in the Vicarage and John Bennett was renting 46 acres of the glebe, for which the Kilns, formerly the Abbot's Barn, were the farm buildings. At this time, John Bennett junior rented and lived at the 42 acre Burley Farm, just up the gated road in Linton parish and the two farms may have been worked together. The rest of the glebe was in five different hands.

Thomas Berriman of Brookhouse rented five acres of glebe adjacent to his land in Bythan and Foxley at the eastern parish boundary; Henry Jenks of Avenbury Court had a small area in Debdale then called Deborah's Wall; Edward West who farmed the Hide in Stanford Bishop had two acres that bordered his land; James Edwards of Upper Venn incorporated 'Ladies Acre' with his farm; and two acres of wood at Cusop were retained in hand by Edmund Higginson. As to the Kilns, this could refer to lime kilns on the site especially as Lyme Paddock is just across the road, otherwise it may apply to brick kilns. There is no obvious sign or tradition of either. In 1851, the house was occupied by a farm labourer, Edward Brown and his family; 20 years later it was the home of another farm worker, John Evans, his wife Charlotte and their four children.

The glebe always appeared high on Avenbury taxation lists, because it included the value of the tithe or tenth part of the profit of the produce for the whole parish. We find in 1663, John Hackett assessed for the glebe and tithes at £48 which was double the assessment of John Brown of Little Froome who was the largest landholder in the parish. In 1777, Mr Hayles was assessed at £23 17s 4d for the glebe and tithe, while Richard West of Little Froome was listed at £14 for his property and Richard Corbett of Hopton at £12. The glebe and tithes passed from John Hackett to Richard Corbett at the end of the 17th century and appear to have remained with the Corbett family for more than a century, although an Avenbury parish rate of 1771 assessed Mr Hayles for the Glebe. In 1793 they passed to Ralph Cope Hopton and others, and the land tax return of 1798 shows Mr Hopton and Mr Thomas Price as the holders. By 1812 the Barnebys and Mr Price were listed as the owners. An abstract of title reveals that in 1815, one third part of the Rectory of Avenbury was purchased for £3,666 13s 4d, which means that the whole of the rectory comprising vicarage, glebe and tithes had the considerable capital value of £11,000.[11] The land tax return of 1831 showed Edmund Higginson as the sole owner when his assessment was £23 14s 4d.

The glebe was always around 60 acres, principally arable, and in early days this was the church's share of the community's land and would have been similar in size to the village farms. The greatest income for the rector and the church would have been from the tithe payments due from the whole area to which they ministered. With the passage of time village farms changed in size, the result of inheritance, partition, merging, sale, purchase, marriage and other factors. The glebe land remained the same as it belonged to an institution; consequently its extent in 1840 would be closer than that of other farms to the early pattern of landholding in the parish.

The Last Avenbury Vicarage

The third Vicarage, for which we know the site, is today called the Old Vicarage and stands between the ruined church and Avenbury Court. It was built in 1854 on land belonging to John Freeman which was part of the Court Farm, and had been chosen 'as a site for a Parsonage House'. Possibly John Freeman, who lived at Gaines in the nearby parish of Whitbourne, initially provided both the land and money to erect the house. On the 15th of March 1855 the Governors of the Bounty of Queen Anne for the augmentation of the maintenance of Poor Clergy paid John Freeman £130 for:

> 'All that messuage or dwelling house with the buildings, yards, gardens and land thereto adjoining and belonging and therewith occupied containing altogether half an acre or thereabouts ...bounded on the south by a public highway leading from Bromyard Downs to the town of Ledbury, on the west and north by other land of the said John Freeman and on the east by land of the Representatives of the late Very Reverend Charles Scott Luxmore, decd. late Dean of St Asaph ... Which messuage or dwelling house and buildings have lately been erected and are in the occupation of the Reverend James Archibald the vicar of the said vicarage and church of Avenbury'.[12]

The Rev John Shepherd was appointed to the living of Avenbury in 1859 and this was the childhood home of his son Edward Henry who was to be the last vicar of Avenbury.

Queen Anne's Bounty was established in 1704 by an Act of Parliament which renounced the Crown's rights to certain church income and applied it instead to the augmentation of poor livings. Parishes such as Avenbury, Bredenbury and

Avenbury Vicarage built in 1854 and with a Victorian postbox at the gate.
Howard Painter

Stanford Bishop with small rural populations all benefited from the fund. Apparently the sum of £200 had been allocated by the Governors for an augmentation of the vicarage or church of Avenbury.

The new Vicarage is now 145 years old and a delightful medium sized house; built of stone with dressed stone quoins around the windows and doors, and a large central chimney, it has been modernised but little altered. The stone stable and outbuildings were built at the same time as the house but are of plainer construction. The Governors of Queen Anne's Bounty purchased an adjacent acre of land for the Vicarage in 1873, which lay on the south-west side of the house and garden and was also part of Avenbury Court then belonging to Miss Frances Hooper of Tenby, Pembroke. A few years later in 1881, another acre was added to the Parsonage site by Edward Luxmore, the owner of Brookhouse Farm which had land to the east of the Vicarage. Recently another plot of adjacent land has been purchased and the site extends from the road to the river Frome.

For the Rev John Wilson who was vicar here in 1891, the stipend was £102 with a new vicarage built in 1854 and 9 acres of land. Whitbourne, a parish to the north-east of Bromyard, which was of similar size; but with a population of 745, (Avenbury at this time, had a population of 371) was able to pay their Rector over £500 a year and provide a large house with 34 acres of glebe. In 1919 the - Ecclesiastical Commissioners made a grant of £95 to the benefice of Avenbury to be paid to the Rev Edward Henry Archer-Shepherd as long as he should remain vicar here. If he remained for another four years he would be eligible for an additional pension of £75. In the 1920s efforts were made to raise the stipend of Avenbury to £200, however the writing was already on the wall. In 1920 in a letter to the *Hereford Times* Mr Archer-Shepherd wrote:

> 'The decision of the Bishop that the parish church should eventually be closed will come as a surprise to very many; but they, at least, will have no right to complain who by neglect of their parish church have contributed to that decision.'

The vicar complained bitterly of small congregations and lack of support. His late father was appointed to Avenbury in 1859 and had been a notable and popular preacher at his previous church, All Saints in Worcester. When he first came to this parish the congregation rose to some 80 people but within a short time dropped to its more regular number of seven to 15 parishioners.

Another factor that contributed to the low income of the church must be the absence, for several centuries of a resident lord of the manor. Furthermore by 1900 many of the larger farms were tenanted and landlords would have contributed to the upkeep of the parish church near their residence. The Rev E H Archer-Shepherd explained in another letter to the *Hereford Times* that the largest landowners, the Worcester Consolidated Municipal Charities, were not allowed to contribute to any Denominational object and other landowners had either sold or were trying to sell their farms.

For many centuries members of local and important families, including the Avenbury knight, had been buried and commemorated in Avenbury Church, contributing at the same time to the fabric and upkeep of this institution. No doubt people were still being buried here but they no longer had the resources of earlier generations.

Finally the church here had a role to fill so long as it was a focus for the parishioners. The Court had long since abdicated a duty of care in the manor, but the upkeep of roads, law and order and concern for the poor and needy had unified the farmers in maintaining local government that met and worked within the vestry. The 19th century found these duties being removed to unions of parishes and county districts which met elsewhere, frequently in Bromyard and Hereford. Although local government in Avenbury had always liaised and united with a larger area, the basic responsibility had been parochial and this was no longer so. The support system for Avenbury Church had withered away.

After the death of the Rev E H Archer-Shepherd, the last vicar of Avenbury, the Vicarage was sold by the Ecclesiastical Commissioners for England. In May 1932, Charles Edward Hughes who was the manager of Lloyds Bank in Bromyard and lived at that time in the Bank House purchased the property for £540 and came to live here. Mr Hughes sold the Old Vicarage in 1950 to the Skipp family who still live in the property.

What remains of Avenbury Church in 1999.
Howard Painter

The early 13th-century tower arch of Avenbury Church in 1999.
Howard Painter

TABLE 5

RECTORS, VICARS AND PATRONS OF THE CHURCH OF AVENBURY

RECTORS		PATRONS
Hugh of Mappenoure	c1199	Osbert of Avenbury
Gilbert de Bourghill	1277	Osbert of Avenbury
Roger le Rous	1313	Elinor le Rous
R Petit		Elinor or John le Rous
VICARS		
William Tokye	1320	Abbot & Convent of Dore
Thomas Webbe of Bromyard		"
Peter le Smyth	1349	"
William de Stocton	1360	"
Walter of Glazeley	1380	"
Thomas le Webbe	1383	"
Walter Parker	1409	"
John ap Reece	1411	"
David de Hay	1417	"
John Alleyne	1431	"
Nicholas Baron		"
Ralph Hurletone	1506	"
Hugh Martyn	1510	Bishop of Hereford
Henry Smith	1514	Abbot & Convent of Dore
John Longford	1515	"
George Borwych	1529	"
Roger Field	1563	The Crown*
Richard Hope	1574	"
Richard Evans		"
Richard Wilkes	1626	"
Humphrey Barber	1642	"
Phineas Jackson	1661	"
Thomas Kettelby	1668	"
John Walker	1698	"
John Jennings	1713	"
Joseph Taylor	1752	"
John Mogridge	1783	"
Richard Lloyd	1796	"
Charles Maund	1831	"
R H Williams	d1849	"
James Archibald	1851	"
John Shepherd	1859	Rev Arthur Childe
Robert Polwhele	1867	John Freeman
John Wilson	1878	Mrs Childe Freeman
E H Archer-Shepherd	1897	
	d1931	

*The Crown retained the right to appoint the incumbent of Avenbury.
Compiled from John Duncumb, *Collections towards the History and Antiquities of the County of Hereford* (1812); *The Registers of the bishops of Hereford*; Parish registers and trade directories for Herefordshire

Chapter 6

Landowners and Farmers

'I, therefore, Sir must apply to you for what is observable in your parish, and which the most diligent Enquirer cannot find out without the Information of knowing and judicious Men; who live either on the spot, or in the nearest Neighbourhood'.

HRO *'Letter from R Walwyn to Dr Roberts at Ross'* (1749)

In the past the inhabitants of parishes were bound together by parochial duties and the shared responsibilities of raising levies, taxes and tithes imposed on their properties. Of particular interest are the Militia Assessments of 1663 and the Hearth Tax Return of late 1665, which record the names of many of the 17th-century Avenbury families. These can be followed by the Land Tax Records, which for Avenbury date from the late 18th century and show different landholding families in the parish. Finally the Tithe Schedule of 1840 lists all the properties, owners and occupiers within the parish at that time.

Hereford Militia Assessments 1663

The Militia Acts of 1662 and 1663, permitted the king to appoint lords lieutenant and deputy lieutenants for each county to commission officers, to lead musters and to conduct military operations. Property owners within counties were responsible for providing horse and foot-soldiers, arms, ammunition, cartage and supplies. In Herefordshire, properties were charged within their respective parishes and the yearly value of each property was the basis of the assessment; that is the rate at which the premises could be honestly leased. The raters were usually chosen from the more substantial farmers who were responsible for making the valuation, which in Herefordshire was in the region of 3s an acre, dependent on the fertility and use of the land. The annual value for the whole county averaged 3s 4d per acre. The Avenbury raters were Richard Corbett, Robert Charlott and Richard Hancock (or Handcox) and they appear to have made their list in an ordered way round the parish, starting with John Browne at Little Froome and finishing with the land at Hopton.[1]

TABLE 6

AVENBURY AND HOPTON SOLLERS MILITIA ASSESSMENTS 1663			
	£	s	d
John Brown gent or his tenant	24	00	00
Thomas Crowther for the Mills	12	00	00
Henry Pitt	21	00	00
John Conney (Cunney)	6	00	00
Edward Porter for Birchingfeld	6	00	00
Anthony Rowden gent or his tenant	6	00	00
Alexander Gretton Esq or his tenant	6	00	00
Philip Bennett	3	00	00
William Sherriff for the Heath	21	00	00
John Michell for Burberies	12	00	00
John Ball gent or his tenant	9	00	00
Richard Corbett	9	00	00
John Hackett Esq for Glebe and Tithes	48	00	00
Edward Shepard for the Brookhouse	27	00	00
Mr Stitch for the Lower Venn	27	00	00
John Broome gent and his tenant William Sherriff	18	00	00
Richard Handcox gent	6	00	00
John Pembridge gent and his tenants	18	00	00
Mrs Katherine Selly (Scilly) widow	6	00	00
Thomas Taylor	3	00	00
John Farley gent for his brother Richard's lands	1	00	00
Robert Charlett gent	21	00	00
John Farley for his brother Wm's lands	12	00	00
John Love and John Pembridge gent	1	00	00
Roger Woodyate	6	00	00
William Bennett	3	00	00
Anne Corbett widow	3	00	00
Rowland Rea	1	00	00
William Lucas	2	00	00
Gilbert Nicholett Esq and his tenant	36	00	00
John Browne gent de Hall Court*	3	00	00
Rich Corbett or his tenant George Gough	3	00	00
William Caldow (Caldwell)	2	00	00
Charge	**383**	**00**	**00**

'This appears by the Table of Contributions Rule to be att halfe value.'
*Hall Court is in Bishop's Frome

Herefordshire Hearth Tax

This tax was levied at the rate of 1s a hearth for each half year on the occupiers of all houses except the very poor, and was taken from Michaelmas (29th September) 1662 to Lady Day (25th March) 1689. It was an unpopular tax and if the occupier failed to complete a return the constable was empowered to enter the house and count the hearths. The window tax which was imposed later was more acceptable because windows could be counted from outside the house. The 1665 Hearth Tax lists for Herefordshire are on micro-film at the Herefordshire Record Office and show some of the same people as the Militia Assessments of 1663. The 1663 Militia Assessment was on owners of land although from the Avenbury list it seems it could be paid by the tenants, no doubt by an agreement in the lease. The Hearth Tax was on the occupiers of houses and where the same people pay both they could be owner-occupiers.[2]

TABLE 7

AVENBURY AND HOPTON SOLLERS HEARTH TAX RETURNS 1665

	No. of Hearths
Gilbert Nicholett Esq	IX
Robert Charlott	V
Richard Corbett	V
Roger Woodyate	I
James Powell	III
Nicolas Evans	I
John Cunny	I
Henry Pytt	V
George South	I
Thomas Taylor	I
Thomas Bridges	I
William Colwall or Caldwell	I
Mr. Hughes farmer	IV
William Sherriffe	II
William Browne	II
Edward Shepard	II
William Cunny or Coney	II
William ffarlow gent	IIII
Mr Brownes	VIII
Thomas Wall	II
Joseph Woodroffe	V
Thomas Crowther	I
William Lucas	I
Richard Hancox and Katheryn Slee (1 stopt up)	IV
John Lowe or Love	I

However this list of 26 householders is not complete and the Lady Day return for 1664 in the Public Record Office shows 84 charged hearths, 31 charged houses and 52 total houses in Avenbury parish, which means that in 1664 twenty one occupiers were exempt on the grounds of poverty and possibly a similar number in 1665. The names of the Avenbury property owners and residents at this point in time helps to show some of the people and families that were associated with the parish in the mid-17th century.

TABLE 8

ESTATE OWNERS AND HEARTHS 1663-1665

	Estate Owners	Hearths*	Property Value £
1	John Hackett for glebe and tithes		48
2	Gilbert Nicholett for Hopton	9	36
3	Edward Shepard for Brookhouse	2	27
4	Mr Stitch for Lower Venn		27
5	John Brown for Little Froome	8	24
6	Henry Pytt (Noakes)	5	21
7	William Sherriff for the Heath	4	21
8	Robert Charlott (Cusop)	5	21
9	John Pembridge (Upper Venn)		18
10	John Broome and Wm Sherriff (Court)		18
11	John ffarley for brother Wm land	3?	12
12	Thomas Crowther for the Mills	1	12
13	John Michell for Burberies		12
14	John Ball or his tenant		9
15	Richard Corbett (the Greeve)		9
16	John Conney		6
17	Edward Porter for Birchingfield		6
18	Anthony Rowden or his tenant (Sawbury)		6
19	Alexander Gretton or his tenant (Hackley)		6
20	Richard Handcox (Munderfield)	4 (stopt up 1)	6
21	Mrs Katherine Selly, widow (Munderfield)	4	6
22	Roger Woodyate	1	6
23	Philip Bennett		3
24	Richard Brown de Hall Court		3
25	Thomas Taylor	1	3
26	Anne Corbett widow		3
27	William Bennett		3
28	Richard Corbett or his tenant George Gough		3

29	William Caldow (Caldwell)	1	2
30	William Lucas	1	2 10s
31	Rowland Rea		1 10s
32	John Love & John Pembridge gent.	1	1
33	John ffarley for his brother's lands (Richard ffarley)		1

*hearths if they can be identified

1. John Hackett for glebe and tithes, which attracted the highest assessment in Avenbury; for it represented not only the 60 acres of glebe but also the tithes or tenth part of the profits of the whole parish. This is the only entry for John Hackett in Herefordshire and he may have lived in another county; his wife Susannah appears with him for an indenture regarding Avenbury tithes in 1666.
2. Gilbert Nicholett of Hopton Sollers was High Sheriff of Herefordshire in 1668; his forbears had lived at Hopton and his son inherited the estate after his death in 1690.
3. Edward Shepard was the occupier of Brookhouse; his house with two chimneys was rebuilt around 1800.
4. Mr Stitch the owner of Lower Venn appears to be the Henry Stitch Esq who had a considerable estate in Stanford Regis which could have bordered Lower Venn. His assessment there of £82 10s represented half of that manor.
5. John Browne of Little Froome Manor was a member of an important Herefordshire family who had lived at Little Froome for generations; two of his ancestors had served in Parliament in the 14th century.
6. Henry Pytt was surely the son of Henry Pytt of the Noakes who died in 1661.
7. William Sheriff of the Heath was the owner occupier and evidently a large farmer for he rented another farm from John Broome, gentleman. The rented property could have been Avenbury Court, for the manor of Avenbury was said to have belonged to the Berrington family of Stoke Lacy at one time and Margaret Berrington married a John Brome.[3]
8. Robert Charlott probably lived at Cusop, where a widow Sarah Charlott was living at the end of the century. Several members of this family were commemorated by memorial slabs in the church between 1658-1696.
9. John Pembridge may have owned Upper Venn for this was a large and important farm and would have been in the higher range of property valuations. Elinora Pembridge was buried in Avenbury Church in 1665.
10. John Broome and his tenant William Sherriff. As mentioned at number 7 this may have been Avenbury Court and previously a Berrington property. A John Broome also had estates at Ewithington and Wolferlow in Herefordshire.

11. John, Richard and William ffarley. The family owned the Burgess in the 17th century which could be the house with three hearths in 1665.

12. Thomas Crowther for the Mills, surely Little Froome Mill, which as later documents show had three mills, that is three pairs of stones under one roof. The Mill, like the tithes, represented an income other than from just agriculture for milling was a service industry for the whole community. Thomas Crowther had one hearth.

13. John Michell for Burberies which one surmises was Nurburys.

14. John Ball could be the John Ball gent who also had property in Bromyard - borough, Linton and Bredenbury and was a considerable landowner.

15. Richard Corbett who had five chimneys. This would have been a large house possibly the Parsonage or perhaps the Greeve with which the family were associated for so many years. Richard Corbett, gentleman was buried in 1689 and Jane his widow 'and last wife of John Creswell, gentleman' was buried in 1697. The Corbett surname is known to have spanned nearly five centuries, for in 1514 the bishop of Hereford granted an Indulgence for contributions to the support of Richard Corbet of Avenbury 'ruined by fire'. There are still - Corbetts in the district.

16. John Conney perhaps of Rough Mintridge. In 1661 'Elizabeth the wife of John Conney de Kyrple (Keephill, Winslow)' died and John Conney also had a property in Winslow. Both John and William Conney occupied houses in Avenbury in 1665 and William and Elizabeth Conney produced a son, William, in 1661.

17. Edward Porter for Birchingfield; that would be Birchyfield.

18. Anthony Rowden or his tenant. It would seem that this was a property that lay on the edge of the parish; probably Sawbury Hill and Wiggall which had belonged to the le Moigne family of Rowden who were the ancestors of Anthony Rowden.

19. Alexander Gretton Esq or his tenant. Alexander Gretton was Clerk of the Spicery to both Charles I and Charles II and married Sarah Rumney of Suckley in Worcestershire. The Rumneys were an important family and this may have been an estate that Sarah brought to the marriage and is thought to be Hackley.[4]

20. Richard Handcox, gentleman died in 1682 and he appears quite frequently in Quarter Sessions records of the mid-17th century when he was serving Avenbury, probably as constable. He was one of the 1663 raters for the parish. The family lived at Munderfield Court and his mother was Mrs Katherine Selly who appears as Katherine Slee in 1665 when she shared her house with her son.

21. Mrs Katherine Selly, with her son Richard Handcox, had a house with four hearths of which one was 'stopt up'. In 1690, the twin sons of Richard and Maria Sely were baptised and within a few days were buried.
22. Roger Woodyate had one hearth and was probably the owner and occupier of his property; he died in 1672 leaving his estate to his son Edward who married Maria Lowe or Love of Avenbury. The Woodyate family remained in the parish certainly until 1727 when another Edward Woodyate was churchwarden.
23. Philip Bennett was assessed for £3 as was William Bennett; the family remained in the parish and served as parish officers.
24. Richard Browne of Hall Court in Bishop's Frome. This would appear to be the 29 acres called Fox Leasow on the boundary south-east of Hopton which was described as part of Tricketts Farm in 1840.
25. Thomas Taylor had one hearth.
26. Anne Corbett widow.
27. William Bennett.
28. Richard Corbett let his land to George Gough. This may have been a smallholding to the south of the parish, as like William Caldow's small property, it was listed at the conclusion of Avenbury parish and after Hopton Sollers.
29. William Caldow who was surely the William Caldwell with one hearth.
30. William Lucas with an assessment of £2 10s appears with one hearth.
31. Rowland Rea
32. John Love or Lowe (his daughter married Edward Woodyate) and John Pembridge gent. John Pembridge also had an estate valued at £18 surmised as Upper Venn, while John Love had one hearth and may have been the tenant of Mr Pembridge's other property.
33. John ffarley gentleman for his brother Richard's lands. John, William and Richard were all landowners in Avenbury. William lived at the Burgess and had three hearths; the brothers may have shared William's house. A Mrs Martha Pharley, widow, lived in Bosbury, otherwise these were the only ffarley lands in Herefordshire. William ffarley gentleman, had five children baptised in Avenbury Church between 1665-1671 and he died in 1677.

These later entries are the smaller properties in the parish with correspondingly small houses. While even the large farms are difficult to correlate 350 years later, the smallholdings are often impossible to clearly identify.

A century later, in 1771, another record was made of landowners and farmers with their properties. The list was found with the parish records.

TABLE 9

'A Rate assessed on the Inhabitants of the Parish 1771', and was in order of value:

		£	s	d
Mr Hayles	Glebe	23	17	4
Natt Smith	Brookhouse	17	18	0
Richard West	Little Froome	14	0	0
William Cooke	Munderfield	13	18	0
Richard Corbett	Hopton	12	0	0
Mr Homes	Lower Venn	11	0	0
Edw Davis	Venn	9	19	0
Thomas Taylor	Noakes	9	8	0
Jas Cook	Avenbury (Court)	8	13	8
Jos Hill	Nurburys	8	0	0
Jos Hill	The Hill		6	0
Thos Cook for	the Burgess	7	6	0
Benj Stanford	Heath	7	4	0
Wm Fincher	Hackley	6	12	0
Jn Corbett	Greve	6	5	1
Thos King	Cusop	4	5	0
Jn Weaver		4	0	0
Thos Baylis		4	0	0
Edw Morgan		1	11	6
Mr Colly		1	8	0
Thos Morgan		1	2	0
Thos Wood	Munderfield	1	2	0
Robt Bennit		1	0	0
Jn Brown		1	0	0
Thos White		1	0	0
Benj Dennis			18	0
Alice Hopcott			17	6
Jn Edwards			10	4
Jn Smith			10	0
Fra Loyde			8	0
Jn Godfrey			6	0
Jn Coney			5	6
Jn Vernal			5	6
Thos Viccaridge			4	4
Edw Preece			4	0
Jn Preece			3	2
Wm Nott			2	0
Jn Smith				10

This document records a farm called the Hill, probably Hanging Hill, which lies on the eastern parish boundary. When in 1294, there was an enquiry into a murder which took place on Bringsty Common, now in the parishes of Whitbourne and Linton, John of the Hulle of Avenbury was called as one of the witnesses.[5]

The Land Tax

From the end of the 18th century onwards the Land Tax helps to tell the story of Avenbury properties. Some farms can be traced from 1798 if their Land Tax remained the same. The glebe and tithes was always the most valuable property, with the Brookhouse next.

TABLE 10 THE LAND TAX OF 1831

In 1831 the situation shown by the land tax was:[6]

Property	owner	£	s	d
Glebe and Tythes	E. Higginson	23	14	4½
Brookhouse	Mr Cayley	17	18	0
Munderfield Court	Mr Cooke	14	14	2
Hopton Sollers	Richard Allison	12	0	0
Lower Venn	Mr Rogers (late)	11	00	0
Little Froome	William Wall	10	00	0
Upper Venn	E Higginson	9	19	0
Noakes	F Williams	9	8	0
Avenbury Court	John Freeman	8	13	0
Nurburys	William Wall	8	00	0
Heath	Mr Cooke	7	4	0
Birchyfield	Mr Wight	6	12	0
Greeve	Dr Walker	6	5	5½
Burgess	Dr Walker	5	14	0
Cusop	Richard Barneby	4	5	0
Little Froome Mill	W Wall	4	0	0
Hackley	Mr Wight	2	8	0
Goodships	Mr Philpotts	2	0	0
	Mrs P Bray	1	6	0
Copton	Josh Went	I	2	6
Munderfield	Mrs Morse	1	2	0
Northfields	Andrew Maund (late)	1	1	0
Pt Tricketts	John Brown	I	0	0
Copton Fields	Vernall Family (6x2s 11d)		17	6
Stocks	Mr Rogers (late)		13	0
Hanging Hill	John Bennett		6	0

Commutation of Tithes 1840

> 'Corbett the present Impropriator intends making application to Parliament for leave to sell all the Tithes great and small to the propriators of the different estates and offers the vicar an advance of £5 per Ann for his Concurrence'.
>
> John Mogridge, vicar of Avenbury *c*1783[7]

Tithes were for the majority of farmers a proverbial 'thorn in the flesh' and represented one tenth of their annual profit. There were predial tithes payable on fruits of the earth such as corn, hay, timber, fruit and other crops; mixed or agistment tithes payable on animal products such as colts, lambs, calves, wool, milk, eggs and honey; and personal tithes payable on the clear gains of a man's labour and industry and they were levied on the profits of milling and fishing and similar activities. These were divided into the great tithes due from grain, hay and wood and usually paid to the rector of the parish and the small tithes payable for animal products and due to the vicar. These had customarily been paid in kind, hence the need for a large tithe barn.

The Tithe Commutation Act was passed in 1836 to commute tithes in kind and substitute a fluctuating money payment known as a corn rent adjusted each year on the basis of the seven year average price of wheat, barley and oats. The important distinction on land was that arable land was tithed at about one-fifth of the value of the annual rent, whilst grassland was tithed at about one-eighth of the rent; hop ground in Avenbury was allotted an extraordinary charge of 6s per acre. Tithe schedules and maps were drawn up for each parish in order to empower the Tithe Commutation Act and were completed in a relatively short time. The Avenbury schedule dates from 1840 and lists every landowner, tenant, field and crop. It is an invaluable record of the parish at that time and provides the basis for subsequent research.

The Act was also designed to provide the incumbent with a reasonable and reliable stipend, but as we know in Avenbury the tithe was in the hands of impropriators:

> 'for as it is apprehended the whole Vicarial Tythes of Avenbury at that time could not be valued at more than Thirty pounds per Ann. Plantations of Hops have flourished so prodigiously within the last Fifty years in this parish that the Tythe of Hops and Cyder only is normally worth, one hundred and Fifty pounds'.
>
> John Mogridge, vicar of Avenbury *c*1783[8]

The report by the commissioners in 1840 explained that:

Edmund Higginson of Saltmarsh is the owner of all the tithes of the lands in the parish subject to tithes except one third part of the Lower Venn 170 acres and the Stocks 85 acres both the property of Thomas Pargeter of Foxcoat, Co Worcester. The said Thomas Pargeter is the owner of the said one third part of the tithes of the two estates called the Venn and the Stocks. It is agreed that £420 shall be paid to Edmund Higginson from all lands in the parish subject to tithe including the glebe, the rent charge of which shall be fixed at £10 and apportioned exclusively upon the said glebe. The annual sum of £12 15s shall be paid to Thomas Pargeter for the said 1/3rd of tithes of the Venn and the Stocks.

The whole parish of Avenbury contains	3,178 acres
Subject to tithe are	2,832 acres
Arable land subject to tithe is	1,103 acres
Meadow land subject to tithe is	1,537 acres
Woodland	31 acres
Hop ground subject to tithe is	131 acres

The tithes of the following lands are discharged and exempt from payment of tithes by Declaration of a merger:

Hackley 108 acres by Declaration of August 1839 signed by the Rev Thomas Price, Thomas Philip Payne Wight Esq, Edward Werge Hervey Esq and Marianne his wife, Maria Wight, spinster and Eliza Jane Wight, spinster.

Greeve Farm 120 acres and Burgess Farm 133 acres signed 17th September 1839 by Charlotte Walker, spinster.

The Glebelands if not in the hands of the owners amount to 61 acres and belong to Edmund Higginson.

Gross rent charges payable to the tithe owners in lieu of tithes

to Edmund Higginson	£420 00s
to Thomas Pargeter	£12 15s
total	**£432 15s**

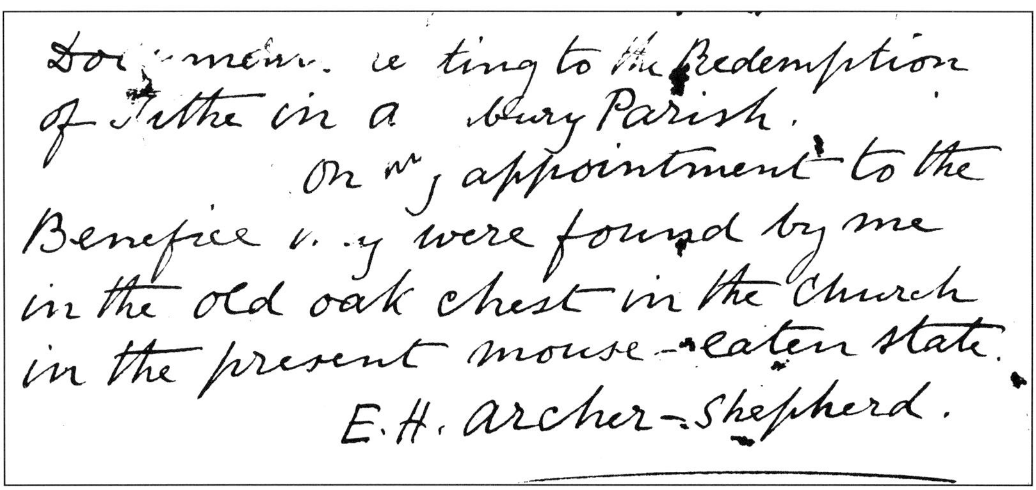
Do ments ting to the Redemption
of ithe in a bury Parish.
On my appointment to the
Benefice y were found by me
in the old oak chest in the Church
in the present mouse-eaten state.
E. H. Archer-Shepherd.

Document regarding tithe redemption.

The annual tithe payments due to the impropriators represented a considerable capital investment on their part. Delabere Walker purchased the tithes of the Greeve in 1800, for which he paid £350 and a few years later in 1815 he purchased the tithes of the Burgess for £700; the Declaration of 1839 was made by his daughter Charlotte Walker. In 1815 one third part of the rectory of Avenbury which included both the tithes and the glebeland was purchased by Richard Barneby for £3,666 13s 4d. This means that the whole was worth £11,000. What salary the vicar received at this time was not mentioned but in 1867 the Rev Robert Polwhele was paid annually £100, with a residence and nine acres of glebe.

The tithe map and schedule are to be the yardstick by which the Avenbury properties are considered in the next section, for this is the only record that exists whereby every farm, field and each cottage is measured and the owners, tenants and occupants recorded. Although it would be satisfying to be able to compare the size of farms in 1663 and 1840, it is impossible because we do not know to what extent land changed hands to make larger and smaller units and in some cases, farms have disappeared altogether.

TABLE 11

PROPERTIES IN AVENBURY AT THE TIME OF THE TITHE MAP OF 1840

Property	No. on tithe map	Owner	Occupier	Acreage
Hopton		Richard Allison	William Holloway	
Broach Cottage	453			total 319
Brookhouse		Rev C Scott Luxmore	Thomas Berriman	
Bythan				
Church Bank Cottage	146			total 303
Little Frome		William Wall	Edward West	238
Mill				16
Nurburys				40
Blacksmith's shop & cottage	528			
				total 294
Munderfield Court		Benjamin Saunders	Robert Dent	
Castle House	405			
house	364			
house	490			
house	525			
				total 286

Lower Venn		Thomas Pargeter	Mary Payne	172
The Stocks			Mary Fidoe	86
Gunsmiths cottage	517			
(now Stocks Cottage)				
Chestnuts	519			
				total 258
The Burgess		Charlotte Walker	Sarah Derry	132
cottage	527			
The Greeve				113
				total 245
Upper Venn		Edmund Higginson	James Edwards	180
Vicarage	148		Rev William R Haddy	
Glebe: The Kilns			John Bennett	46
land only			Thomas Berriman	5
land only			Henry Jenks	3
land only			Edward West	2
in hand				2
land only			James Edwards	1
				total 239
Hackley		Thomas Philip Payne	James Evans	80
Birchyfield		Wight		66
Rough Mintridge				41
Limekilns, Pencombe Lane			John Radford	16
				total 203
The Heath		John Henry Cooke	Robert Hancock	
cottage in Stoke Lane	357	Joseph and Charles Cooke		total 198
Avenbury Court		John Freeman	Henry Jenks	
house & cottage,	514			
Munderfield Row				
Pound Cottage	185			total 191
Noakes		Francis Williams	William Green	189
Cusop		Elizabeth Barneby	William Hill	141
Sawbury Hill		John Turner Beresford	William Gillam	
Red Hill Cottage				total 78
Goodships		Thomas Philpotts	Ann Williams	35
Fox Leasow (land only)		John Brown	in hand	29
Tanners Field (land only)		Richard Brown	in hand	20
Northfields		Mary Ann Maund	John Williams	15

Coopers Green (with Avenbury Court)		Rev Richard Williams	Henry Jenks	12
Wiggall		William Grape	John Weaver in hand	9 2 total 11
land only **house**	94-100 99	John Cooke	in hand James Walwyn	10
Leasow		Charles Dutton	James Nash	10
Hanging Hill (no house, farmed with the Kilns)		William Towers	John Bennett	10
land only	331-334	Mark Davies	in hand	10
Yewtree **Frensham**	504 484	Joseph Went	in hand Thomas Edwards	total 10
Birch Hall	 382	Betty Smith	Peter Pitt Mary Bull	9 2 total 11
land only	335-9	Thomas Haywood	in hand	8
Copton Field Farm (now Copton Farm)		James Vernall	in hand	7
now Copton Field	473-6	William Vernall	Peter Pitt & Thomas Stallard	6
Holly Bush		Jane Lloyd	Peter Pitt	6
Growlands	462	Mary Vernall	in hand	5
Growlands	467	John Vernall	in hand	5
land only	470-72	William Johnson	in hand	5
land only	477-78	Thomas Brooks	Joseph Went	4
Greeve Coppice		Henry Jenks	in hand	4
house	522	John Gurney	in hand	3
Ashbed Orles		Mary Paine	in hand Mary Fidoe	3
four houses (now Long Cottage) **land** **house**	384 383	John Oakey	John Hadley, Thomas Morton and others in hand William Jenks	 3

Claypits	375	John Tyler	in hand	4
two houses	363	James Gurney	Mary Evans	3
Wake House	257	Ann Wilcox	Henry Jenks	2
house	351	William Wright	Richard Davies	2
orchard	488	Ann Lloyd	Joseph Went	2
plock	492	William Jenks	in hand	1
part of Ox Leasow		Trustees of St Katherine's Charity Ledbury	Robert Dent	1
house	355	William Vernalls	in hand	1

Houses or cottages and or garden or land below one acre, in 1840.

Property	**No on tithe map**	**Owner**	**Occupier**
cottage	25	John Walker	William Green
opposite Pound House (two cottages)	152	Thomas West	Thomas Draper and others
house	352	William Davies	in hand
orchard	353	Richard Badham	Joseph Stallard
garden	356	Ann Taylor	Richard Cooke
house	354	John Brooks	in hand
house	365	Richard Hill	Ann Gardner
The Perns	400	Thomas Woodyate	in hand
School House	401	John Griffiths	in hand
house	402	James Bough	in hand
Vinetree	511	Price	James Soley
Hawthorn Cottage	518	James Edwards	in hand

What has happened to these former Avenbury families? Some died and left no living descendants, some moved to near-by parishes or further afield in this country, whilst others began a new life abroad. Fortunately with the aid of records, family traditions and remembered history it is becoming easier for people to trace their ancestors and their roots. Herefordshire Record Office, Herefordshire Family History Society, Bromyard Heritage Centre, local libraries and the Bromyard and District Local History Society regularly receive enquiries from people tracing their family in this part of the country. Consequently visitors from all over the world come here looking for the homes of their forbears.

The information in this chapter, together with other records relating to Avenbury enables us to consider the parish during recent centuries.

Avenbury churchyard and the ruined church about 1990. *Charles Grant*

Chapter 7

The Domesday Manors after 1600

'In the early days of June the walk through the fields from Bromyard to Avenbury is a continuous picture of real rural beauty. The little river Frome, deeply winding through rich alluvial meadows covered by heavy crops of grass, supplies the central line of beauty in a sinuous course of curves. Gently rising slopes, well timbered with great trees, limit the landscape, showing on their sunny sides broad fields of corn still green, with here and there a hop-yard, whose luxuriant growth of darker foliage tells of the fatness of the land.'

James Johnston, *The Finding of St Augustine's Chair (1898), 10*

Between the Domesday survey of Avenbury with its associated manors and the tithe survey of the parish, 754 years had passed. In 1840 it was possible for the first time to see an accurate acreage of the farms in the parish.

FARMS THAT EVOLVED FROM THE DOMESDAY MANORS

Avenbury Court	191 acres
Brookhouse with Bythan	303 acres
Upper Venn	180 acres
Lower Venn	172 acres
The Stocks	86 acres
Little Froome	238 acres
Little Froome Mill	16 acres
Nurburys	40 acres
Hopton Sollers	319 acres
Noakes	189 acres
Sawbury Hill	78 acres
Wiggall	11 acres

These manorial properties which comprise some 1823 acres, were of superior status and so occur in national records. Therefore we can partially fill in those intervening years.

Avenbury Court

It was seen in Chapter 4 that Avenbury Court and Brookhouse were in the hands of the Berrington family in the 16th century. Margaret Berrington, a daughter of Robert Berrington, married John, a son of William Brome or Broome of Withington in Herefordshire. John Broome of Avenbury died in August 1610.[1]

Map 8

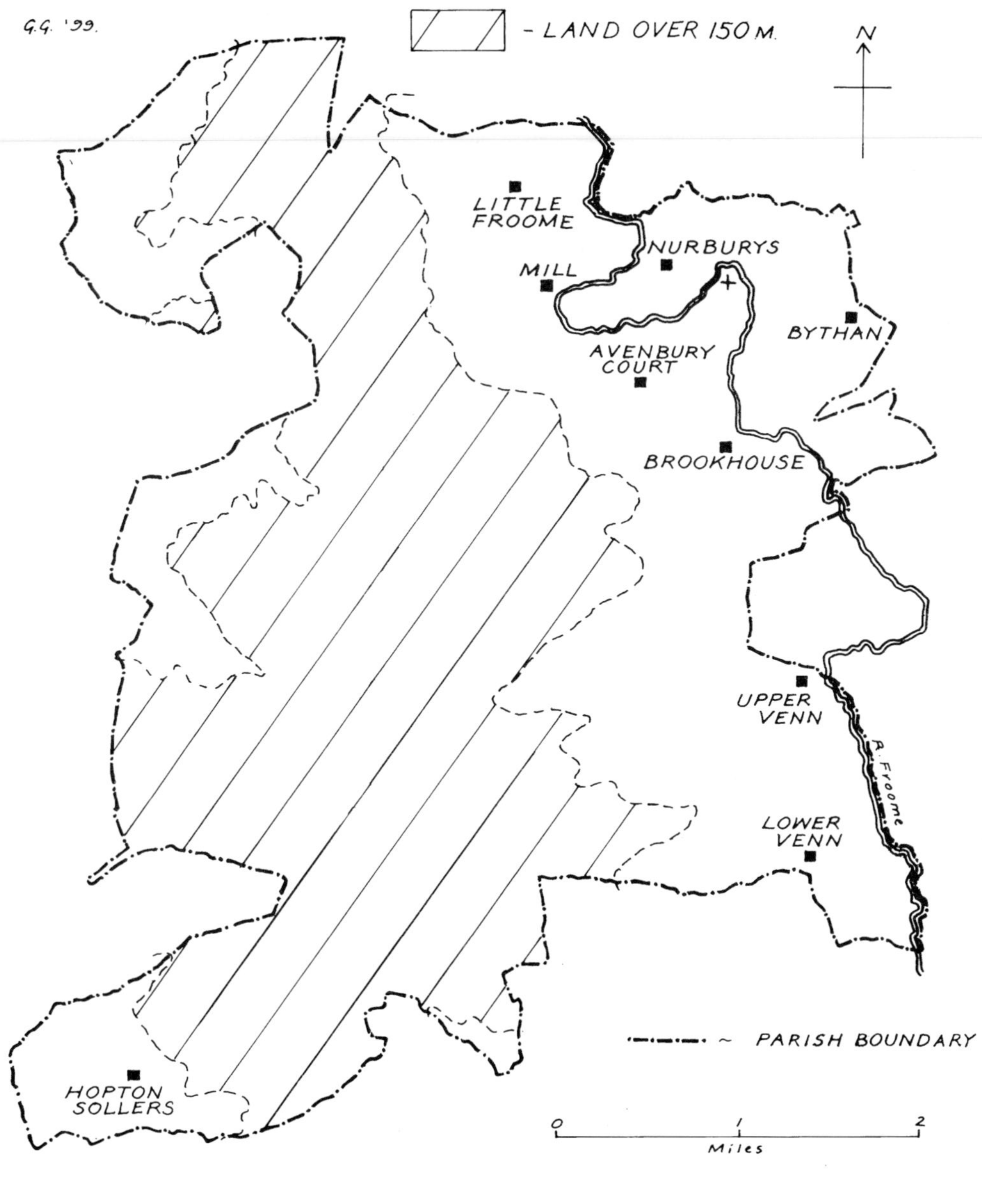

THE DOMESDAY MANORS OF AVENBURY, LITTLE FROOME, VENN AND HOPTON SOLLERS.

Avenbury Court (from Brookhouse). *Howard Painter*

Avenbury Court from the north around 1980. The trees in the foreground are growing on the banks of the river Frome.

The hop kilns and Avenbury Court 1998.
Howard Painter

John and Margaret may well have lived at Avenbury Court and perhaps built the present house. A later John Broome and his tenant William Sherriff appear in the 1663 Militia Assessments for Avenbury, apparently for this property.

The large house of Avenbury Court was built as an L-shaped stone house in about 1600 and has very heavy ceiling beams in the downstairs rooms. There was later a considerable modernisation and partial rebuilding when the original, heavy gable roof was replaced by a hipped roof, and much of the upper storey was rebuilt in brick. There is a large vaulted cellar which extends beneath the parlour and dining room, and the house had an outside kitchen with a bake-oven. The large timber-framed granary over a stone-based barn and the adjoining circular brick hop kilns, alongside the house, date from about 1870-80. There is a fine range of 19th-century farm buildings across the road from the house and they incorporate an earlier stone barn. There must have been a farm fire here in 1898 for the church registers record the death of James Mansell aged 52 years, burnt to death in a barn at Avenbury Court.

John Freeman of Gaines in Whitbourne owned Avenbury Court in 1840, the property having belonged to his grandfather before him. Apparently the farm had belonged to a Mr Gardiner who exchanged it with the Freeman family for property they held in Stoke Lacy.[2] There was a Nathaniel Gardiner at the Court in 1754 and he may be the Mr Gardiner referred to. The last John Freeman of Gaines died in 1870, his family having lived in Whitbourne since 1690 when they built their mansion house at Gaines.[3] As we saw in Chapter 5, John Freeman gave land and money for the last Avenbury vicarage built in 1854. Avenbury Court was

Hop kilns after conversion to a dwelling 1998.
Howard Painter

Avenbury Court hopyard 1905. This photograph shows both hoppickers and visitors. The tally sticks recorded the number of bushels picked.
Bromyard Local History Society Collection

sold to J B Hooper for £7,000 in 1871 by the trustees of the Gaines Estate and then, within a short time and for the same sum, to Miss Frances Hooper of Tenby, Pembroke. The trustees of the Municipal Charities in the City of Worcester[4] (later called The Worcester Consolidated Municipal Charities) acquired this and other Avenbury farms around 1878. The trustees have recently sold Avenbury Court in several lots to different buyers, and part of the land has been added to Brookhouse, whilst the house and buildings are being developed and modernised.

Mr. Thos Adams bushelling at Avenbury Court hopyard.
Bromyard Local History Society Collection

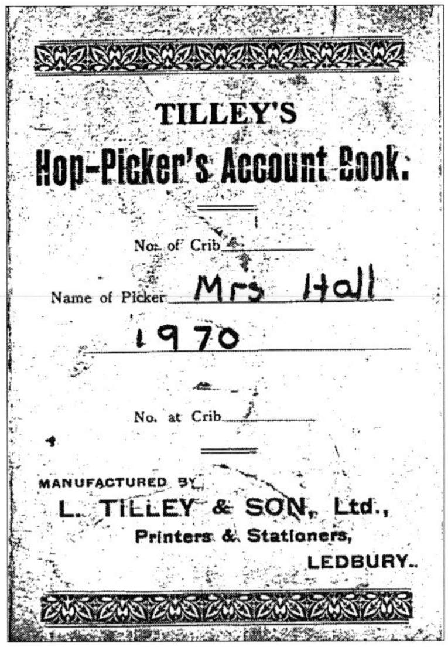

The Court was called Avenbury House in 1851 when 73 year old Henry Jenks was the tenant farmer sharing the house with two elderly sisters, a 37 year old niece and three general servants. The older generation of Jenks had all been born in Grendon Bishop where the family were well established and they were related to Mr Jenks the tanner in Pump Street, Bromyard. Twenty years later the name of the property was again Avenbury Court and Edwin Morris farmed the 150 acres with two labourers and a boy; his household was small with himself, his wife Mary and a domestic and a farm servant living in.

Thomas Adams and his wife Mary came to the Court from Pembrokeshire around 1886. They had a large family. When their son Thos (Thomas) was old enough to farm on his own they rented Lower House, Stanford Bishop, which was another property in the hands of the Worcester Consolidated Municipal Charities. On retirement Thomas and Mary moved to Down House near Bromyard with three daughters, and Thos took over Avenbury Court with his wife Frances. Thos Adams was a well respected and admired farmer, who was particularly noted for his skill at growing hops. When he retired he built a bungalow on the Ledbury Road above the Court and his family still visit Avenbury and Bromyard.

Brookhouse with Bythan and Church Banks

In about 1650 Dr Edward Stillingfleet, bishop of Worcester, purchased Brookhouse from the Berringtons and at the same time acquired Mintridge in Stoke Lacy. Edward Shepard farmed Brookhouse as tenant in 1663 when his estate was valued at £27 and was the second largest farm in Avenbury. In 1665 his house was taxed on two hearths. Brookhouse and Mintridge

Brookhouse, July 1999.
Howard Painter

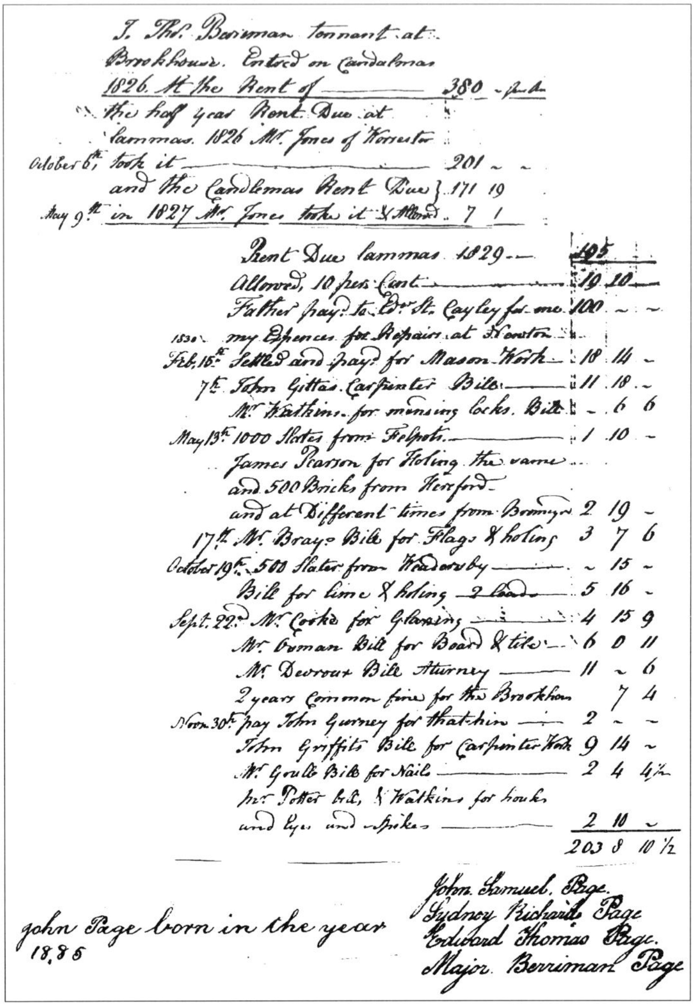
I. Thos. Berriman tennant at
Brookhouse. Entred on Candalmas
1826. At the Rent of —— 380 - pr an
the half year Rent Due at
Lammas. 1826 Mr. Jones of Worcester
October 6th, took it —— 201 - -
and the Candlemas Rent Due } 171 19
May 9th in 1827 Mr. Jones took it & Allowed 7 1
Rent Due Lammas 1829 — 195
Allowed, 10 per Cent —— 19 10 —
Father payd to Edw. St. Cayley for me 100 - -
1830 my Expences for Repairs at Newton
Feb. 15th Settled and payd for Mason Work — 18 14 -
7th John Gittas Carpenter Bill —— 11 18 -
Mr. Watkins for mensing locks. Bill - 6 6
May 13th 1000 Slates from Felpots —— 1 10 -
James Pearson for Holing the same
and 500 Bricks from Hereford
and at Different times from Bromyard 2 19 -
17th Mr. Brays Bill for Flags & holing 3 7 6
October 19th 500 Slates from Woodersby —— - 15 -
Bill for lime & holing 2 loads —— 5 16 -
Sept. 22nd Mr. Cooke for Glasing —— 4 15 9
Mr. Osman Bill for Board & tile —— 6 0 11
Mr. Devrout Bill Atturney —— 11 - 6
2 years Common fine for the Brookhouse 7 4
Novm 30th pay John Gurney for thatchin —— 2 - -
John Griffits Bill for Carpenter Work 9 14 -
Mr. Goulds Bill for Nails —— 2 4 4½
Mr. Potter bill, & Watkins for hooks
and Eyes and Spikes —— 2 10 -
203 8 10½
John Samuel Page.
Sydney Richard Page
Edward Thomas Page.
Major Berriman Page
john Page born in the year
18,85

Extracts from the farm diary of Thomas Berriman of Brookhouse, Avenbury. The diary begins

'I Thos. Berriman tennant at Brookhouse. Ent(e)red on Candlemas 1826. At the rent of (£)380 per annum'

Thomas Berriman, the eldest son of Thomas and Sarah Berriman, was born in Lockton, Yorkshire in 1792. He married Sarah Wright also from Yorkshire in 1815. Their three children Mary, William and John were all baptised in Lockton. The family moved to Avenbury and took the tenancy of Brookhouse in 1826. Thomas appears to have farmed here successfully, for in 1846 he was able to lend money on mortgage to Benjamin Wall of the Scar Farm, Linton, Bromyard and purchased that property in 1854. Thomas died at the Scar in 1872, his wife Sarah having died there two years earlier; they were both buried at Avenbury. John their youngest son continued to farm at the Scar and died there in 1894; his wife was Jane Wood and she died in 1887. John and Jane Berriman were buried at Stanford Bishop.

Before her marriage to John Berriman, Jane had a daughter Mary Jane Wood who was brought up as a Berriman; she was to marry Thomas, the son of Richard Page and his wife Jemima. At the time of his death in 1876, Richard Page was the owner of the small estate called Northfields in Avenbury. Mary Jane and Thomas Page moved to the Herefordshire House in Stanford Bishop, an inn close to the Scar Farm, and remained there for the rest of their days. They had five children all of whom lived locally. Their eldest son Major Berriman Page was given both the Berriman name and also that of his paternal grandmother Jemima Major.

The diary is today in the keeping of Thomas Berriman's descendant John Page who has recently retired from farming at the Hill House Farm, Norton, Bromyard, Herefordshire.

Brookhouse 1998 from the back garden
Howard Painter

both remained with the Stillingfleet family. Bishop Edward was succeeded in turn by his son Edward, dean of Worcester, by his grandson Edward, a prebendary of Worcester, and finally in 1798 by his granddaughter Elizabeth Stillingfleet. She married John Cayley of Yorkshire. Sometime between 1835 and 1840 their son, Edward Stillingfleet Cayley, sold the properties to the Rev Charles Scott Luxmore[5], who had been vicar of Bromyard 1822-1834. His daughters, the Misses Luxmore, were the probable donors in 1862 of land near the church in Bromyard for the site of a National School, which was duly built and known as St Peter's School.[6] Luxmore's first tenant at Brookhouse was Thomas Berriman. This was the time of the survey (1840) and at that point Brookhouse, at 303 acres, was still the second largest farm in the parish.

Returning to tenants, Francis Smith was farming Brookhouse in 1747 and he was followed by Nathaniel Smith, both of whom were active parish officers. There was on the south wall of Avenbury Church a marble tablet to:

> 'the memory of Mr Nathaniel Smith, late of the Brookhouse, in this parish who died 13th of December, 1804, aged 25 years'.[7]

A Miss Smith remained farming at Brookhouse to be followed by Mr Walker, tenant to Mr Cayley in 1812. Edward West of Little Froome then took over the tenancy. By 1831 Thomas Berriman was the tenant and he was still there when the Rev Charles Scott Luxmore purchased the property.

The present house appears to have been built by one of the Stillingfleet family whilst the Smith family lived here . A sale notice of 1840 describes:

> 'The HOUSE consists of a substantial modern Brick and Stone-built Edifice, covered with Slate, with all convenient and necessary Rooms and offices convertible (at a small expense) into an excellent Residence.'

It is a pleasant comfortable house of two storeys with attics, and as the name suggests is close by the river Frome. Of particular interest is the large two-storey brick barn built with almost immediate access to the back door of the farmhouse. This 18th-century building must have housed a valuable commodity, perhaps corn awaiting sale or it could have been a malting house for barley. It was designed to carry a considerable weight on the upper storey.

Bromyard sheep market in the 1920s.
Bromyard Local History Society Collection

"It used to be said that a farmer called Philpot of the Brookhouse, Avenbury, has had as many as a thousand sheep at Bromyard fair at one time." *Bromyard: A Local History (1970), 55*

The tenant in 1851, Stephen Philpotts, who had been born in Bromyard parish in 1817, farmed 330 acres and employed seven labourers. The household consisted of himself and his wife Ann, two young sons, an 18 year old cousin Catherine Couch and three general servants who were all male. Twenty years later Stephen was still farming Brookhouse, but his first wife must have died because he was remarried to Eliza and had a nine year old son; his 82 year old mother lived with them, also a niece of 15 described as a servant, and a bailiff, William Berriman perhaps the son of Thomas Berriman, a former tenant.

The Luxmore family retained the property until 1911 and in that year sold it to the then tenant, Frederick John Cook, for £4,966. The farm covered 342 acres principally in Avenbury although there was some land in the adjacent parish of Linton. Other Luxmore properties were sold in the same year and included: Newton Farm in Stoke Lacy and Winslow which was purchased by James Farmer Parker; Goodships Farm in Avenbury purchased by Francis Whitsey Williams of Bromyard; and Mintridge Farm in the parishes of Stoke Lacy and Avenbury which was conveyed to Clara Hodges.[8]

Frederick John Cook, who was born around 1846, was the son of Thomas Cook who farmed at Upper Norton near Bromyard. They were descendants of the Cooke family who farmed and lived at Munderfield Court for several generations (see Chapter 8). He died at home in 1912, and by his will made provision for his widow to continue farming at Brookhouse. After her death the property was to be divided equally between their four sons and three daughters. His widow Eliza Ann died before 1928 and three of their children were then residing in the farmhouse: Elizabeth who had in 1913 married Philip Henry Smith, but was now widowed, and two sons John Farmer Cook and Alfred James Cook. Of the remainder of the family, Tom was farming at New House in Bodenham and Hubert was farming at Merrifields, Stoke Lacy; May had married Leslie Farmer Parker of Cheyney Court, Bishop's Frome, and Elsie had married John Perry Pudge of Broadfield Court in the same parish. What a farming family! Many of their descendants still live and farm in the district.

Frederick John Cook of Brookhouse *c*1846-1912.

Eliza Ann, the wife of Frederick John Cook, with two of their daughters. Elsie later married John Perry Pudge and May was to marry Farmer Parker. Photograph taken before 1928

In 1928 Brookhouse, with 342 acres, was put up for auction at the Hop Pole, Bromyard and subsequently purchased by two of the Cook brothers, Alfred and John. Within 7 years the property was sold for £7,150 to John Heath Agnew who was living at the Falcon Inn, Bromyard. Mr Heath Agnew, whom many people can still remember, and who has since published books on Herefordshire history, made many minor alterations to the house. In 1940 he sold fields to the north of the farm to the neighbouring Oliver family, and when the Brookhouse next came on the market in 1942, it included only 309 acres and sold for £11,500 to the Herefordshire Fruit Company whose registered office was the Mansion House, Hereford. In the post-war years the value of farmland rapidly appreciated and mortgages were available at less than 5% interest. When in 1947 the Herefordshire Fruit Company relinquished the property, it comprised only

Hoppicking at Brookhouse. Elsie Cook is booking and her brother Hubert Cook is bushelling.
Bromyard Local History Society Collection

BROOK HOUSE

2 MILES FROM BROMYARD.

To be Sold by Auction, by

BENTLEY, HOBBS & MYTTON

at the BROOK HOUSE, on

THURSDAY & FRIDAY, 16th & 17th FEBRUARY, 1928

By direction of the Executors of the late MR. F. J. COOK, commencing at **11** a.m. each day.

76 CATTLE

Viz.: 10 Hereford Heifers and Cows and Calves, 9 Hereford and Shorthorn Heifers and Cows in calf, 3 fresh Barrens, fat Hereford Cow, 4 fresh 2-year-old Hereford Heifers, 5 Bullocks 18 months old, 25 Yearling Heifers and Bullocks, 8 Rearing Calves, and Pedigree Hereford Bull, "*Pershore Boy Blue*"

145 SHEEP

85 Cross-bred Ewes in yean, 6 Barren Ewes, 52 Store Tegs, and **2** Pure-bred Oxford Rams.

9 HORSES

7 Cart Mares and Gelding, Black Cob and Pony.

8 PIGS, 60 FOWLS

PONY, GOVERNESS CAR and HARNESS, GEARING,

The whole of the Excellent

AGRICULTURAL IMPLEMENTS

(by the Best Makers)

3 capital Drays, Harvest Trolley, Waggon, 3 Carts, *Massey Harris* Binder, *Bamford's* Swath Turner, 2 Mowing Machines, 3 Horse Rakes. Cambridge and Hop Rolls, *Wallace's* Manure Drill, 2 Hop Washers, *Weeks'* Powdering Machine, *Weeks'* Fruit Sprayer, Corn Drills, Ploughs, Harrows, Scuffles, *Pilter* 15-tine lever Cultivator, Scales and Weights, Hop Cribs, *Robinson's* Destronite Hop Powder, *McDougall's* Hop Wash, Hop Sacks, *Hearson's* Incubator, Portable Wood Poultry Houses, Anthracite Coal, Garden Roll, Potatoes.

MACHINERY

Tangye 6 H.P. Oil Engine, *Lister's* 6 H.P. Portable Oil Engine, *Clipper* Chaff Machine, *Bamford's* No. 2 Corn Mill, Iron Shafting and Pulley Wheels, Belting, &c.; 1.400 GALLONS OF CIDER, Empty Casks, a portion of the Antique and Modern Household

FURNITURE

Oak Hall Stand, Mahogany Extending Dining Table, Mahogany Chiffoniere, Mahogany frame Single Chairs, Oak China Cupboard, Overmantels, Easy and Occasional Chairs, Mahogany Occasional Tables, Oak Bureau, Eight-day Grandfather Clock, Oak and painted Chests with drawers, Old Oak Hanging Press, Painted Bedroom Suites, Dressing and Washing Tables, Iron and Wood Bedsteads, Feather Beds, Carpets, Kitchen Articles, Deal Top Tables, Old Oak Dresser, Cooking Utensils; DAIRY ARTICLES: *The New Lister* E.I. Separator, *Llewellyn's* End-over-End Churn, *Lister's* Butter Worker, Scales and Weights, Dairy Utensils and other Effects.

ORDER OF SALE.—FIRST DAY, Thursday, 16th February: Agricultural Implements, Machinery, Cider, Sheep, Cattle, Pigs and Horses.
SECOND DAY, Friday, 17th February: Poultry, Poultry Appliances, Household Furniture.

Mrs. Harborne, Falcon Hotel, Bromyard, will supply Refreshments.

Catalogues can be obtained of the Auctioneers, Worcester, Bromyard and Pershore.

Record Printing Works, Bromyard

Page of sale catalogue for Brook House, Avenbury 1928.

12lb baskets of Mushrooms picked at Brookhouse and then taken by train from Bromyard to Birmingham.

Flooded meadows on drive to Brookhouse 1920s.

Hop picking at Brookhouse 1920s.

Hay making at Brookhouse, Alfred Cook centre front.

Haymaking at Brookhouse *c*1920, John Cook bottom right.

John Perry Pudge	Hubert Cook	Alfred Cook	John Cook	Leslie Parker	Tom Cook
Eliza Ann Cook (Granny Cook)		Elsie Pudge	Elizabeth Smith	Mary (May) Parker	Granny Parker or Aunt Jones

The plough team at Brookhouse.

Horses.

		Lot		No.
27	6	153	"BONNY," bay cart mare, aged, good worker	1
28	17	6 154	"BLACKBIRD," black ditto	2
32	.	6 155	"DARBY," bay ditto	3
30	9	156	"SNIP," dark brown ditto	4
7	7	157	"FLOWER," dark chestnut ditto	5
33	12	158	"CAPTAIN," chestnut cart gelding, 6 years old, ditto	6
26	5	159	"SMILER," bay cart mare, 6 years old	7
16	16	160	"NIGGER," black cob gelding, 6 years old, quiet to ride and has been driven	8

Turn Out.

		Lot		No.
10	10	161	"JUDY," bay mare pony, aged, quiet to ride and drive	9
11	11	162	Varnished Governess Car with rubber tyres, lamps, cushions, &c., *by Jones, Hereford*	
3	10	163	Set of black brass mounted harness	

Brookhouse sale, February 1928.

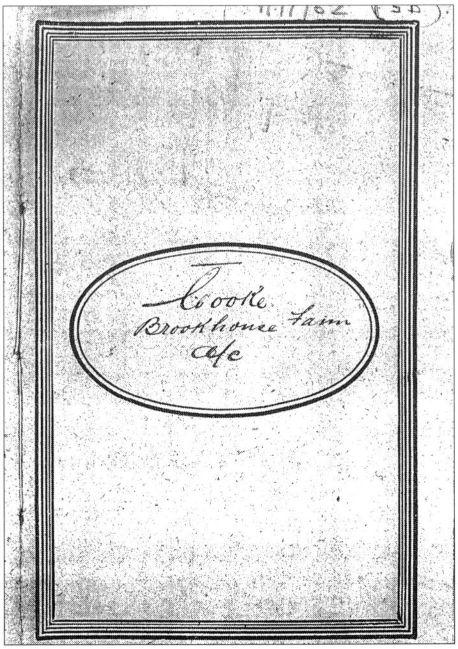

1877	£	s	d
13 bus of Beans @ 5/6	3	11	6
7768 Coal	12	7	1
77 June 14 bullocks	"	"	"
" at £11-10 ea	161	"	"
June 14 6 Heifer &	"	"	"
" Calves @ £12/10	75	"	"
2 Turnip Manure	13	"	"
2do Hop do	16	"	"
Poles	30	"	"
Waggon	"	"	"
Hop Bushel	"	"	"
Hop Cotte 9 tons	4	19	"
2 Colts at 35 ea	70	"	"
Cash —	200	"	"
12 pieces of Sacking	"	"	"
at 18/	10	16	"

231 acres for which William Phillips of Worcestershire paid £16,000. The remaining 78 acres surrounded Bythan to the east of the parish and included 34 acres called Upper and Lower Foxley. Some of this land has recently been bought back by the present owners and Brookhouse is now very similar in size to the 303 acres of 1840.

Bythan

This is an unusual name that means 'within the valley'.The house is approached by a long drive from the Avenbury Lane and lies on the eastern parish boundary at the 500 foot contour level with breathtaking views. Most records show the property as being part of Brookhouse, but it may at one time have been an independent holding. This was a small timber-framed house built around 1700, the front of which has now been replaced with brick. What is astonishing is the long, post-1840 range of stone, open-fronted buildings which form, with the house, three sides of a large yard. They were probably built by the Luxmores for their tenants the Cook family of Brookhouse, and were used for yarding cattle. In 1851 William Philpotts lived at Bythan with his wife and family of five children between the ages of five and twenty two; he described himself as a farm labourer and may have been a relative of Stephen Philpotts who was then at Brookhouse. Another farm labourer Thomas Benbow was here in 1871 with his wife and a young niece.

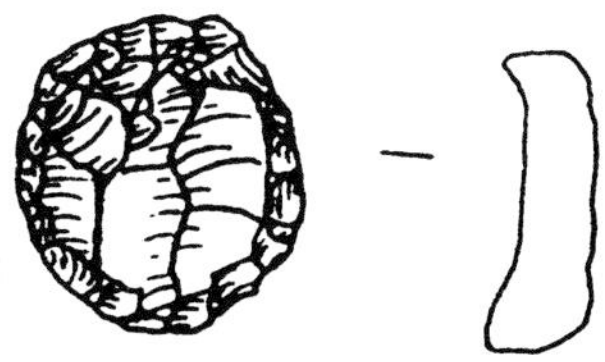

Thumbnail scraper found at Bythan by Deborah Waller. *Drawn by Philippa Bradley*

Bythan, July 1999. *Howard Painter*

The Smith family taken at Church Banks, Avenbury about 1900.
Left to right:- Jim Smith, late of Burley, William, Jim's father, Doris, Jim's sister, Walter, Jim's brother killed in First World War, Hester, Jim's mother, Mrs. Britton, Jim's sister.

Church Banks

In 1840 these were two cottages at the edge of the parish on a track which still runs from the east side of the Avenbury Lane to Pool Hall in the parish of Linton. The cottages were part of the Brookhouse Estate and stood in fields belonging to Brookhouse called Church Banks. The sale catalogue of 1840 described 'all those two newly-erected, stone-built Cottages or Tenements, covered with Slate'. Two farm workers' families were living here in 1851, Joseph Pulling with his wife, a daughter, two sons and a grandson in one cottage, and 21 year old Thomas Dennis in the other. Twenty years later there were again two farm workers' families here, Robert Bishop and his wife Sarah with three daughters, and John Hinksman, his wife Elizabeth and three young children. James (Jim) Henry Smith, who was born in 1888, married Agnes Mary Powell in 1914. They lived at Church Banks when Jim was stockman at Brookhouse. Later, 1900-1930, Jim was churchwarden and bellringer at Avenbury Church. The present single stone house is still called Church Banks and has wonderful views across the Frome valley.

Upper Venn

The Pychard family who resided at Paunton Court in Stanford Regis and at the Venn in Avenbury were in possession of both Upper and Lower Venn in the 16th century, and the family remained the owners of Upper Venn well into the

Upper Venn, Avenbury, 1931.
Royal Commission on the Historical Monuments of England

next century. In 1585, Margaret Pychard of the Venne, widow, made her will which was proved in 1591.[9] This reveals what appears to be a third Venn property as she bequeathed to her son Walter Pychard the 'Little Venne' which she had by lease from John Awbrey of Grendon. Margaret Pychard also left to her son Walter 'all such rentes as shall be due unto me at the tyme of my decease by John Pitchard my sonne for the farme of the Venne'. It would appear that John was renting the (Upper) Venn or part of it from his mother and it was to John that she left the bulk of her goods and stock after her legacies and debts had been discharged.

Margaret's daughter Ann married into the Pembridge family, which may have been a branch of the Pembrugge family of Evesbatch, a small parish to the south of Avenbury, bounded by Acton Beauchamp, Cradley and Bishop's Frome.[10] In 1663 Mr Stitch of Paunton had Lower Venn, and John Pembridge, 'gent' (who was perhaps Margaret Pychard's grandson) and his tenants had an estate valued at £18. This was probably Upper Venn. Elinora Pembridge was buried at Avenbury in 1665.

The Upper Venn Farm, from the south-east, 1943, showing the large 17th-century cottage which was taken down between 1943 and 1950. *H. Tooby and Sons*

Upper Venn 1998. West front.

Howard Painter

The house of the Upper Venn is built on a rocky outcrop which forms a platform several feet above the surrounding land. The present house occupies about half the raised level and a garden (which has now disappeared) at one time filled the remainder. It is quite possible that at other times buildings utilised all this raised area which is unlikely to flood. Nor, despite the surrounding watercourses, does flooding appear to be a problem on the farm. The timber-framed house was built on a stone plinth and on the north side the bedrock shows clearly in the foundation. The original house appears to have been a hall with a cross-wing at each end, probably built around 1600. There have been subsequent additions and alterations and a great deal of brick infill of the timber-framing.

We do not know, at present, who possessed or farmed Upper Venn for the century after 1663. Edward Davis was in occupation before 1771, serving as overseer in that year, churchwarden the following year and overseer again in 1777. The Land Tax return for the end of the 18th century shows the Rev Mr Griffiths as the landlord and Francis Smith as his tenant. Francis Smith was churchwarden for Upper Venn in 1784 and overseer in 1806 (see Chapter 11).

Upper Venn 1998. View from the south.

Howard Painter.

The Rev Mr Griffiths was probably the Thomas Griffiths who in 1778 was appointed to the living of Stoke Lacy as both patron and incumbent; he was the son of the Rev John Griffiths and his wife Ann (a daughter of Bellingham Freeman of Gaines, Whitbourne). Thomas Griffiths married Sarah Brome of Huntington and Withington in Herefordshire. Ann was a considerable heiress and a list of her fortune included money lent to John Fidoe the elder of Little Froome, Avenbury.[11]

By marriage the Griffiths family were related to the Freemans of Gaines, the Barnebys of Brockhampton, the Brome family of Withington and the Higginsons of Buckenhill and Saltmarsh near Bromyard, and no doubt to many more landed and influential Herefordshire families. By 1817 Upper Venn was owned by William Higginson of Saltmarsh, whose niece Elizabeth Bulkeley married John Barneby of Brockhampton. Upper Venn then passed into the hands of Mrs Barneby and was inherited (about 1830) by Edmund Barneby, a great-nephew of William Higginson. Edmund took the name of Higginson and lived at Saltmarsh which he rebuilt in about 1840.[12]

The considerable stone farm buildings of Upper Venn, with king-post roof construction, comprise cowsheds and barns, and were surely built by Edmund Higginson for his tenant James Edwards who was farming here by 1840. James was a Shropshire man born in 1791, and his wife Maline was born in Herefordshire in 1793. In 1851 they had a household of nine, which included Maline's sister, a niece and nephew, a domestic servant and three farm servants. By 1871 the tenancy, then of 220 acres, had passed to William Leake a man of 35 years, and a son of William Leake who had been farming the Burgess in 1851. The younger William was living at Upper Venn with his unmarried sister Jane, who was his housekeeper. Another sister, Mary Todd 'Farmer's wife', with her young daughter, was in the house on the night of the census. She appears to have been the wife of Benjamin Todd of the Burgess; was she visiting or were there marital difficulties? There were three living-in farm servants and 15 year old Mary Hall helped in the house.

Stephen Philpott was 'landowner, farmer, hop grower, and cattle dealer', at Brookhouse and Upper Venn farms in 1876-7 and he was followed at the Upper Venn by William Dorrell. Mr Charles had the farm in the 1930s and his wife was remembered as a shrewd and capable housewife and excellent butter maker. The Tooby family were here by 1940. The 19th-century farm buildings are still in use and there are now extensive modern buildings. Today over a third of the farm acreage is down to corn, 100 acres out of a total of 280. In 1840 the farm covered 179 acres of which 77 acres were arable and ten were planted with hops, but no hops are grown on the farm today. At one time a cart track ran from Upper Venn to Munderfield and another to the Rumney Building in Stanford Bishop, but these ways have now disappeared.

Lower Venn, Avenbury, July 1999. *Howard Painter*

Lower Venn

The large farmhouse of Lower Venn was built as a timber-framed house in the 16th century, but the back and side walls have since been rebuilt in stone and the front plastered and rough cast. Much of this covering was removed during extensive renovation in 1996-7 to show original timber-framing again. The early ceiling beams with wide chamfers can still be seen in the hall (now the dining room), the parlour wing and the kitchen. Further evidence of it being pre-16th century are shown by some long carpenters' marks in the attics, one being ten inches in length and on a smoke-blackened beam. Either this beam was reused from an earlier house or it indicates that at one time the present house was open to the roof. There is a small 17th-century parlour with a moulded beam. There are extensive farm buildings of stone and timber-framing, which include an imposing eight bay barn. There are good hop drying facilities, for today, with 30 acres of hops, this is the largest acreage of the three remaining hop growing farms in the parish.

In 1663 Mr Stitch was assessed at £27 for 'the Lower Venn'. He appears to be the 'Henry Stich esq' who was assessed for £82 l0s in Stanford Regis, where he probably occupied the Paunton Court Estate. Thomas Wood was farming at Lower Venn in 1688 when Roger Robinson of Avenbury wrote in his will 'And for all the rest of my goods and chattles, my debts and funeral expenses discharged, unto my loving kinsman Thomas Wood of the Lower Venn in the parish of Avenbury whom I make executor of my last will'.[13]

The Rogers or Rodgers family who owned Lower Venn in the 18th century, were letting the farm to tenants by 1777, and were probably responsible for the Georgian renovation to the house. A James Rogers was churchwarden in 1708,

Daughters of Thomas and Mary Payne of Lower Venn.

Elizabeth Gillard
Nee Payne
Bt. 14-4-1824 Bromyard.

Anna Maria Payne
Bt. 19-9-1830
Bromyard.

1715, 1716 and 1735 and they may have been father and son. James and Margaret Rogers had a son James baptised at Avenbury in 1707. Two daughters Margaret and Elinor were baptised in 1709 and 1714. John Homes was farming here by the end of the 18th century, to be followed by Edward Davies before 1817, and then by Thomas Cook, and in 1831 by William Woodyate. Mr Rogers was the owner in 1817 and subsequently a William Rogers, who died in 1830 or 1831, when the property was aquired by Thomas Payne. Thomas Payne was born in 1795, the son of an inn-keeper and butcher in Bromyard. He married around 1820-1822 Mary Rogers who was baptised at Avenbury in 1802, the daughter of John and Mary Rogers. Thomas and Mary Payne moved to Lower Venn after 1830 where sadly Thomas died in 1838 following a fall from his horse at Avenbury. Lower Venn then came into the hands of Thomas Pargeter who also owned the adjacent Stocks farm (see below), but Thomas Payne's widow Mary continued to live and farm the 172 acres there. Lower Venn and the Stocks still belonged to Thomas Pargeter in 1840 when Mary Payne was farming 172 acres at Lower Venn and Mary Fidoe 86 acres at the Stocks; two cottages at Munderfield which are now called Stocks

James Edward Payne Bt. 12-4-1835
Avenbury
Son of Thomas & Mary Payne of Lower Venn.

George Gillard
Married Elizabeth Payne 1852.

Cottage and Chestnuts were also on the estate. Mary Payne died in Bromyard in 1879 at the age of 81 years. Her funeral card bore the inscription "Her children arise up, and call her blessed."

In 1851 Henry Davenport was farming 180 acres at Lower Venn, where he lived with his wife Jane, five daughters, three sons and two living-in farm servants.

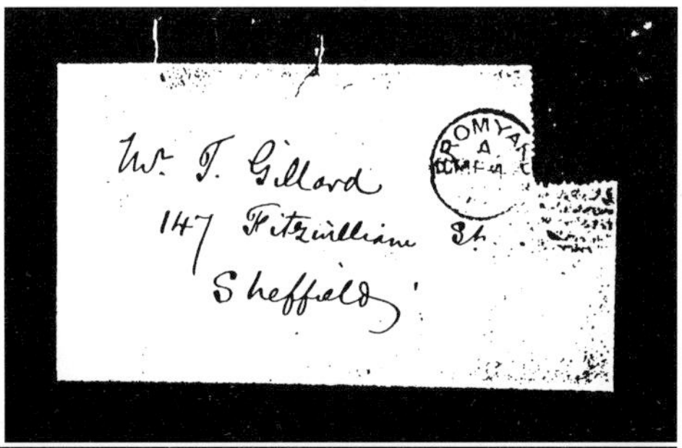

Mr T. Gillard
147 Fitzwilliam St.
Sheffield

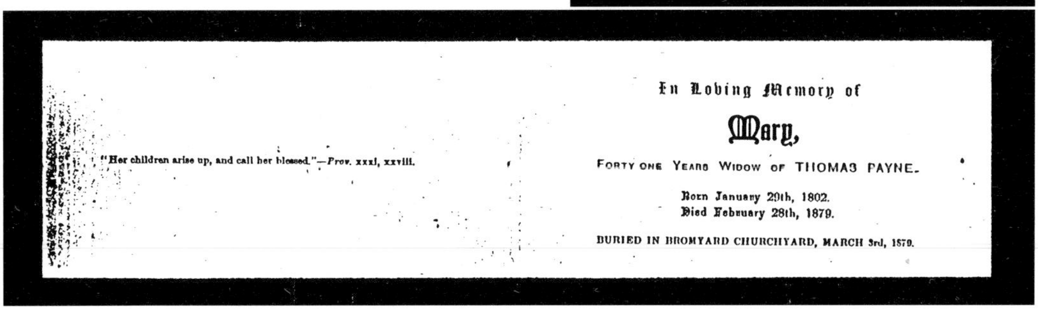

"Her children arise up, and call her blessed."—Prov. xxxi, xxviii.

In Loving Memory of

Mary,

Forty one Years Widow of THOMAS PAYNE.

Born January 29th, 1802.
Died February 28th, 1879.

BURIED IN BROMYARD CHURCHYARD, MARCH 3rd, 1879.

Twenty years later his widow Jane was head of the household and farming 165 acres, assisted by her 19 year old son Thomas and her daughter Caroline's husband, George Yeates. George was 20 years older than his wife and by 1891, Mrs Caroline Yeates (or Yates) was farming Lower Venn. The farm then came into the hands of Mrs Cissie Yates and was later farmed by her daughter Jean who sold it in 1995. This appears to be the only local property to have stayed with the same family since 1851, a connection that was maintained through the female line. In 1995 the acreage was back to 180, made up of 30 acres of hopground, 110 acres of grass and 40 acres of corn.

Munderfield Stocks or The Stocks

Rear view of the Stocks, Avenbury, about 1975.
Phyllis Williams

Stoc, later, stokes or stocks is an old name that can mean 'secondary settlement'. Stocks may thus have been an outlyer to the Venn or Munderfield. An alternative derivation could be from *stocc,* a tree-trunk which was perhaps left standing as a boundary marker or after woodland clearance. In that case the Stocks could be an old boundary area between the Venn and Munderfield. Either meaning makes sense. The stone house dates from about 1800 and there are extensive farm buildings of the same period.

Munderfield Stocks 1998. Hop kiln, farm buildings and farm house.
Howard Painter

The Rodgers family had the Stocks as well as Lower Venn

in 1817, which so far is the earliest reference to the Stocks. William Callow was the tenant there and by 1831 he was followed by Mr Hancox. For a short time the farm belonged to Edward Price of London, but was soon sold to Thomas Pargeter. As mentioned Mrs Mary Fidoe, a 44 year old widow, was farming the 86 acres in 1840 as his tenant. The 1851 census records her as still there, with her 16 year old son and a farm servant, as well as, by chance, a visiting daughter-in-law and granddaughter. In 1871 Richard Hayling, an 87 year old 'farmer of 85 acres employing two labourers and one boy', was there with his son and three servants, to be followed by John Banford and then the Charles family, whom many people can still remember.

It appears to be a myth that families 'in the old days' remained on the same farm for generations. It was true in some cases but appears to have been the exception rather than the rule in the period that we are looking at in Avenbury.

Little Froome

The important and influential Brown family of Bromyard and Little Froome made this their home for several centuries and were responsible for building much of the present house. A branch of the same family lived at Hall Court in Bishop's Frome. The Militia Assessment of 1663 records John Brown, gentleman, having an estate valued at £24 in Avenbury, whilst John Brown of Hall Court had a holding in this parish assessed at £3. Two years later in the Hearth Tax return Mr Brown's house, which would have been Little Froome, had eight hearths - this was a large house. In 1675 this estate belonged to Anthony Brown. He was then a minor, and his maternal grandfather Arthur Weaver of Shropshire was his

Little Froome, Avenbury, 1931.
Royal Commission on the Historical Monuments of England

guardian.[14] Anthony Brown of Avenbury, surely the same, was presented at the Hereford Quarter Sessions in 1693 and upon a bond (recognisance) of £40 bound to be of good behaviour and to appear at the next session. 'If the said Anthony shall refuse so to do. Then you are safely to keep and bring him to the common Gaole of this County.'[15] By 1706 Anthony was running the estate but decided in that year to let both his farm and his 'mansion and manor house called Little Froome' to Edward Fidoe, a yeoman of Fencote, Docklow near Leominster, on a 12 year lease at an annual rent of £90. Anthony retained the use of two rooms in the house, a cellar and also two standings in the new stable for himself and his servants if they came to stay. [16]

The parish registers show several deaths in the family about this period. Richard Brown died in 1670 and Anthony Brown in 1674. Ann, the daughter of Richard and Amphilis Brown, was born and buried in December 1691 and Mrs Jane Brown died in December 1692. Anthony and Sarah Brown had a son John born in June 1700, but sadly Sarah died the following month; Anthony must have remarried because he and his wife Hannah had a son Samuel in 1705. The last two members of the Brown family to possess Little Froome were two brothers, John and Anthony 'who both died young and unmarried about the year 1760'.[17]

However the property had been sold before this, as by 1746 it belonged to Thomas Woodhouse of King's Caple, Herefordshire, whose brother Francis had purchased the adjacent farm of Birchyfield.[18] John Fidoe, surely the son of Edward, was the tenant of both farms and the annual rent for the two properties was £140 with a 21 year lease. Little Froome and Birchyfield were sold by the Woodhouse family to Richard West of Bredenbury in 1768.

Woodhouse Charity

Mr T Woodhouse, by his Will, dated 20th January 1745, and proved at Hereford 14th April 1746, gave to the poor of the borough of Leominster the annual sum of £5, in the following manner, viz.:

> 'I give, devise, and bequeath unto the minister, churchwardens, and overseers of the poor of the borough of Leominster, in the county of Hereford, for the time being, and to their successors, for ever, one yearly sum of £5 of good and lawful money of Great Britain, to be issuing and payable out of all and singular my messuage or tenament, lands and heraditaments, called Little Froome, in the parish of Avenbury, in the county of Hereford, upon the 17th day of July yearly, in memory of my wedding-day with my late dear wife Ann Price, to be distributed amongst the poor of the said borough, with power to distrain upon the said premises for nonpayment of the yearly sum of £5'.

This payment was made by the proprietor of the estate on which it was charged to the overseers of the borough of Leominster till 1816, when Mr West, the then proprietor, who had purchased the estate subject to this incumbrance, refused to continue it, insisting that it was void under the Mortmain Act.[19]

Little Froome 1998. Front aspect. *Howard Painter*

Richard West came to live at Little Froome and regularly served the parish as churchwarden and overseer; his son Edward was born in 1780/81 and inherited the property; he too was, in turn, churchwarden and overseer to Avenbury.

Richard West of Bredenbury 1676-1748

Richard West
of Little Froome
died 1800 married Ann
Cook of Munderfield Court who died 1810

William West
of Bredenbury
died 1807 unmarried

William the younger
of Bredenbury

Richard
of Birchyfield

Edward
of Little Froome

Unfortunately the West family experienced a sad year in 1848 for Edward and his wife Jane died in March of that year aged respectively 69 and 70 years and were followed by their daughter Elizabeth who died at the age of 34 in June. Although Edward and his family were living at Little Froome at the time of their deaths, it was as tenants and not owner occupiers. The property had been sold some years before to William Wall of Worcester who owned a considerable acreage in the Bromyard district and Whitbourne. The reason for the sale appears to have been to pay off debts.

In 1840 the Little Froome estate comprised 294 acres in the parish of Avenbury. John Duncumb in 1812 wrote:

> 'A survey of the manor of Little Froome was taken for Francis Woodhouse, jun. esq. by J. Saunders, in the year 1722; by which it appears that it was considered coextensive with the estate, which then comprised about four hundred acres.'[20]

Little Froome 1998. Front aspect. *Howard Painter*

It is difficult to know where the missing 100 acres may have been without the aid of the 1722 map, but as Birchyfield with Northfields comprising 81 acres were part of the 18th-century estate, they may supply some of the missing land; it was also claimed that a detached area of Avenbury, later annexed to Bredenbury parish, belonged to the manor of Little Froome.

The house at Little Froome was built for an important family and was the heart of a large estate. The earliest part of the present timber-framed and stone house dates from before 1600 (the ceiling beams with seven to eight inch chamfers could be as early as 1550) and is the work of the Brown family who may have built round and extended an even older house on the same site. There is a fine plaster ceiling in the present kitchen and this must originally have been a more important room, probably the family parlour; there are some 17th-century moulded beams with decorative stops both up and down stairs, acquired when the house was remodelled or extended. The West family appears to have been responsible for the Georgian renovations and for the large stone outside kitchen with a lean-to pentice, which is reached from the back door of the house; they may also have been responsible for the addition of the farm office. The house has been modernised and altered since.

The farm buildings are extensive and principally 19th century. A well-built barn has a date slab inscribed 'EW 1819' and records the era of Edward West. There is a gin-ring or horse-engine house where horses were used to pull gearing to thresh corn and do other work; similar buildings can be found on other local farms and demonstrate the importance of corn to the farm economy. An unusual

Horse engine house, Little Froome. July 1999.
Howard Painter

building is the old slaughter house, with a brick front and ceiling beams similar to some of those in the house; was this once the stable? For it stands by the house and drive and may be the 'new stable' in which two standings were reserved for the use of Anthony Brown in 1706. Apparently animals were slaughtered and prepared here ready for marketing until the 1930s. There were of course some good hop kilns and storage buildings, for the Frome Valley was and still is noted for the quality of hops grown in the fertile soil. The brick cowhouse and barn are late 19th century and probably built by the landlord William Wall.

OWNERS AND OCCUPIERS OF LITTLE FROOME AFTER 1575

1575 Richard Brown
1663 John Brown = daughter of Arthur Weaver
1670 Richard Brown decd
1674 Anthony Brown decd
1675 Anthony Brown
1691 Ann daughter of Richard and Amphilis Brown decd
1692 Mrs Jane Brown decd
1700 Anthony and Sarah Brown
1705 Anthony and Hannah Brown
1706 Anthony Brown owner
Edward Fidoe (his tenant)
John and Anthony Brown last of the family to own Little Froome
1746 Thomas Woodhouse owner John Fidoe (his tenant)
1768 Francis Woodhouse
1786 Richard West
1800 Edward West
1840 William Wall owner
Edward West (his tenant)
1848 Edward, Jane and Elizabeth West decd.
1851 John Nott
1867-1890 Richard Allies
1891 James William Pearson
1896-1917 James Farmer Parker
Fred Price
1930-1935 Albert Pettifer
1940 Norman Ernest Paske
The Paske Family

Little Froome Hopyard. Ray Taylor, Harry Paske, Janet Jones, Walter Lloyd, Adam Jones, Michael Paske.
Bromyard Local History Society Collection

Threshing at Little Froome. *Ethel Paske*

A family visiting an Avenbury hopyard about 1910.
Bromyard Local History Society Collection

Loading green sacks of hops at Little Froome.
Bromyard Local History Society Collection

Hoppicking at Little Froome with Bromyard Downs and Church Banks in the background.
Bromyard Local History Society Collection

Bromyard hoppickers in Little Froome hopyard taking a tea break.
Bromyard Local History Society Collection

An enchanting picture of a family picking hops at Little Froome. The children are picking into an umbrella.

Bromyard Local History Society Collection

Mrs. Preece of the White Horse and Mrs. James of the Tan House, Bromyard visit Little Froome hopyard with their children and nieces and nephews.

Bromyard Local History Society Collection

Sheep shearing at Little Froome. *Ethel Paske*

Nurbury's

The name means 'to the north of the fortified place' and could refer to the Saxon 'Agena's fortified place' from which Avenbury takes its name. In 1663 John Michell was assessed £12 for Burburies and this may have been the same property. The Wood family owned and farmed Nurbury's at the beginning of the 18th century and William Wall acquired Nurbury's about 1831. By the time of the tithe survey in 1840 it was a small 40 acre farm and part of the Little Froome Estate. A 'Plan of the Nurbury's Estate in the Parish of Avenbury' was drawn by John Webb, a surveyor of Worcester, in 1832 and shows a large house with a considerable and tidy

Nurbury's 1931.
Royal Commission on the Historical Monuments of England

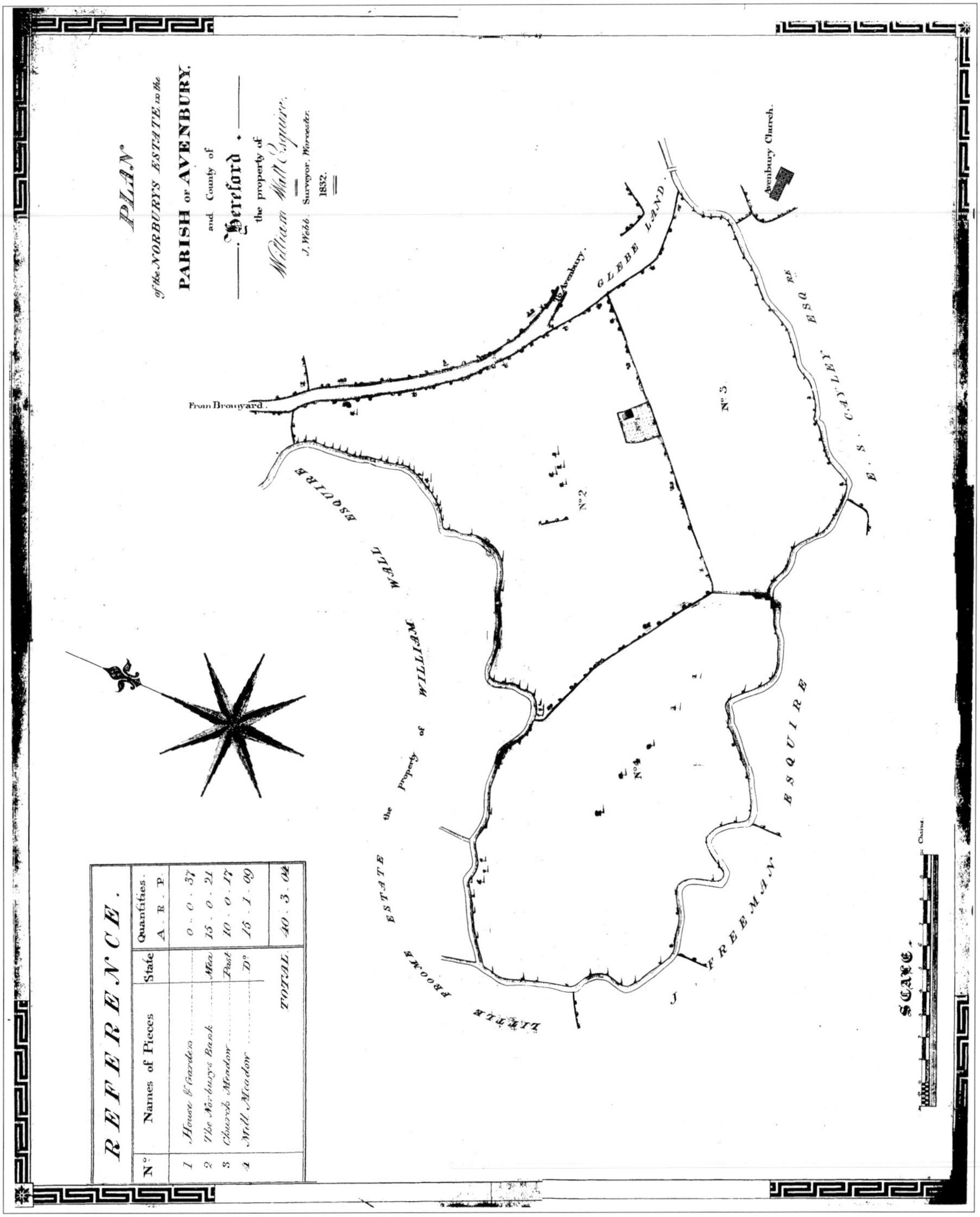
PLAN
of the NORBURYS ESTATE in the
PARISH or AVENBURY,
and County of
Hereford.
the property of
William Wall Esquire.
J. Webb. Surveyor, Worcester.
1832.
Avenbury Church.
From Bromyard
To Avenbury
GLEBE LAND
No 2
No 3
No 4
E. S. CAYLEY ESQ RE
WILLIAM WALL ESQUIRE
LITTLE FROOME ESTATE the property of
J. FREEMAN ESQUIRE
SCALE
Chains
REFFERENCE.
No | Names of Pieces | State | Quantities A. R. P.
1 | House & Garden | | 0 . 0 . 37
2 | The Norburys Bank | Mea | 15 . 0 . 21
3 | Church Meadow | Past | 10 . 0 . 17
4 | Mill Meadow | Do | 15 . 1 . 09
TOTAL | 40 . 3 . 04

garden.[21] The entrance to the property must have been from the Avenbury Lane near the hollow-way that led to the church. Nurbury's is remembered as a small house with a large chimney and was described by *The Royal Commission on Historical Monuments* in 1932 as a timber-framed 17th-century cottage with two original windows with moulded frames and mullions and some moulded ceiling beams. The house was demolished within living memory and the land is now farmed with Little Froome.

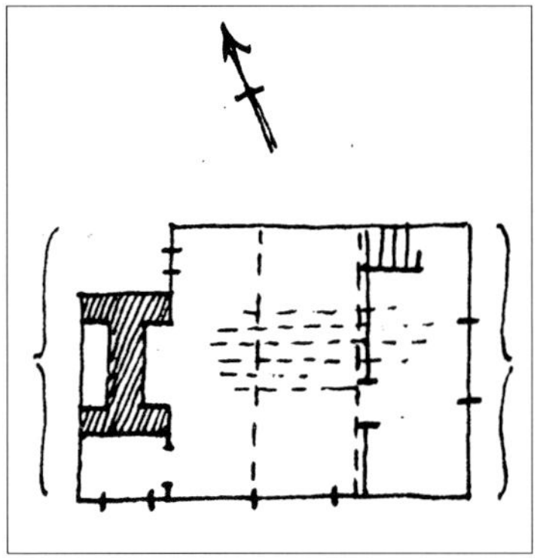

Plan of Nurbury's.
Royal Commission on the Historical Monuments of England

Little Froome Mill otherwise known as **Brand (Burnt) Mill**

The *Domesday Book* records a mill on this manor in 1086, worth 32d, probably on or very close to the same site. It also records for Avenbury 'A mill which pays nothing' but no other mill has yet been traced, so it would appear that the Avenbury Mill which was in the 13th century described as a fulling mill disappeared, and that Little Froome was the only mill that operated for the parish.

The earthworks associated with a water corn mill were extensive and expensive to construct, for in addition to the necessary buildings, a mill pool and mill leat were needed and good stoned access for heavily laden horses and carts. A

Little Froome Mill, 1970s. *Jennifer Weale*

regular and steady supply of water to drive the mill was a paramount need and this flow had to be carefully controlled to avoid damage to the mill machinery. The leat starts to the north of the Little Froome Estate near the boundary with Bromyard and a road may have come off the Avenbury Lane to the Mill, for 'Brandmyll Yate' was a land marker here in 1575. Whatever fire or accident occurred to warrant the name of Brand or Burnt Mill happened a long time ago and the name persisted for centuries.

In 1663 Thomas Crowther was assessed at £12 'for ye Mills'. Brand Mill was part of Little Froome Estate and in 1675 the miller, James Callowhill, had a six year lease of :

> 'all that messuage or dwelling house and all...water corne grist mylls commonly called ye Brand Mylls situate lying and beinge under one roofe in Avenbury.'

There were in 1673 three mills in operation,[22] probably meaning three pairs of millstones. Arthur Weaver who was acting for his grandson, Anthony Brown, agreed that the estate would be responsible for repairing the flood gates, if it became necessary, and also the tiling on the roof. Tiles lessened the risk of fire but were probably more expensive than the usual thatched roof. A century later Thomas Fincher was the miller and tenant and the buildings included a house, barn and stable with 12 acres of land. Around 1800 Richard Smith was the miller and like other occupants of the Mill duly served the parish as churchwarden and overseer.

The tithe map of 1840 shows a house, mill and another substantial farm building which probably comprised a barn and stable. Mrs Jennifer Weale recorded the property in 1971 when she noted that there had been a weir and sluice gate across the river Frome which diverted the water by a long contour leat to the mill; there was a leat back from the mill to the river to prevent flooding and also a by-pass hatch at the point where the leat crossed a small stream which flows into the river a short distance from the mill. The mill was described as a medium-sized red brick building with three floors and a gabled roof of king-post construction, which probably dates from around 1800. There was also a timber-framed and stone barn which appeared of 18th-century construction. The 19th-century brick house was detached from the mill building and at that time there were a number of bake ovens and kitchens pointing to use as a bakery as well as a residence.

The last miller, Mr Harry Mason, who moved to Birmingham, said that he could grind two cwt of corn in an hour and that he was never prevented from milling through shortage of water, but that floods did prevent operation of the machinery. Mr Pettifer, a Bromyard business man, at one time owned Little Froome and he planned to use the mill to make electricity for the town, but the enterprise never came to fruition because it was impossible to use the mill wheel during floods. The old iron water wheel, which was overshot, was removed for scrap during the Second World War. It ran two pairs of stones by an octagonal vertical wooden shaft. By 1971 the building was 'a dangerous ruin'.

Blacksmith's Shop lay at Munderfield on the road near the drive to Munderfield Court.

Hopton Sollers or Upper Hopton (Hopton Sollars)

George Dudgen, who died about 1609, lived with his family at Hopton Sollers in the late 16th century. His daughter and heiress Anne married William Nicholett of the Hill, Eastham, near Tenbury in Worcestershire about seven miles from Bromyard. By this marriage the Dudgen Estate in Avenbury passed to the Nicholetts who came to live at Hopton Sollers and retained the property for nearly 200 years.

William Nicholett of Hopton Sollers indicated in a will dated 18th February 1643 that he wished to be buried in the chancel of Eastham Church 'as near unto my Father and my Mother as conveniently can be'; and he left 20s to the poor of each of the parishes of Avenbury and Eastham. His eldest son William, born in 1617, appears to have inherited most of his property, wearing apparel and a considerable part of the household goods, as well as the responsibility for augmenting the portion of his sister Margaret. The other children were already married and established, Sarah being married to Francis Unett of Castle Frome and Mary to John Barneby. The two sons-in-law were appointed executors to oversee the will. At the time of his death, William senior was in possession of

Hopton Sollers *c*1900. *Morgan Collection*

Three generations of the Parker Family, John, Farmer, Carol and Percy in 1969.
Janet Parker

Hopton Sollers, Wicton in Bredenbury and the Hill at Eastham. Wicton had come to the Nicholett family by the marriage of Anne Rowden of Rowden near Bromyard to William Nicholett of Eastham around 1540. William, who married Anne Dudgen, was their grandson.[23]

William junior died leaving no children, for Nash reports a memorial in Eastham Church to William Nicholett and Anne his wife who departed this life 29th April 1649 and 'died without issue'. Of his four brothers, George, Richard and Andrew died young, and Gilbert, who was born in 1620 and lived at the Hill in Eastham, carried on the line at Hopton Sollers. His son Gilbert junior, the grandson of William and Anne (Dudgen), served in 1668 as High Sheriff of Herefordshire. In 1675 he married Mary Cornwall of Moccas in Herefordshire. Gilbert died in 1690 and Mary in 1702, leaving a son also called Gilbert as their heir at Hopton.

The present fine large stone 17th-century house at Hopton Sollers was built by the Nicholett Family. The nine hearths in the tax return of 1664 were surely of this dwelling. The site is a flat plateau with magnificent views down the valley. Silas Taylor who was a subcommissioner in sequestrations in Herefordshire during the Civil War was also a keen local historian; he travelled widely in the county and writing in about 1655 he described Hopton as 'a town on ye side of ye hill'.[24] Pos-

Hopton Sollers, 1931.
Royal Commission on the Historical Monuments of England

sibly at this date there were still some farmsteads standing that derived from the five village farmers of 1086, for there are, even today, earthworks beside the long drive that ascends from Stoke Lacy and these may well indicate lost buildings.

Gilbert, the son of Gilbert and Mary and later known as Colonel Nicholett, was born in 1680 and was quite young when his parents died. He was to have a distinguished career. He served Queen Anne and was aide-de-camp to the Duke of Marlborough, serving in all his battles except for one when he had leave of absence to get married. His first wife was Theodosia Tomkins of Buckenhill near Bromyard, but sadly she died at the age of 23 in 1708 and was buried in Hereford Cathedral. Gilbert made a second marriage the following year to a very young woman, who was in her early teens, Ann Mary Christiana Doyge of Brussels, whose father was auditor to the Emperor of Germany. By Ann Mary he fortunately had a son and heir, Gilbert the third, for Colonel Nicholett too died young at

Hopton Sollers 1998. *Howard Painter*

Hopton Sollers 1998, south front. *Howard Painter*

the age of 33 in 1713. His widow remarried and her second husband was John Skynner of Walton in Bishop's Frome, and she was buried in Bishop's Frome Church in 1770 at the age of 74.

The Nicholett family do not appear to have been active in Avenbury itself, seldom if ever taking a parish office, even of churchwarden; it would seem that they attended the church of Stoke Lacy. At the Quarter Sessions in 1679, Gilbert Nicholett appealed against a claim that he should assist in the repair of ways in Avenbury. He said that he had always and at his own expense repaired the ways to Hopton without assistance from the parish. The court declared that he ought not to be charged and discharged him for the future from any claim on his premises.[25]

Gilbert Nicholett the third was born in 1710 and in about 1738 he married Elizabeth Stephens of Bromtrees Hall in Bishop's Frome. She was the daughter of Richard and Elizabeth Stephens who had built a new house on the site around 1722 and had established an estate of some 165 acres.[26] Gilbert and Elizabeth moved to Bromtrees Hall shortly after their marriage and their son Gilbert, born in 1749, was described as of Hopton Sollers and Bromtrees Hall and afterwards of Pill House, Barnstaple, Devon. Gilbert the fourth married a West Country bride and his family moved south. The estate at Hopton was sold about 1778 to John Clark of Devon, who shortly afterwards sold it to James Cooke and by 1812 it belonged to the Liverpool merchant Richard Allison (*c*1748-1835). This Richard married Elizabeth the daughter of William Dowding of Worcester in about 1787 and thereby acquired Great Wacton near Bredenbury. There was a marriage agreement in 1786, to which John Freeman was party, to raise £2,000 for the child

Green hops being levelled in the hopkiln at Hopton Sollers in 1985 by Farmer Parker.
Farmer Parker

The dried hops being baled by Edward Partridge, Farmer's grandfather in the same year.
Farmer Parker

Augering out holes ready for apple trees 1998. *Farmer Parker*

Planting and guarding apple trees 1998. *Farmer Parker*

Hopton Sollers no longer grows hops, and is now growing 80 acres of cider apples.

View of Hopton Sollers. *Farmer Parker*

or children of Richard Allison and his wife, Elizabeth (Dowding). Their son Richard lived from 1790 to 1874.[27]

During the 18th century the house of Hopton Sollers was extensively modernised and altered, following dilapidations or possibly a fire. The roof was completely replaced, new windows inserted, the staircase was moved and a new one added, and a corridor was constructed upstairs to serve the bedrooms. Later, in the 1800s, a model range of buildings which included stables, wainhouse, barn, horse-engine house and other farm buildings was constructed to augment the

Hopton Sollers horse engine house 1998. *Howard Painter*

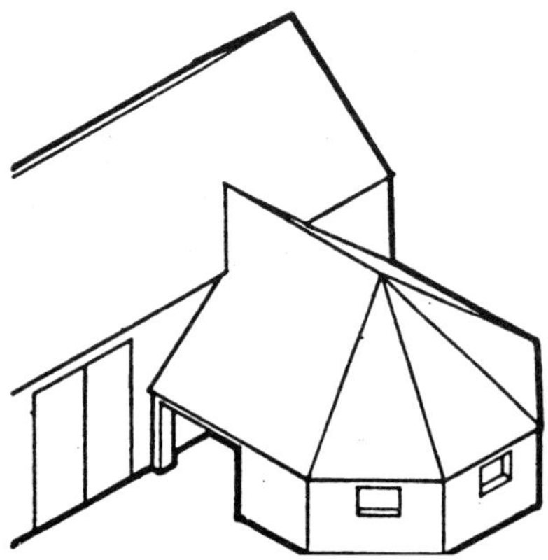

Half-octagonal horse engine house on side of barn.

large 17th-century eight bay corn and threshing barn. Nineteen acres of hops were grown here in 1840 and the extensive hop drying and storing facilities of several periods are particularly interesting.

William Holloway was the tenant in 1840 when this was the largest farm in the parish, covering 319 acres. William was born in Worcestershire, and he and his wife Ann had two grown-up children living with them at Hopton in 1851; their five male farm labourers also lived in the house and Ann Pilliner, a 20 year old house servant was their only domestic help. By 1871, their son Benjamin was farming Hopton with 350 acres; he and his wife had four young children under the age of seven, two house servants, a governess and two farm workers in their large household. William Holloway, probably another son, was farming at Hackley. Benjamin Holloway farmed Hopton for many years and was active in the parish, serving on the committee to establish the school at Munderfield. Edward Price was here in 1940 and Mr John Parker and his family have been at Hopton Sollers since 1952.

OWNERS AND OCCUPIERS OF HOPTON SOLLERS after 1600

George Dudgen of Hopton Sollers = Margaret
d1609
William Nicholett = Ann Dudgen
d1643 d after 1649
Mary Baskerville of Pontrilus 1= Gilbert Nicholett =2 Mary Thomas
Gilbert Nicholett =1675 Mary Cornwall of Moccas
High Sheriff 1668-9 d1690 d1702
Theodosia Tomkins 1= Gilbert Nicholett =2 Ann Doyge
of Buckenhill 1685-1708 1680-1713 m1709 1696-1770
Gilbert Nicholett = Elizabeth Stephens of Bromtrees Hall
1710-1778 1718-1801
Gilbert Nicholett = Elizabeth Reader of Devon
1749-1796
1778 John Clarke of Devon
James Cooke
1812 Richard Allison of Liverpool
by 1840 William Holloway
by 1870 Benjamin Holloway
1940 Edward Price
1952 John Parker
The Parker Family

Noakes

Noakes was in the hands of William Brown in 1347 and apparently remained in the ownership of that family who lived at Little Froome. The *Visitation of Herefordshire 1569* records on page 45 that there was around 1580 a Richard Heydey of Noxe or Nox, Herefordshire. Richard married Dorothy a daughter of John Rompeney of Suckley and she was the widow of Richard Browne. He could well have had a lease of Noakes as a result of the marriage. Nearly 300 years later

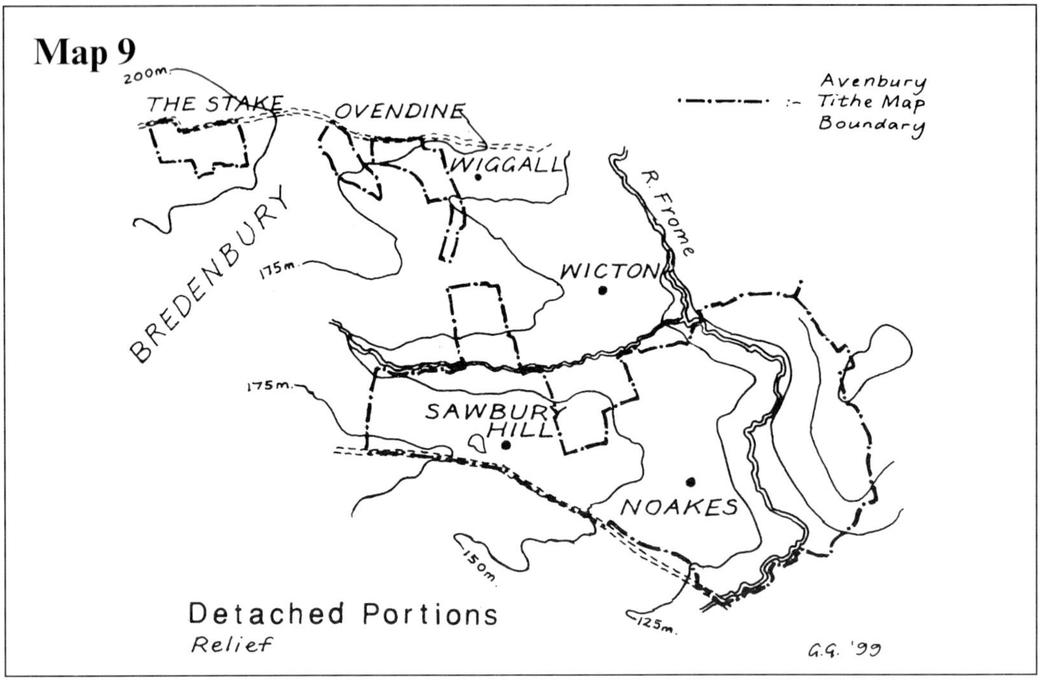

the Brown family were still or again involved with Noakes. In 1670 Anne Pitt of Noakes, widow, devised in her will 'the lease and all my estate, title, term of years yet to come and unexpired ...granted of the messuage or tenament and ffarme called the Noakes....by one Anthony Browne and Richard Browne gents. unto me the said Anne for the tearme of one and twentie yeares if the said Richard Browne shall soe longe live or for some longer tearme' to her brother-in-law James Pitt of Felton, Herefordshire.[28]

Noakes 1998. *Howard Painter*

The Pitt family were at Noakes for some generations for in 1661 'Henry Pytt of the Noke' died and was buried at Avenbury Church. Another Henry Pitt, probably his son, had an estate assessed at £21 in 1663, and in 1665 Henry Pitt paid tax on five hearths. This 'Henry Pitt the elder of Noakes' died in 1666, leaving his widow Anne his executrix and principal beneficiary, with legacies to his sons Henry, Rowland and Richard, to his married daughters Anne ffloyde, Elizabeth Joyner, Rachael Drewe and Sarah Kinge, and to his unmarried daughters Susannah and Joan. To his brother James he left 'All that one meadowe or piece or parcel of meadow......being within the parish of Bromyard.... called and known by the name of Brann Mill Meadowe'. The value of his goods, cattles and chattels added up to over £183, which included books worth 10s and his wearing apparel worth £3, a considerable item when three bedsteads, a feather bed and flock bed were only valued at £3. His room by room inventory included parlour, buttery, hall, kitchen and some seven upstairs rooms. Part of this house dating from the 16th century still stands.

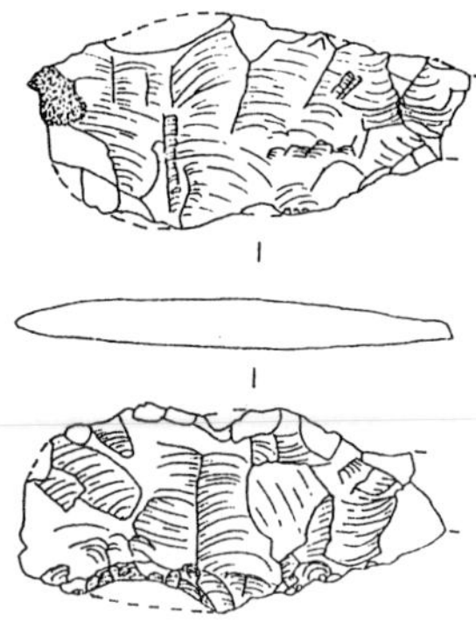

Leaf shaped arrow head found at Noakes by - Deborah Waller. *Drawn by Philippa Bradley*

Henry Pitt, his eldest son, died shortly afterwards and his widow Anne died in 1670. In her will she left 2s 6d to be distributed amongst the poorer of the inhabitants of the parish of Avenbury, and furniture, beds, sheets, dishes and other household goods and farm stock to various members of the family together with money bequests. Her inventory added up to £136. Her daughter Joan, as yet unmarried, received the residue of her estate and was with Anne's brother Philip Andrews, an executor of the will.

The Morse family owned the Noakes in the mid-18th century and they probably added the Georgian front wing to the house. By 1790 Mrs Mary Davis, previously a widowed Mrs Morse, was living at the Noakes with her son William and his family; William was the 'only surviving son and heir of William Morse decd.' and he died in 1811, leaving sons John and Edward and daughters Anna Maria and Kate.[29] His will directed that the Noakes should be sold to pay his expenses and debts, his son John was to inherit Wiggall in Avenbury (now in - Bredenbury) and Bolter's Close in Bredenbury, and the remainder of his estate was to be divided equally between the four children. Andrew Maund purchased the Noakes in 1815 but perhaps he could not raise the money as five years later Francis Williams of Wichenford in Worcestershire became the owner. Later Noakes became part of the Bredenbury Estate.

During this period many different tenants were recorded in various documents and returns: Charles Davis in 1736, George Maund in 1759 and 1783, and Mr Raybold 1805 and 1817 (William Raybold of the Noakes together with William White living at the same place were named as trustees for the management

Noakes 1998. *Howard Painter*

of William Morse's estate after his death in 1811). William Green who was unmarried was here before 1835, and in 1851 he was farming 195 acres at the Noakes with seven labourers and a boy. He had living in a housekeeper and house servant, his waggoner, waggoner's boy and a farmservant. Joseph Corbett 'farmer, hop grower and cattle dealer' was at the Noakes by 1867 and his son, another Joseph, by 1891. By this last date the ancient estate and manor of Noakes which had for centuries been a detached part of the parish of Avenbury had been transferred (in 1882) to the parish of Bredenbury.

Sawbury Hill 1998. *Howard Painter*

Sawbury Hill

This small manor came into the hands of John le Moigne of Rowden around 1243 and remained part of the Rowden Estate until it was purchased by Edmund Higginson of Saltmarsh Castle near Bromyard in 1858. Sawbury Hill subsequently became allied to the Bredenbury Estate.

In 1691 Anthony Rowden of Rowden made a will devising Sawbury Hill (then in the tenure of William Baker) together with other property (which included Hill House and Ganderland in the township of Winslow) to trustees.[30] The Herefordshire Militia Assessments for 1663 show that Anthony Rowden, gent of Rowden, was valued for £6 in Avenbury, in Winslow for £10, in Bredenbury for £3 5s, in Bromyard borough for £1 l0s and in Thornbury with Rowden for £28. His was a considerable estate.

Anthony Rowden born in 1629, was twice married, first to Sybille Cassey, and then to Jane Chetle of Worcester, but remained childless. Jane was executrix of Anthony Rowden's will and one of his trustees. She later married Francis Bridges of Tibberton in Worcestershire. Mary Rowden, Anthony's sister, who married John Barneby of Brockhampton, was the Rowden heiress and her grand-daughter Mary Briggenshaw married Edward Cope Hopton of Canon Frome,

Sawbury Hill 1998. *Howard Painter*

Herefordshire. By 1734, Sawbury Hill and other Avenbury properties were in the hands of Richard Cope Hopton of Canon Frome, the son of Edward and Mary. At that time Sawbury covered 74 acres.[31]

Mr Vale was farming here in 1805, and the next known occupier was Joseph Gillam who also farmed the Hill House. By 1840 Sawbury Hill belonged to John Beresford Turner who owned the nearby 49 acre Hill House farm in Winslow parish. William Gillam rented Sawbury Hill farm and John Gillam rented Hill House, on opposite sides of the Leominster Road out of Bromyard. In 1851 Mrs Gillam, an elderly widow, was farming Sawbury with her son John, while the waggoner and waggoner's boy both lived in the house, as did a farm servant and house servant. The two farms were purchased by Edmund Higginson from Septimus Holmes Godson in 1858. Thomas Parlour was at Sawbury in 1867 and in 1871 he described himself as farmer of 131 acres, employing three labourers. George Nutt was farming Sawbury by 1891, but by then, in fact in 1882, Sawbury Hill together with Noakes and Wiggall had already been transferred to the parish of Bredenbury.

A comfortable three-storey Georgian farmhouse, built in stone around 1760, now stands on the site and may have been built by the Cope Hopton family. There are extensive farm buildings, which include an impressive eight bay stone and timber-framed barn. These form a courtyard complex between the house and the road. There are slight earthworks that could indicate a moated house site here in medieval times and a field by the house was still called 'fish pool piece' in 1840.

DESCENT OF SAWBURY HILL AFTER 1600

Anthony Rowden = Ann, daughter of Maurice Berkeley
1540-1622
Richard Rowden = Mary Bushell of Broadmaston, Gloucestershire
1566-1651
Edward Rowden = Anne Pembrugge of Wellington, Herefordshire
1601-1656 1604-1704 buried at Bromyard

Anthony Rowden 1629-1691
= 1 Sybille Cassey d1678
= 2 Jane Chetle of Worcester
(she remarried Francis Bridges of Tibberton, Worcestershire)

Mary Rowden 1630-1721
= John Barneby of Brockhampton

Anne Barneby = Timothy Briggenshawe
Mary Briggenshawe, heiress of Rowden = Edward Cope Hopton
Richard Cope Hopton d 1810
His cousin Rev William Parsons, assumed name of Hopton 1817
1840 John Beresford Turner
1858 Edmund Higginson of Saltmarsh Castle

Wiggal

Wiggall built in 1841 by Thomas Purser.
Howard Painter

This was another detached portion of Avenbury and lies near Sawbury Hill of which it may have been a part. The unusual name appears to derive from the personal name Wicga and means 'Wicga's Hill'; the nearby Wicton Farm probably means 'Wicga's settlement'.[32] There are 30 acres at the northern extremity of the detached Avenbury lands lying on the road which runs from Bredenbury to Rowden, which may also have belonged to Anthony Rowden and his ancestors. In 1840 there were 11 acres at Wiggall belonging to William Grape, nine acres at the Stake belonging to William Crump and nine and a half acres at the Leasow which belonged to Charles Dutton. Wiggall had certainly been included with the property of Anthony Rowden's trustees in 1705.[33]

There was also, a farm called **Overdine** or **The Birches** which was described in 1790 'all which premises are in Avenbury, and were heretofore reputed to be part of the manor of Little Froome'.[34] This may take us back to 1086 when Hugh, the brother and sub-tenant of Roger Lacy, held both the manor of Little Froome and Sawbury.

Richard Bufton purchased Wiggall from the Cope Hoptons in 1736 'to hold of the chief lord of the fee by rents and services due'.[35] Richard was unable to repay the mortgage and sold the property to Humphrey Cooke of Upper Sapey in 1778. Wiggall then comprised a messuage, cottage, barn, stable, fold, garden and two orchards with six acres of land, three acres of meadow and two acres of pasture and was sold to William West of Bredenbury in 1808.[36]

William West purchased other small properties in the vicinity including the Birches and Overdine; he took down cottages, buildings and fences and threw them into one. By 1811 Wiggall together with Bolter's Close in Bredenbury were in the hands of William Morse of Noakes, for in that year he left these properties to his son John (see Noakes page 129).

Before 1840, Wiggall became the property of William Plumtre Grape. Plumtre Grape was a surgeon of Bromyard and lived for a time prior to 1836 in the maltster's house opposite the Falcon Inn. In 1837, he purchased Bolter's Close, a small farm in Bredenbury, and possibly at the same time Wiggall, as there is an estate map of the two properties dated 1839 which now hangs at Wiggall. The house at Bolter's Close was then standing but there was no building at Wiggall. The 1841 census report for Bredenbury shows William Plumtre Grape of 'independent mean' living at Bolter's Close with Thomas Purser, farmer, then aged 35 years and his wife Martha and Joseph Philpott a farm worker. When William Plumtre Grape sold Bolter's Close in 1845, the conveyance stated that the house, stable and buildings there had recently been rebuilt.

The present house at Wiggall was also built at this time in stone and brick and with a datestone inscribed '1841 TP' which initials must stand for Thomas Purser. It is rectangular in shape and on three storeys, with two principal rooms on each floor and a service lean-to at the rear of the ground floor. A barn, stable, cowhouse and pigscots were built at the same time and together they present a very useful small farming complex standing by the road from Bredenbury to Rowden. Thomas and Martha Purser, both of whom were born in Pershore, were still living there in 1851, and William Plumtre Grape a 'retired medical man' was lodging with them; a young house servant Sarah Phillips aged 15 helped to look after them all.

The household must later have moved to Bromyard for when Plumtre Grape died there in 1866 at the age of 85, he appointed his old servant Thomas Purser and his son Thomas Henry Purser both of whom were then living with him, to be executors of his will. To Thomas Purser with whom he had lived at Wiggall, he left four parcels of land in Bredenbury 'formerly part of Bolter's Close' and in the occupation of Sarah Cave, as well as a piece of arable land in the parish of Bromyard called Lloyd's Acre, together with all his money, securities, furniture and personal estate. To Thomas Henry

Wiggall built in 1841 by Thomas Purser.
Howard Painter

Purser the son he left £4,000 and a parcel of meadow called Highwell and the Old Orchard, both in the parish of Bromyard, together with all his remaining real estate.

Thomas Purser died at Bromyard in 1872, leaving to his wife Martha his house and premises in Pershore, and also the yearly sum of £25 payable out of the rent of Wiggall which was then in the occupation of Sarah Cave (who must have been farming Wiggall with the four parcels of land from Bolter's Close). To his son Thomas Henry he left 'all my messuage, buildings, garden and premises situate in the town of Bromyard in which I now reside and all my lands adjoining thereto called Haylings Orchard'. Thomas Henry was also to have Wiggall and the Pershore property after the death of Martha Purser, who died in Bromyard in 1890 at the age of 89.

Thomas Henry Purser, who had served as a colonel in the Herefordshire Rifle Volunteers, had lived until his death in 1928 at Bird's Eye, Highwell in Bromyard, which could have also been the final home of William Plumtre Grape and Henry and Martha Purser. He left his considerable estate between his four children Rose Gertrude, Beatrice Mary, Henry and Edmund George, with a slight indulgence towards Rose 'as some recompense to her for the years during which she has cared for me and her mother and for having been thus prevented from securing a position such as my other three children have been able to provide for themselves'.

Wiggall, described as 'all that freehold farmhouse with buildings and 17 acres, two roods and 34 perches of land,' was sold by the Pursers in 1929 for £700 to William Smith, and in 1933 it was purchased by the Evans Family of Wacton. They still own the property and live in the delightful house built by Thomas and Martha Purser to be their home in 1841, more than 150 years ago.[37]

Chapter 8

Other Farms in Avenbury Parish after 1600

> 'In my young days most of the farmers rode to market on strong, short-legged horses, two or three in company - neighbour fashion - talking of cattle, corn or orchard crops, and later in the day meeting again at market dinner, to learn the latest London news or country gossip.'
>
> James Johnston, *The Finding of St Augustine's Chair* (1898), 3

The remaining larger farms in the parish have not left such complete records as the Domesday manors, but their history can be traced to a lesser extent. In 1840 they comprised some 1107 acres and were in order of size:

Munderfield Court	286 acres
The Heath	198 acres
Cusop	141 acres
Burgess	132 acres
Greeve	113 acres
Hackley	80 acres
Birchyfield	66 acres
Rough Mintridge	41 acres
Goodships	35 acres
Northfields	15 acres

These larger farms all have descriptive names relating to position, terrain, other natural features or an early farmer, and in most cases will have been farms or clusters of holdings which were established if not by 1086 then certainly within the next two centuries; the farmhouses of today are probably on or very close to the sites of medieval settlements.

The land in the parish is fertile, with medium to heavy soil and suitable for all grain crops which today can average over three tonnes to the acre. Hops do very well although the acreage devoted to the crop has diminished considerably over the last few years. It is an expensive crop to establish with the cost of poles and wire supports, and it needs a high input of fertiliser and sprays, moreover, today's markets are unsure and competitive with no assured return at the end of the season. The ground is on the heavy side for root crops but potatoes are grown. Grass is a prime crop and stock do well in Avenbury.

Most of the farmhouses date from the 17th century and there are a few barns from this period. There are some fine farm complexes that were built as a result of the prosperous period of the 'High Farming' years of the mid-19th century. Corn

Map 10

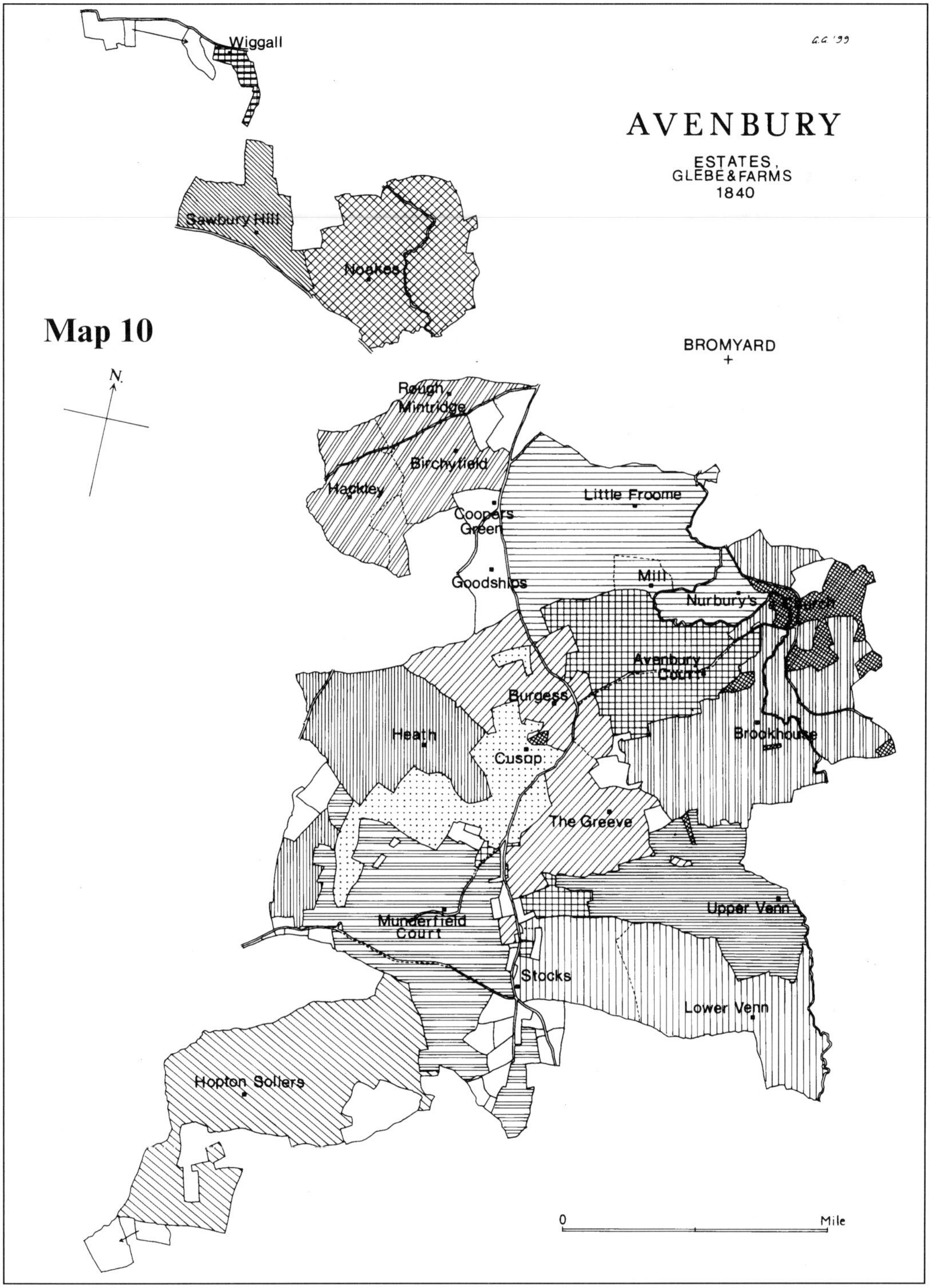
G.G. '99
AVENBURY
ESTATES,
GLEBE & FARMS
1840
BROMYARD
N.
Wiggall
Sawbury Hill
Noakes
Rough
Mintridge
Birchyfield
Hackley
Little Froome
Coopers
Green
Goodships
Mill
Nurbury's
Church
Avenbury
Court
Burgess
Heath
Cusop
Brookhouse
The Greeve
Upper Venn
Munderfield
Court
Stocks
Lower Venn
Hopton Sollers
0
Mile

prices were high and the larger corn growing farms such as Hopton Sollers, Little Froome and Munderfield Court added a horse-engine house, often called a gin-ring, to their large corn barns to help with the threshing and other work. The horse-engine was later replaced by the oil or petrol engine. Other farms used the horse-engine outside in the stack yard without a protective building. Many farm buildings date from this period after 1800 and include stables, cowhouses, hop kilns and barns, which must in some cases have replaced earlier structures.

Farm and other houses also benefited from periods of prosperity or new landlords. Sawbury Hill and the Heath were both rebuilt about 1770 and Birchyfield around 1810. The farmhouses of the Burgess and the Greeve were both extended between 1815 and 1869 and at about the same time many houses were refronted, extended and renovated in brick or stone, instead of the traditional timber-framing.

James Johnston describing the buildings that he had seen on a walk from Bromyard to Avenbury and Stanford Bishop in the mid-19th century wrote in 1898:

> 'Fifty years ago most of the farm homesteads were old half-timbered houses, chequered black and white, with barns that far exceeded them in size: fronting the deeply littered foldyard, fenced with a square of pigsties, cowhouses and stables, thick-thatched and walled with strong wattle-work and thick mortar.'[1]

Munderfield Court

The place-name derives from *felde* which means 'open land' and it is thought that the name was given to an area which had been cleared for arable or stock farming; the significance of *Munder* has long been agonised over, but it is now thought to be an Anglo-Saxon personal name Munda so here we have 'Munda's cleared land'.[2] There are two Munderfields in the Bromyard district: Munderfield Harold in Winslow parish was an important estate in medieval times and was at Domesday held by a *radman* or 'riding man' who owed a superior service to his overlord. The Avenbury Munderfield was probably an integral estate at an early date and could have supported a number of farming families in the Saxon and Norman periods. The remains of house platforms which could indicate a community here at one time lay in the orchard south-east of the farmhouse and on the west side of the old road that goes south from the house. They were seen when the Bromyard and District Local History Society visited Munderfield in 1972.

The field names of 1840 may indicate that the cleared land was for stock farming: Ox Leasow, Cow Pasture, Stirkey (stirks were young cattle) and Witherley which may derive from 'wether', another name for a ram. A list of field names for Munderfield which appeared on a conveyance of 1856 included: Milch (milk) Meadow, Stable Orchard, Sweet Greens, Sterkey, Upper Cow Leasow, Ox

Leasow Croft, Witherley and also those several pieces of Arable Land in a Common Field called Castle Field and also that piece of land enclosed out of Crays (another name for a crow) Field at the bottom of Castle Field. Another interesting field name was St Mary's Close of 12 acres and there was a cottage and garden called Vine Yard in the occupation of John Brown which was surely the attractive cottage near the Stocks Farm today called Vine Tree Cottage.[3] There was also at Munderfield in Ox Leasow an acre of land called Beggar's Meadow in two separate parcels which had at some time been given to St Katherine's Hospital in Ledbury and for which the tenant of Munderfield Farm paid £1 annual rent.[4]

John Hancox of Munderfield, Avenbury made his will on the 22nd February 1598.[5] He had taken out a lease for a house and land at Munderfield in 1577 which was to continue after his death for another 80 years, so long as his wife Anne and his sons Richard and John should survive him. After his wife's death or remarriage the remaining years of the lease were to pass to his four children George, John, William and Dowty. The lease had cost John Hancox more than £140 and as he had not that value 'in goods or otherwise' he charged his son Richard who was his executor, to pay legacies to the remainder of the children. His furniture he left principally to his wife Anne. It would seem that the family continued to farm at Munderfield. A Richard Handcox appeared in the Quarter Sessions records of the mid-17th century when he was serving office as constable and he was also one of the parish raters in 1663.

The Militia Assessments for 1663 show Richard Handcox with an estate valued at £6 and in 1665 he shared his house of four hearths with his mother Mrs Katherine (Catherine) Selly who also had an estate worth £6. Mrs Selly (Sely) of Munderfield, widow, died in January 1677 and her son Richard administered her small estate of £8 18s 6d. This was comprised principally of personal and household goods, but she did have £2 18s 0d owing to her for rent. One of the appraisers of her estate was Edward Mason and the inventory of Thomas Mason of Munderfield dated 18th October 1676 has also survived. Thomas lived in a house with a parlour, hall, buttery and dayhouse (dairy) and rooms over the parlour, hall and dayhouse. The value of his livestock was £11 13s 4d, the corn and hay £7 6s 8d, and his hops £5, the total estate being worth £33 18s. The present house at Munderfield Court is large and Catherine Selly appeared to live in only part of it although her son Richard certainly shared the house in 1665. Where the Mason family lived is not at present known.

The next known occupiers of Munderfield Court were the Cooke or Cook family who were active in Avenbury certainly from 1733 when William Cooke was churchwarden and for several generations after. William Cooke the elder, gentleman, was born about 1670, the son of William and Joyce Cooke of Avenbury. He married in 1715, a widow, Ann Hallings of Stoke Lacy and died in 1738. Their eldest son another William inherited the property at Munderfield at the young age of 22, when he was already married to Mary Gardener of Much Cowarne. This William was churchwarden in 1747 and 1754. Father and son and possibly

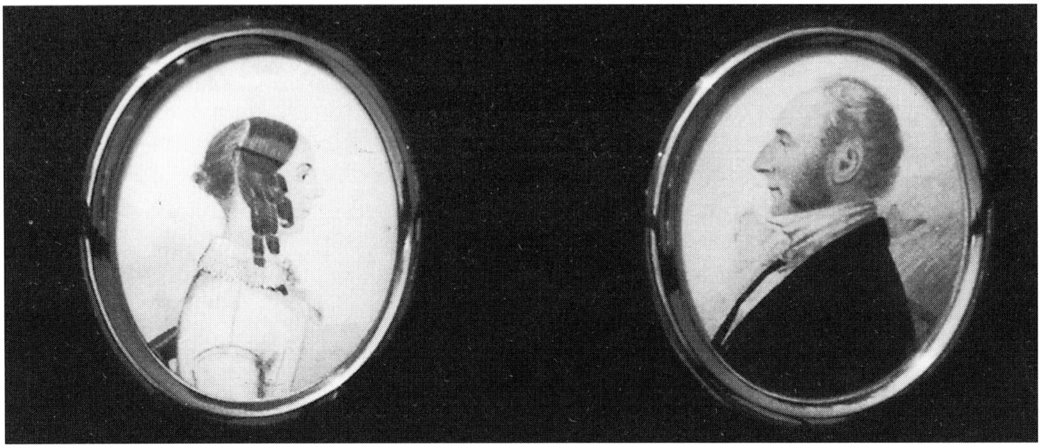

John Cook b. Avenbury 1772, married Ann Weeks (b.1779) 1797

Howard Painter

This beautiful sampler was worked by Rebecca Cook of Bromyard in 1786, when she was aged 10. Rebecca was a granddaughter of William and Mary Cook of Munderfield Court, Avenbury. *Howard Painter*

grandson served as overseers in 1736, 1743, 1750 and 1758 and William Cooke junior was overseer 'for Munderfield' in 1767, 1774 and 1786. The marriage of William and Mary was fruitful for between 1737 and 1758 they had 18 children all of whom appear to have been christened at Avenbury Church. William Cooke died in 1776, to be survived by his widow Mary and ten of their children: namely William, Thomas, James, John, Edward, Ann (the wife of Richard West of Little Froome), Jane (the wife of Nathaniel Smith probably of Brookhouse), Elinor (the wife of William Phillips), Margary and Sarah. From 1764 there was a Thomas Cook at Avenbury Court and in 1794 a James Cook at Hopton; the Cook family farmed and occupied

THE COOK(E) FAMILY OF AVENBURY AND BROMYARD

William Cook = Joyce buried 1707 Avenbury

William Cook = (1715) Ann Hallinge bp 1693
died 1738 at Munderfield Court

William Cook = (1736) Mary Gardner of Much Cowarne
died 1776 at Munderfield Court

John Cook = (1771) Rebecca Smith of Bromyard
bp 1747 — died 1778
died 1815
he became a chandler in Bromyard

John Cook = (1797) Ann Weeks
1772-1841 he was a chandler of Bromyard — died 1831

John Cook = (1841) Jane Gardner
1805-1874 — of Bishop's Frome
he was a chandler — died 1876
of Bromyard.

Thomas Cooke = Eliza
bp1808
farmed at Norton,
Bromyard

John Gardner Cook = (1870) Sarah Mytton
1842-1876 — died 1922

Sarah Cook = (1895) Walter Painter

Frederick John Cook = c1876 Elizabeth Parker
1846-1912
of Brookhouse, Avenbury

Thomas bp 1878 of Brookhouse Avenbury
Alfred James bp 1880
Hubert bp 1882 of Brookhouse Avenbury
John Farmer bp 1884
Elizabeth bp 1886
Mary bp 1887
Elsie bp 1889

most of the larger farms in the parish at various times. As late as 1935 direct descendants of the Cooke family of Munderfield Court were farming at Brookhouse.

Robert Dent farmed the estate after the Cooke family and he appears in the tithe schedule of 1840 as tenant of 286 acres which belonged to Benjamin Saunders of Bromsgrove. Robert Dent was born in 1772. In 1851 he described himself as a farmer of 285 acres, employing seven labourers. He and his wife Ann

Thomas Cook born around 1808, a great grandson of William and Mary Cook of Munderfield Court and the father of Frederick John Cook (*c*1846-1912) of - Brookhouse.

had a grown-up son and daughter living at home with a house servant and two of their labourers living in.

By 1871 a younger man of 30, Stephen Philpott perhaps a son of Stephen Philpott of Brookhouse, had taken the lease. He and his wife Anne had a large household of nine, with two young children, Anne's father (Peter Hyde, also a farmer), her sister, a domestic servant and two farm servants. Henry Thomas followed Stephen Philpott towards the end of the century. The Eckley family came to Munderfield Court in 1900 and the fourth generation of that family are still farming here.

The house at Munderfield bears the stamp of several generations. There is considerable timber-work of the early 17th century including two ovolo moulded beams in the kitchen similar to those in Little Froome farmhouse and one ceiling beam with wide chamfers which could be 16th century, and there are early roof timbers. The plan of the house suggests a date before 1650 and there are signs of internal timber-framing and

Redvers Eckley in the hopyard at Munderfield Court.
Bromyard Local History Society Collection

Hops from Munderfield Court being carried by Frome Valley Transport.
Bromyard Local History Society Collection

an external section which is now hidden by the roof of a rear extension. The Cook family made their mark in the 18th century with an ambitious renovation of new hipped roof, new windows and fireplaces, and consequently the house, especially from the outside, looks misleadingly Georgian. An intriguing feature, which is the result of the house being built into a bank, is the raised small front garden, beneath which are goose pens and dog kennels; the cellar is entered at ground level from the farmyard.

The stone farm buildings are impressive and although some look older, they appear to date from after 1840 as the present lay out is quite different to that on the tithe map. They were probably built by the landlord Benjamin Saunders of Bromsgrove in Worcestershire, for his tenant Robert Dent. One by the house

Munderfield Court July 1999. *Howard Painter*

Munderfield Court, cellar beneath house. *Howard Painter*

Barn at Munderfield Court with 12 square stone pillars. *Howard Painter*

incorporates an outside kitchen, cider mill and press, with hop drying facilities and storage for grain on the upper floor. This building was subsequently extended in brick for further hop kilns, but they are now disused as hops are no longer grown on the farm. There is an unusual open hay or corn barn with a slate roof supported by 12 square stone pillars and a magnificent 12 bay barn built of stone externally with a brick lining. Attached to the rear of the barn is a gin-ring, which contained gearing pulled by horses to work a threshing machine and other farm machinery. There is an excellent range of buildings opposite the house which includes stables and further away a wain house and cowshed.

In 1840 there were four more dwellings on the Munderfield Estate: Castle House in Castle Field which stood just down Stoke Lane near the crossroads, a cottage further down Stoke Lane, a cottage on the small road that leads to Growland Farm, and Stone Cottage on the Munderfield Road. Of these only Stone Cottage still stands. There is no history of a castle at Munderfield but the ground here is over 200 metres (650 feet), the highest in the parish, and this may have suggested an ideal castle or defended site. Alternatively the name could derive from *caestel* 'a heap of stones', possibly denoting an old ruined building or fortification.

The Heath

The farm name derives from the heather plant, which appears to indicate that this area was left uncultivated at one time. There is a field on the west boundary of the farm called Chance Moor which may have been moorland used for chasing or hunting. In 1840 the Heath belonged to John, Joseph and Charles Cooke, and Robert Hancock was their tenant. It was the fifth largest farm in the parish and the farm buildings were probably the most extensive in Avenbury; there was also a cottage in Stoke Lane which has now disappeared.

In 1620 Edward Lane of Hopton Sollers left to 'Henry Boyce of the Heath and his poore wiefe & children one whoope of Momcorne' (a measure of mixed corn). The Boyce family, whose family home may have been the Heath, are recorded in the parish between 1589 and 1707. Henry Boyce as a sidesman signed the 1628 Avenbury terrier; while Richard Boyce had been a signatory to the terriers of 1589 and 1619. Richard Boyce of Avenbury left a will dated 1637 leaving legacies to his daughter Alice Woodyate and to her son Edward and the remainder of his goods, cattle and chattels dead or alive to his wife Alice. Alice died in January 1639 leaving many legacies including 10s for the poor of the parish of Avenbury. Richard Boyce may have been her second husband, for she left money to her son John Sheppard and his children, and like her late husband she left legacies to members of the Woodyate family; the principal beneficiary and executor of her will was her son-in-law Thomas Conney, whose family we meet again farming other properties in the parish.[6]

By 1663 'William Sherriff for the Heath' was assessed £21 on his estate and in 1665 he was listed with two hearths. William Sherriff, senior, died in 1671 and in the same year Richard Sherriff was guardian of Avenbury Church. Richard's wife Frances was buried at Avenbury in 1705. A Richard Sherriff was either road surveyor or constable for Avenbury and in 1681 he appealed at the Quarter Sessions to be reimbursed for his expenses on behalf of the parish. (See Chapter 11)

A description of the property in 1733, described:

> 'All that messuage or tenament and ffarme situate lying and being in Avenbury in the county of Hereford, commonly called or known by the name of the Heath now in the tenure of Mary Norris or her undertenant or undertenants. And all dovehouses barns stables gardens orchards lands....to the said messuage....belonging or in anyway appertaining situate lying and being in Avenbury aforesid.'[7]

Miss Norris was living in Worcester in 1730 and died sometime before 1737. After her death there was a report in chancery to decide her next of kin. She was the daughter of Thomas Norris of Eye, Herefordshire and his wife Frances, nee James. Apparently, before the age of consent for marriage but with the consent of her mother, Mary had agreed to marry 'one Mr Herbert', but before the year was out changed her mind 'and never afterwards married on that account'. As she was the only child of Thomas Norris, her estate was deemed to descend through her father's three sisters: Sarah who had married Edmund Weaver, Mary who had married Miles Blount and Jane who had died unmarried. The heirs of Mary Norris were adjudged to be three. The first two were Sarah and Ann Weaver, spinster daughters and coheirs of Richard Weaver late of Hereford, who had been the son of Sarah and Edmund Weaver. The third was John Blount of Orleton, Herefordshire, son of Thomas Blount (who had married Mary Mostyn of Flint in Wales) and grandson of Mary and Miles Blount.[8]

In 1737 the Misses Weaver and John Blount sold the Heath (then in the tenancy of John Corbett) to John Fidoe of Little Froome for £1,200, who sold in turn to William Davis of Bromyard for £1,600 in 1763. William Davis and his wife Ann also had considerable property in Hereford, Bromyard and Much Cowarne, but by 1770 they owed some £3,670 to several creditors and in 1772 sold the Heath to Luke Stanford of Leominster for £2,700. The Stanford family retained the farm until after 1800 and were followed by Mrs Stephens and then a Mr Hyde.

Joseph Harris of Henwick House near Worcester appears to be the next owner. In 1821 he released the Heath to his cousin Mary, her husband William Cooke and their seven sons. Mary died in 1824, Joseph Harris died in 1832 (by his will confirming that the farm was for the use of his cousin's seven sons) and William Cooke of Orleton upon Teme, Worcestershire, died in 1837. Thereafter the Heath was in the hands of Francis, Thomas, William, John, Henry, Joseph and Charles Cooke. The survivors or their heirs sold the farm in 1865 to John Birchley for £5,574. The Birchley family owned the Heath for 64 years making many improvements which are still appreciated by those farming there today.

Farm buildings at the Heath, Avenbury. Stables and cow house *c*1900.

James Pearson and his wife Mary were farming the 199 acres in 1851 with the help of three agricultural labourers and a house servant all living in. William Yeates from Kimbolton near Leominster was farming here in 1871 with two labourers. William was probably the brother of George Yeates (another Leominster man) then married to Caroline Davenport of Lower Venn and in 1871 farming there with the Davenport family. William was a widower with nine children aged between eight and 26 years old. He managed the farm with the help of his eldest three sons, one of whom was a saddler, and his two eldest daughters, who acted as housemaid and dairy maid, while the four younger children were described as 'scholars'.

The present range of brick farm buildings were built about 1900 following a fire on the premises. John Birchley's son William Birchley sold the Heath in 1929 to Mr and Mrs John Hodges of Church House, Stoke Lacy. John Hodges was born in 1887 and in 1921, married Daisy Adnet from Cowarne House in Stoke Lacy. Today the old title deeds for the Heath are appropriately kept in the leather travelling case which was Daisy's gift to her husband on their wedding day. John and Daisy's son, another John, continued to farm the 200 acres at the Heath and now the next generation of the Hodges Family are living here.

Reception after the wedding in 1921 of Daisy Helen Adney with John Hodges. Daisy and John moved to the Heath in 1929.

The Heath, Avenbury.

John Hodges about 6 years old.

Standard Fordson 1940s. Heath, Avenbury.

John Hodges rolling the lawn *c*1938. Heath, Avenbury.

The Heath 1999. *Howard Painter*

The present comfortable brick Georgian farmhouse was built around 1770, quite probably by the Davis family. Otherwise it was the work of the Stanford family. Part of the earlier timber-framed house (perhaps the home of the Boyce family) was retained in the new building and now this *c*1550 timber-framed wing has been converted into a most attractive dwelling overlooking the lake for the use of Mrs Hodges senior. There are very extensive farm buildings of several periods, including two square hop kilns.

Cusop

The farm is on high land to the west of the Munderfield road, and the name offers difficulties. There is a parish of the same name on the western boundary of Herefordshire which was in 1086 spelt *Cheweshope* and it has been suggested that that name derives from a Welsh stream name *Cyr* which means 'chickens' and from the word *hop* 'secluded valley'.[9] The Rev W Morgan in about 1923 wrote 'There seems to be very little doubt that the name (Cusop) is derived from the Welsh Saint Cewedd, and hope which signifies a valley or hill'.[10] It is said that if it rains on St Cewydd's feast day, July 1st, then it will rain for 40 days, and Rev W Morgan claimed that Saint Cewydd is the Welsh equivalent of Saint Swithun. The Avenbury Cusop may be a descriptive name, or, it may have been named from an early farmer who came to Avenbury from Cusop parish; it is less likely to have been named from the Welsh saint.

The farm was spelt *Kewsopp* in 1694 when it was the home of Sarah Charlott, the elder, a widow. The Charlott family were important in the parish during the 17th century and the deaths of several members were commemorated in the parish church. These included William Charlott 1658, another William Charlott 1671 and his wife Mary 1672; Mary and Elizabeth in 1678, and our Sarah Charlott, widow, in 1696.[11] Then there was 'Rebeccah ye daughter of Mrs Mary Charlott of Bromyard widdow was buried in ye chancel of Avenbury October 3(r)d 1691'. Finally Mrs Sarah Charlott, another Sarah, 'of ye towne of Bromyard', married Richard Hide of Hopton Wafre in Shropshire in Avenbury Church in 1708.[12]

Cusop from the rear 1998. *Howard Painter*

Robert Charlott had an estate valued at £21 in 1663, one of the highest valuations in the parish, and five hearths in 1665. He died in 1682 and Sarah the elder may have been his widow. She made her will in 1694 and died in 1696, leaving household goods and personal effects of considerable value. 'Her wearing Apparell and money in purse' amounted to £10 and her household goods were worth £65 l0s. The growing and stored corn with implements of husbandry came to £54 and her cattle, horses and livestock were worth £116 l0s; Sarah also had £51 lent out, a total of nearly £300. She made bequests to her daughter-in-law Mary Charlott, 'widdow and relict of my sonn William Charlott', her grandaughter Joanna who was the daughter of William and Mary, her brother John Skinner of Ledbury, clothier, and her kinsman Richard Gamond 'who lately did dwell and Inhabit with me'. Others to receive bequests included Margery Williams of Bromyard widow, Rebecca Ashby widow of Worcester, Patience Crump of

Monmouth and Thomas Turner, Isabell Mason and Mary Good, three of her servants. She left money to all her servants living with her at the time of her decease as well as 20s to the poor of Avenbury. Finally all her goods, chattels, rights, plate and personal estate of whatever kind went to 'my well beloved grandchild Sarah Charlott the eldest liveing daughter of them the said William Charlott decd. and Mary Charlott'. Sarah was also made executrix of her will.[13]

Cusop, side view 1998. *Howard Painter*

Sarah lived in the farmhouse which still stands today, and it has altered little over the last three centuries. Cusop farmhouse was built around 1600 and is a lovely example of the period. It is a medium sized, timber-framed house with a cross wing, two storeys with cellar and attics and a warm, comfortable atmosphere. The house was given a new front in brick about 1800 and this was probably the work of Thomas King who was the owner-occupier of Cusop at the

Cusop, Georgian front 1998. *Howard Painter*

beginning of the 19th century. The King family had been in Avenbury for some years and were farming Cusop as tenants before 1768. Thomas King of Castle Frome married Jane Wanklin of Ashperton at Avenbury Church in 1706 and a Thomas King was an Avenbury churchwarden in 1760. The family were probably descended from William King who in the late 17th century married Sarah, a daughter of Henry and Anne Pytt of the Noakes.

Thomas King sold Cusop before 1819 and the property belonged to Mr Ricketts for many years and was let to Robert Merriman. Richard Barneby was the owner by 1831 and in 1840 Cusop belonged to Elizabeth Barneby when William Hill was her tenant. After 1840 the service wing was extended to provide hop drying and storage facilities and other farm buildings were added. William Newman and his wife Ann were here in 1851, and in 1871 James Hill a widower farmed the 150 acres with four men, a boy and a housekeeper to look after them all.

Cusop later came into the hands of Major Arthur Price Knott who sold it in 1910 with 145 acres and three cottages to Annie Mary Eckley of Witsetts, Stoke Prior, Leominster. Twenty-six years later in 1936, Mrs R H Eckley put the farm on the market with two brick built cottages.[14] John Edward Thomas and his wife Marguerite purchased Cusop in 1939 and their daughter Mrs Dorothy Masters still lives here, with two more generations of her family living in a house nearby at Munderfield.

The Burgess *c*1600 timber-framed house enclosed between 19th-century front and stone service wing.
Howard Painter

The Burgess

This is an unusual farm name and possibly derives from the birch tree which may at one time have been grown as a crop for a local industry such as tanning or could have grown naturally in the area. The large farmhouse stands on the high ridge above 154 metres (500 feet) just off the Ledbury Road and close to the lane that leads to Avenbury Court and the church. At its core this is a timber-framed house of around 1600 which was enlarged and partially enveloped by a later residence in the 19th century. A stone

Side view of the Burgess showing 19th-century front wing; *c*1600 timber-framed house and service wing. *Howard Painter*

staircase with iron balusters and mahogany handrail ascends three floors to the top storey. The farm buildings today are extensive and like the house indicate periods of farming prosperity on fertile soil. A map of the property with the Greeve in 1815 shows a small farmhouse and farm building, and the tithe map shows no change. By 1869 however there had been a transformation. The sale notice for June 2nd accompanied by a map of the 247 acres of the Burgess and Greeve Estates says 'The buildings consist of A Superior Dwelling House, substantially erected on the Burgess Estate some years ago, but never completely finished internally.'[15]

In the 17th century the Burgess was the home of William ffarley, otherwise Farley, gentleman who in 1665 had three hearths. Three members of the family appear in the assessment for 1663, as John Farley, gentleman, was named as responsible for the payment of £12 for his brother William's lands and £1 for his brother Richard's lands. Between 1665 and 1671, Elizabeth, Rowland, Bertha, Edward and Francisca, the children of William ffarley were baptised at Avenbury Church. John Farley was buried in 1675, William in 1677 and Rowland in 1682. In a title deed of 1698 relating to the Burgess and Down House, near Bromyard, Benjamin ffarley claimed to be the son and heir of William ffarley late of the Burgess, deceased, by Mary his wife. The family property in Avenbury had been sold and the money lent out with the yearly profits and interest to be paid during her lifetime to Mary, Benjamin's mother. Thereafter the capital was to be called in for the use of Benjamin and his intended wife Eleanor Harris of Middlesex. There is no record of who purchased the Burgess at that time.[16]

The Burgess, 19th-century front of house. *Howard Painter*

An indenture dated December 1761 made between John Freeman the elder, Esq of Clifton in the county of Gloucester and others including the Rev Ralph Hopton, vicar of Bishop's Frome, charged a 'farm and lands called Burgess, in the parish of Avenbury' with a yearly rent charge of £15 for the maintenance of a schoolmaster at Bishop's Frome. This endowment was known as Freeman's Charity.[17] John Freeman the younger of Bristol had in 1759 married Abigail, the daughter of John and Abigail Freeman of Gaines in Whitbourne, the families perhaps being related. Abigail's marriage portion was considerable and there was an agreement to buy freehold lands which would be settled on any children of the marriage. The Burgess may have been part of the lands purchased.

Thomas Cooke, probably a member of the Munderfield Court Family, appears to have purchased the farm before 1777, when he was paying £7 6s 'for the Burgess' in 'A rate assessed on the inhabitants of the parish'; and in 1798 Thomas Cooke was the owner-occupier paying land tax of £5 14s. Thomas Cooke was still living here in 1805 when he took Phebe Harbour as a parish apprentice. At the time of the Charity Commissioners' reports 1815-1839, the £15 charged on the property, for the benefit of the schoolmaster of Bishop's Frome, was still being paid from the Burgess which then belonged to Mr Walker and was in the occupation of Mr Derry.

Mr Walker was probably Mr Delabere Walker who was born in 1763 of a large family and became a physician and surgeon in Bromyard. He and his wife Meliora had several children who were baptised in Bromyard Church between 1795 and 1804. Meliora must have died shortly after, for in 1810 Delabere Walker

Windows at The Burgess.
Howard Painter

married a widow Mrs Charlotte Sophia Vicars. Mr Walker and his family then came to live in Avenbury. He had acquired the Greeve before 1798 and by 1812 was farming the two properties together. In 1815, as noted in Chapter 7, he exchanged land with John Freeman of Gaines who then owned Avenbury Court (this accounts for the 1815 map of the farm) and after that he purchased the tithes of the Burgess for £700.[18] In 1824 when he was living at the Burgess, he made over 'All that messuage or farmhouse with the barns, stables and outbuildings commonly called the Burgess' with 125 acres of land for the use of himself for his lifetime and then for his daughter Charlotte who was born in 1800. By 1831 Mr Walker was letting the farm to Joseph Tibbatts and in 1838 was living in Birmingham where he died, leaving everything to his daughter Charlotte. His descendants still live and farm in the Bromyard district and have in their possession a ledger book relating to his patients with their treatments.[19]

In 1840 Charlotte Walker was the landlord and Sarah Derry (either the widow or daughter of the late Thomas Derry) her tenant. After this date the house and buildings of the Burgess were considerably improved, and in 1851 William Leake was the tenant farmer with 247 acres and two labourers; he had three sons and a daughter living at home and two servants living in. Twenty years later Benjamin Todd was the farmer of the same acreage but with six labourers, two boys and a domestic servant; his father William shared the house and he was a 'gentleman'. Charlotte Walker died between 1867-9 and after her death the Burgess and the Greeve were sold. Benjamin Todd, the tenant of the Burgess paid £5,000 for his farm, which he sold nine years later to the trustees of the Municipal Charities in the City of Worcester for £8,500. Today, 120 years later, the Worcester Municipal Charities are still the landlords and their tenants the Turner family have been at the Burgess since before 1940.[20]

Windows at The Burgess.
Howard Painter

Jack Corbett taking a bull to market from the Burgess.

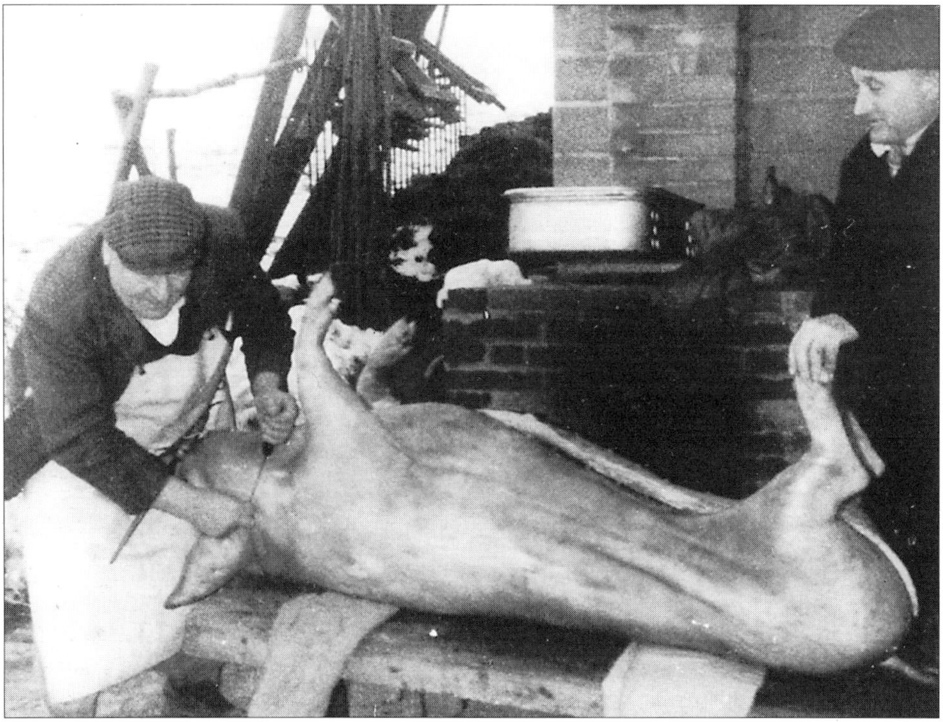

Mr. Frank Turner of the Burgess, Avenbury near Bromyard, butchering a pig in about 1960, with Mr. Tom Bloomfield of Sherford Street, Bromyard.

Bromyard Local History Society Collection

The wedding of Frank Turner of the Burgess and Joan Wall, at St. Peter's Church, Bromyard about 1950. Frank's mother, Mrs. Turner of the Burgess, seated on left. The two older bridesmaids are thought to be Frank's sisters.

Burgess Farm, Avenbury 1950s. A winning horse.
Left to right:- Bernard Smith, trainer, Gerald Morgan, jockey, Sam Turner, owner.

The Greeve

The Greeve is an unusual name which could derive from *graefe* which means 'a grove or thicket' but one look at the site of the old farmhouse and the name suggests a similar Old English word *graef* which has the totally different meaning of 'a grave or pit'. For although on high land, the farmstead (which has now disappeared) stood in a quite pronounced hollow. On the tithe map the house and farm buildings were similar in extent to those of Cusop and the Burgess.

The Corbett family was associated with the Greeve for many generations and this may have been the farm of Richard Corbett who was assessed for £9 in 1663 and in 1665 was taxed for five hearths, indicating a large and recently built house. John Corbett was the owner occupier of the Greeve in 1777 when his parish tax was £6 5s 1d.

Mr Delabere Walker had acquired the 70 acres farm by 1798 from Elizabeth Williams of Bromyard. He had also purchased 14 acres from Mrs Wood of Wick, Worcestershire. John Corbett remained here for some years as a tenant. Later Delabere Walker farmed the property himself together with the Burgess and it is difficult to know in which farmhouse he lived. In 1805 he took Mary Foxall as parish apprentice 'at the Grieve' and served the offices of overseer in 1806 and churchwarden the following year, again for the Greeve.

In 1840, the owner, also of the Burgess, was Charlotte Walker with Sarah Derry her tenant, and in subsequent years the house and buildings were much extended. After the death of Miss Walker, the Greeve together with the Burgess were sold. They were in the tenancy of Benjamin Todd. The homestead was described as 'A house on the Greeve Estate (capable of conversion into cottages) with outbuildings to the same respectively.' The house and buildings have been pulled down during later years, but a considerable amount of stone remains on the site, together with two pools, one of which has a strong retaining wall. The land of the Greeve is farmed today with the Burgess as it has been for some 180 years.

Hackley, Birchyfield, Rough Mintridge and Limekilns

These all belonged in 1840 to Thomas Philip Payne Wight who lived at - Tedstone Court, Tedstone Delamere and had another property in Bromyard.[21] Richard Wight purchased Birchyfield in 1810 and may have acquired the remainder of his Avenbury estate at around the same time. Hackley was let to James Evans, and John Radford farmed the remaining land. The estate covered just over 200 acres in Avenbury and formed a small island at the north-west corner of the parish surrounded by Keephill, Winslow and Stoke Lacy; the Hackley Brook here marks the western boundary of the parish.

Hackley was recorded in 1231 as *Hakel* which means a 'hook' and could derive from the shape of the Hackley Brook or from the lie of the land both of which could be regarded as hook like.[22] An alternative explanation for the unusual name could be the presence at one time of a 'hackle' or 'fish weir' on the brook. This would have comprised a barrier of wattle set across the current to produce an

Hackley 1998. *Howard Painter*

eddy in which fish could be caught.[23] It may be no coincidence that the neighbouring Keephill (earlier *Cuple*) appears to derive from the word *cupe* which means 'a coop or basket' probably for catching fish. There was at one time a mill here for in 1231, Amfelisa, the widow of William of Staunton, sought from John of Croft, one third of a mill at Hackley in Avenbury as her dower, and a 'Wash Wiere' was recorded near Hackley Bridge in 1674.[24] *Wash* could describe 'swampy land' or 'rush of water' and a *weir* was usually associated with a fish or a mill weir.

Staircase at Hackley 1931. *Royal Commission on the Historical Monuments of England*

The house at Hackley is unusual and interesting and dates from about 1620. Built into a bank the back door is on the ground floor, whilst the front door is on the first floor. It has a two-room plan on three storeys with attics, and the large central chimney serves all of the house's five fireplaces. Alongside the chimney, from ground-floor to attic, is a spectacular spiral timber staircase with moulded posts, stair rail and turned balusters. Other houses in the parish may well have had similar stairs but so often they have been removed and replaced during a Georgian or Victorian renovation. To match the staircase there is a flourish of carved

Hackley, outside kitchen and barn. 1998. *Howard Painter*

ovolo mouldings which surround the doorways and are on the beams above the stone fireplaces. On the ground floor, there is also one exposed ovolo moulded beam, whereas the other ceiling beams in the house have been covered. The house is timber-framed beneath the external weather-boarding which was probably added in the late 19th century. Internally the walls are plastered except for the first floor drawing room which has been stripped to show close set timbers. There is a brick and stone vaulted cellar which is entered from the ground floor and extends beneath the front garden. The roof was altered in Georgian times to give more room on the top storey and two lateral gables were added.

There is a late 17th-century timber-framed outside kitchen with a very large chimney, opposite the back door. The building was extended in stone during the 19th century to give room for hop drying and storage, a cider mill, and grain storage. The upper storey of this multi-purpose building provides nesting boxes for doves. The fine timber-framed barn was built at the same time as the house, about 1620, and was extended later that century and again by Mr Payne Wight after 1840, for a plan of Hackley made in 1871 shows more extensive buildings than appear on the tithe map.

This property must have been of some importance, for Silas Taylor in his description of Avenbury in 1655 listed Hackley as a sub-heading but for some reason failed to complete the entry. Records for it, however, are sparse; the house was built by a prosperous man and yet we know little about the early history. Charles Robinson in 1872 mentioned Hackley with Pencombe, when he quoted the 17th-century Herefordshire historian Blount, 'Hackley had also a chapel, and the Rector of Pencombe receives 6s 8d yearly from the chapel yard'.[25] To date no other record has been found of this 6s 8d although a stone building at Hackley is referred to as the old chapel. The following items are recorded in two Pencombe terriers. The first is undated but appears earlier than 1615:

> 'Item we present that there is belonging to our said parsonage one close containing by estimation three acres lying at Hacklett Bridge in the parish of Avenbury'.

The second is dated 5th February 1639 and reports:

> 'Item one pasture at Hackleyes brook containing about three acres lying between the said brook and the highway there on the north and lands in the tenure Thomas Browne of Hackleyes aforesaid on all other parts'.[26]

The tithe map shows, at Hackley, a meadow called Chapel Hill and adjoining it Lady Meadow. There was a Hakeleye recorded in the Pencombe manorial rolls 1357-1442, so if this was the Avenbury Hackley it must have been an outlier of Pencombe manor.[27] Hackley could have been part of Little Froome Estate and was possibly included with the lands and tenements held by John Browne of Frome (Little Froome) in 1431 for which he owed not military service but 100s a year.[28]

Hackley appears to be the property, valued at £6, which was in the hands of Alexander Gretton in 1663. Alexander Gretton Esq who served both Charles I and Charles II as clerk to the Spicery, was the husband of Sarah Rumney of Suckley. Sarah's brother, Paul Rumney, married Joyce the daughter and heiress of

Sheep washing at Hackley.
Bromyard Local History Society Collection

Threshing at Hackley 1935.
Bromyard Local History Society Collection

William Brown of Bosbury in Herefordshire. An earlier Rumney, Dorothy the daughter of John Rumney, had around 1580 married Richard Browne of Little Froome. An indenture of 1647 refers to an unidentified property in Avenbury which was inherited by Mary and Dorothy, daughters of Richard Rumney. Mary had married Morgan Evans, a yeoman, and Dorothy, her unmarried sister lived with them in the house with lands that had been the inheritance of their father.[29]

Thomas Hill 'of Hackley' made his will in April 1700 and apart from a few other family legacies left his 'goods and chattels and, all whatsoever I do posess' to his brother Richard Hill. Thomas left stock, crops and goods worth £127 5s, quite a large sum; he had four oxen, four cows, 15 young stock, a mare and two colts, seven sheep, five pigs, poultry, growing corn and harvested corn with hay and straw, and he was growing hops. William ffincher was at Hackley in 1770 and he was churchwarden in 1771 and 1783. A farming family from Scotland, Patrick and Janet Gilmour and their four sons, were at Hackley in 1851 and farmed 171 acres with eight labourers, three of whom lived in the farmhouse. William Holloway was farmer and hop grower at Hackley by 1871. His was a household of ten: William and his wife Mary, their four children and a nephew who was living with them, with two domestic and two farming servants in the house. William appears to be the son of William Holloway who farmed at Hopton in 1851, and his nephew Benjamin was probably the son of Benjamin Holloway who by 1871 had taken over at Hopton.

Birchyfield (Birchyfields) was in 1840 'Birchy Field Farm' and in 1663 'Birchingfield' (and would appear to be so named from the birch tree). The spelling may derive from *bircen* 'growing with birch trees' or perhaps 'overgrown with birch trees'.[30] Edward Porter owned the property at that date.

Richard Corbett of Birchenfield, yeoman, made his will in June 1697, at which time he had five children: James, Mathew, Richard, John and Rebecca to whom he left five shillings each. The remainder of his money, goods and stock he left to his wife Elizabeth for her lifetime, leaving her to dispose of what remained at the time of her death between the children 'as she shall judge convenient'. Richard left an estate worth £75 12s which included household furniture and provisions with two oxen, five other cattle, a cow and a horse, pigs, poultry and sheep, growing corn and implements of husbandry.

Birchyfield later came into the hands of Packington Tomkins of Buckenhill near Bromyard, to be sold in 1746 to Francis Woodhouse whose brother Thomas had purchased Little Froome Manor. The two properties were by 1755 farmed together and let to John Fidoe who paid an annual rent of £140 on a 21 year lease. Richard West the son of Richard West of Bredenbury bought the whole estate from the Woodhouse family in 1768 and came to live at Little Froome. He immediately sold 21 acres called Northfields which were then part of Birchyfield farm:

> 'all of which adjoin and are part of a farm called Birchyfield and lye in Avenbury, now in the tenure of John Fidoe bounded by the roadways leading from Cowpers Green to Flaggoners Green and from Pencombe to Bromyard and the lands of Richard West on all other parts'.[31]

Birchyfield 1998. *Howard Painter*

As Birchyfield covered 66 acres at the time of the tithe survey in 1840, the farm must have been larger when it belonged to the Woodhouse family. However in 1795 Richard West repurchased Northfields and a house and buildings 'lately erected on the premises', but they were on the market again in 1805. By then his son Richard was living at Birchyfield and he may have built part of the present fine gentleman's residence.

Birchyfield stable block 1998.
Howard Painter

As we saw, Richard Wight had purchased Birchyfield by 1810 and he may have lived here, his family retaining the property until 1842. John Kempson was the next known owner and occupier and he died in 1852 when Keephill in Winslow was also part of his estate. His son and heir, another John Kempson, died unmarried in 1867 leaving 'no lawful issue' and the Birchyfield Estate was inherited by another branch of the Kempson family.[32] *Kelly's Directory* for 1891 describes that:

> 'Birchy Field, the residence of Frederick Robertson Kempson esq. J. P. is a fine modern structure of freestone, commanding an extensive and beautiful view of the surrounding country'.

A 'Plan of the Birchy Field Estate situate in the Parishes of Avenbury, Bromyard and Stoke Lacy, Herefordshire' of 1871 shows:

Hackley	172 acres	0 roods	32 perches
Birchy Field	40 acres	0 roods	38 perches
Keephill	116 acres	0 roods	16 perches
Total Quantity	**412 acres**	**2 roods**	**33 perches*** [33]

*These old measurements were: 40 perches = 1 rood and 4 roods = 1 acre

The house at Birchyfield was not always lived in by the owner and his family and was at times occupied by tenants. The St John family were living here at the time of the 1881 census. Beauchamp St John and his wife Ellen were 36 and 33 years old respectively; they had eight children between the ages of four months and 11 years. Their staff of eight comprised: a governess, nurse, under-nurse, house/parlour-maid, cook, groom/gardener, assistant housemaid and assistant nursemaid. Recently a descendant of Emma Dew, who was the children's 26 year old nurse at that time, contacted the Bromyard and District Local History Society. She told us that Emma Dew from Fownhope gave blood to Mrs St John when she had a baby, presumably this was an early blood transfusion. The family were very grateful and gave her a gift of money which enabled her to invest in a pharmacy business in Worcester. Emma died in 1924 at Evenlay, St Dunstan Crescent in Worcester.

The Kempson family lived at Birchyfield for many decades and there are family memorials in Stoke Lacy Church. Frederick Kempson was a well known Herefordshire architect who designed many public buildings including the National School (St Peter's) in Bromyard which was built in 1862. Whitegates, a large house just down the road from Birchyfield, was built by Lucy Kempson, probably to Frederick's plans. In 1923 John Espen Knott, then living at Down Manor just outside Bromyard, purchased the Birchyfield Estate including Keephill and Hackley from Frederick Kempson who was by then living in Cornwall. Lt Col John Knott CMG, DSO and his family at Birchyfield are still remembered locally. Part of the estate remains with the same family but Birchyfield house and farm now belong to the Stephenson family.

The house at Birchyfield is a good example of a Georgian gentleman's residence of the smaller kind. The main part of the house is of large cut stone and plastered with a moulded cornice. The principal doorway has a slab hood supported by fluted pillars. The outbuildings are extensive and include stables and coach house of the same period and style as the house.

Mr. and Mrs. Herbert Knott in the blackcurrant field at Birchyfield about 1950.
Bromyard Local History Society Collection

Rough Mintridge is an unexplained name but the second element may derive from *ric* which could denote a raised linear feature of some kind.[34] There is another Mintridge Farm in Stoke Lacy parish, but whether they share similar features from which they were named or comprised one estate of which Rough Mintridge was an outlier is at present unknown. Rough may indicate overgrown ground as opposed to cultivated land.

Lawrence d'Abitot was involved with lands at Rough Mintridge in Avenbury in 1262-71 and a few years later with Noakes in Avenbury.[35] Possibly he was one of the heirs, by marriage, of Adam de Botyler or Adam Butler who was in possession of the manor of Rowden, near Bromyard in 1170. John le Moigne of Rowden held Sawbury in Avenbury in 1242 and by 1300 Lawrence d'Abitot, by the right of his wife Lucy, held the neighbouring estate of Noakes (see pages 45, 46, 47).[36]

The Conny Family seem to have lived at Rough Mintridge during the 17th century and appear in parish records and registers with various name spellings. In 1663 John Conney had an estate in Avenbury worth £6 and the Hearth Tax return of 1665 shows John Cunny with one hearth. Elizabeth the wife of John Conney of Kyple (Keephill, Winslow) died in 1662 and Thomas Cunney in 1664; John Coney was a

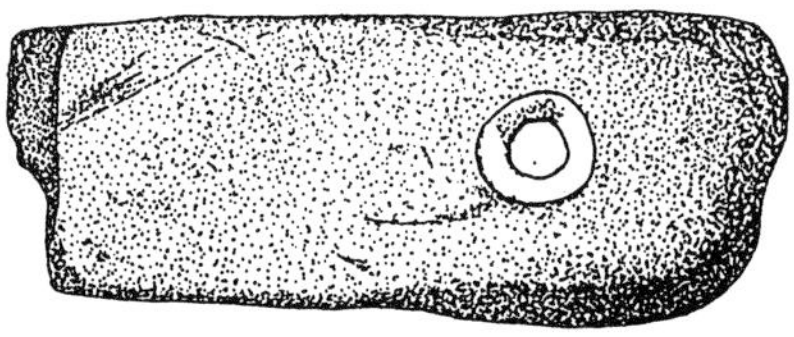

Broken perforated Whetstone found at Hackley by Deborah Waller.

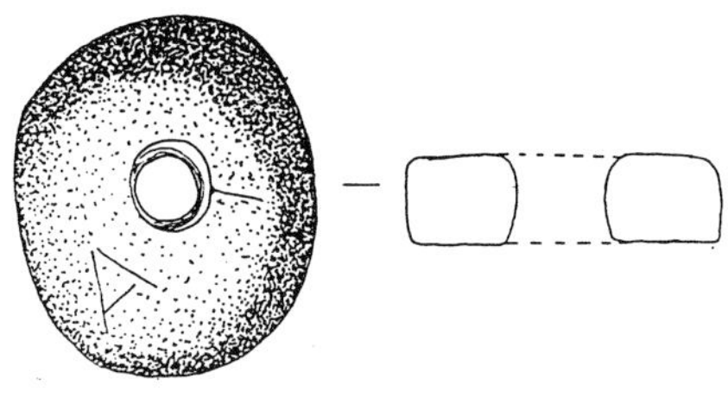

Pre-historic spindle wheel found at Rough Mintridge by Deborah Waller.

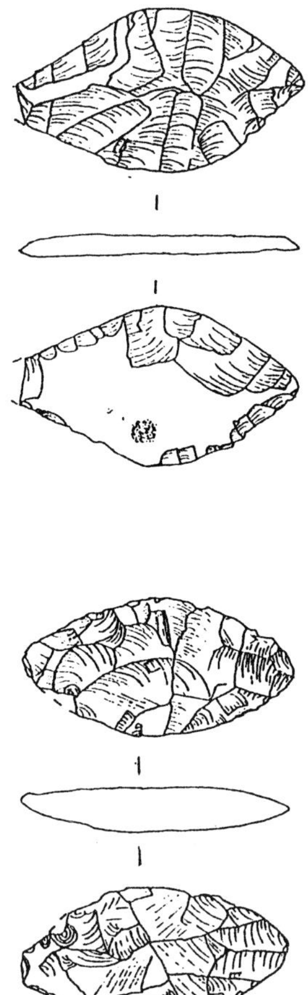

Two leaf shaped arrow heads found at Rough Mintridge by Deborah Waller.

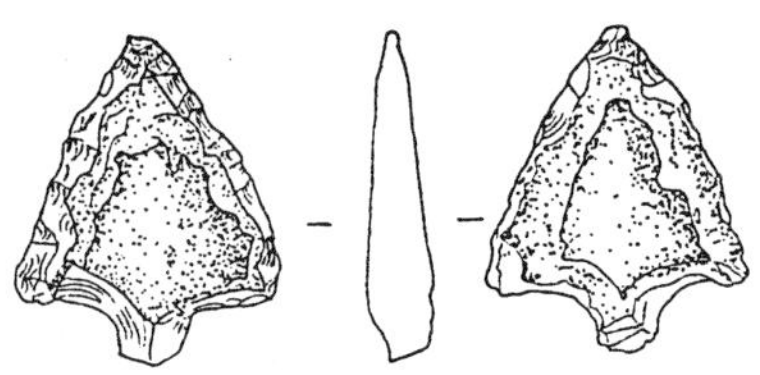

Barbed and tanged arrow head found at Rough Mintridge by - Deborah Waller.

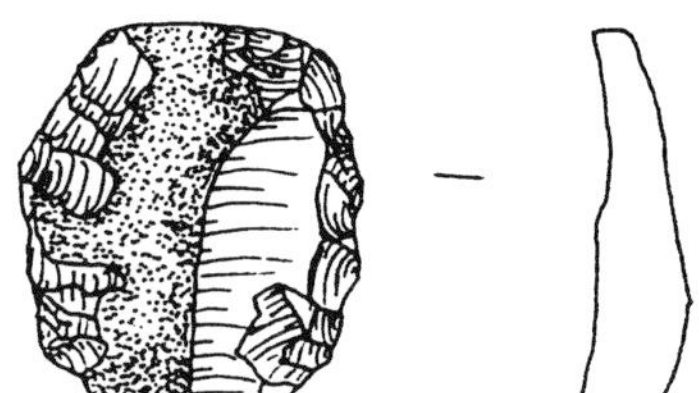

Flint side scraper found at Rough Mintridge by Deborah Waller.

All Drawn by Philippa Bradley

Rough Mintridge 1998. *Howard Painter*

guardian or churchwarden of Avenbury Church in 1673-4. John Conny of Rough Mintridge, yeoman, made his will in 1689 and left amongst other bequests, 12d to his kinsmen John and William Conny to buy gloves. His goods and stock were valued at £69 19s and included three beds, four oxen, four cows and seven other cattle, a mare and colt, pigs and sheep with corn, pulse and pease 'growing in the ground', and after small legacies John left his estate to his wife Margaret. In the next century, John Coney married Mary Barber of Avenbury on 15th January 1708, and their daughter Mary was born on the last day of September the same year.

The stone house and buildings date from around 1800 and would appear to have been built for a tenant. William Morris, a farm bailiff, with his wife Elizabeth, seven children and a 12 year old farm servant Edward Godin, occupied the house in 1851. Twenty years later an Avenbury man, Richard Corbett 'farmer of 70 acres', lived here with his wife Ellen, six children, a domestic servant and farm servant.

Limekilns was in 1840 a smallholding of 16 acres with a house and garden. It was reached by a farm track off the Pencombe Lane which continued from Hackley apparently to thc Hereford Road. As the name indicates, this was the site of a lime burning kiln and the burnt lime was used to improve the soil. Upper Venn Farm also had Limekiln fields and the Kilns in Avenbury Lane may have been for the same purpose.

Mr. and Mrs. Bevan of Rough Mintridge with their family.
Bromyard Local History Society Collection

Goodships 1998. *Howard Painter*

Goodships

In 1840 Goodships was a 35 acre farm which belonged to Thomas Philpott of Suckley who rented the property to Ann Williams. The name is unusual for why should there be a 'good ship' on this high land at the edge of the parish. The name appears to derive from *goodcheps* which means 'good market', from the Anglo-Saxon *caep* 'trade, merchandise, market' and there was in about 1285 a Gilbert Godchep who had three stalls in Bromyard Market Place.[37] The farm stands at the junction of the roads from Hereford and Ledbury as they approach Bromyard at Flaggoner's Green which is considered to have been the hundredal meeting place of Plegelgate hundred. Trade would certainly have been a feature at folkmoots and meetings of the hundred, and the day would have been regarded as a social occasion by the families of the district with possibly 1,000 people gathered here.

Thomas Philpott, senior had purchased from Richard West in 1800:

> 'All those two closes, pieces and parcels of arable land called by the several names of Goodcheps and the six acres by copy containing together twenty six acres ....And also all that piece or parcel of pasture land and ground on part wherof oak trees are growing...containing eight acres...which said parcels of land adjoin together and formerly were part of the lands and grounds of a certain capital messuage and farm called Little Froome'.[38]

Mr. Jones of the Goodships with his pony and trap and son Sam.
Bromyard Local History Society Collection

Adam Jones with his team, haymaking at the Goodships.
Bromyard Local History Society Collection

No house is mentioned at the time and the present stone house dates from around 1800 and was probably built by Thomas Philpott. There is a separate stone kitchen with a bread oven and chamber above, and good farm buildings of the same period.

The Mrs Ann Williams who was living here in 1840, already aged 67, described herself in 1851, as the farmer of 30 acres with one agricultural labourer who lived in. Also at home were her son Edward and a lodger Robert Price, a 63 year old cattle dealer. Twenty years later Jane Williams lived here with her two daughters and a farm servant. Recently the modernised and enlarged property has been used for a successful fish farming business and popular health centre.

Northfields

This was another small farm in 1840 which had been recently established by purchasing land from a larger property and building a house on the site. Before 1768, Northfields Greater and Lesser and Pool Croft formed a 21 acre portion of Birchyfield. Richard West, who bought Birchyfield and Little Froome in that year, sold the 21 acres to James Stone of Grendon Manor in Grendon Bishop. Northfields then came into the hands of Thomas Colly of Bromyard and 23 years later was sold to George Pitt, a Bromyard butcher, who in 1795 sold the property, by now with a 'lately erected' house and buildings, back to Richard West of Birchyfield. The little farm came on the market again in 1805 when Andrew Maund, a

Northfields, front of house 1998. *Howard Painter*

Northfields, roadside barn and rear of house 1998. *Howard Painter*

Bromyard builder acquired 'a cottage with a large garden...and adjacent to the road...containing in all 11½ acres'; he later purchased another six acres called Northfields Leasow.[39]

By the time of his death around 1829, Andrew Maund was a large property owner in the counties of Worcester, Hereford, Brecon and Monmouth, and his daughter Mary Ann Maund, then of the Tithings, Worcester, was his heir to this estate. Mary Ann came to live at Northfields and in 1851 described herself as a 'Land and house proprietor'. She later shared her house with her niece Elizabeth, the daughter of Charles Oxenham Aveline of Cheltenham. Elizabeth inherited her aunt's estate and married Henry Maybery of Brecon.

Chapter 9

Smaller Holdings in the Parish in 1840

'Naturally the memory was more relied on, and proportionately, strengthened by constant practice, so that in all disputed questions concerning custom, right of road, foot-paths through land, or land boundaries, the aged peasant would give the clearest evidence and such as was seldom disputed.'

James Johnston, *The Finding of St Augustine's Chair* (1898), 4

Fox Leasow 29 acres and **Tanners Field** 20 acres

These 49 acres were on the southern parish boundary of Avenbury and in the respective ownership of John Brown of Hall Court and Richard Brown of Bromtree's Hall, both in the parish of Bishop's Frome.

Lands called the Foxe in Bishop's Frome were recorded with the 16th-century surveys relating to *Herefordshire Chantries and other Religious Foundations*, the documents now being in the Public Record Office. A transcription in Hereford Cathedral Archives records that lands called the Foxe in the tenure of Katherine Fitz Nurse had been given to a priest in the service of the chantry of St Mary in the church of Bishop's Frome and after the Dissolution had been with other

Snow on the Ledbury Road near Munderfield 1947.
Bromyard Local History Society Collection

property (including Dovehills in Stanford Regis now in the parish of Bishop's Frome) granted to John Harford and John Farley.[1]

By 1663 John Brown of Hall Court had land in Avenbury assessed at £3, which was probably Fox Leasow. The 50 acres may at one time have been part of Hopton, and both Hopton and Bromtrees Hall were sold by the Nicholett family in 1786.

Cooper's Green

The smallholding was also known as Cowper's Green which could mean 'cowkeeper's green' and it lay across the Hereford Road from Goodships. The 12 acres belonged in 1840 to the Rev Richard Williams who rented the house and land to Henry Jenks of Avenbury Court. Henry probably farmed the land with the Court and the 19th-century stone dwelling may well have been occupied by one of his workers. In 1851 two farmworkers' families occupied a cottage called Cooper's Green Cottage, which may have been a double dwelling, or perhaps the cottage on Corbett's Piece took the same name. Joseph Harbour and Joseph Smith were the two farmworkers in 1851 and Richard Town and Thomas Vernalls were there with their families in 1871.

Family wedding group following the wedding of Alice (Bonnie) Powell and Alfred Hall at St. Peters Church, Bromyard. Taken at the White House, Avenbury. August 1935.

Corbett's Piece

This was an 11 acre field evidently named after a member of the Corbett family. John Cooke was the owner-occupier in 1840 and the cottage there was occupied by James Walwyn.

Hanging Hill

The ten acre holding was also called the Hill and belonged in 1840 to William Towers. It was farmed by John Bennett who rented five acres of glebe nearby and lived at Burley Farm just over the parish boundary in Linton.

Charlie Phillips who lived for some years at the White Cottages, stringing hops at Little Froome.
Bromyard Local History Society Collection

Copton Field Farm now **Copton Farm**

The name means 'settlement or farm at the top of a hill' and the 40 acre farm was at Stocks Cross, Munderfield. In 1824, John Vernall the owner was assessed for land tax at 17s 6d. Within four years he had divided his farm into six parts between members of his family, each of whom subsequently paid 2s 11d in land tax. In 1835 William, James, John and Thomas Vernall were living in the parish and three of their properties were called Copton Field. A Joseph Went had a property called Copton.

Was this the property called Little Copton Field comprising a house with a shop (possibly a blacksmith's), garden, meadow, hopground and eight acres of arable being 'in or near Munderfield' which was left by William Cooke the elder of Munderfield to his infant grandson Richard in 1738?[2] Richard Cooke became a baker in Bromyard. He died in 1764 at the age of 26, leaving a widow and two young children.

The present stone house with a slate roof at Copton Farm, dates from around 1840, and a small barn was built at about the same time. In 1900, Copton Field, a farmhouse with seven acres 'for many years in the occupation of James

Copton Farm, garden front 1998. *Howard Painter*

Vernall' was sold to James Baskerville of Munderfield for £440.[3] The property was later purchased by the Thomas family and from about 1938 to 1948 Mrs John Thomas kept Munderfield Post Office on the premises. The Post Office then moved nearer to Munderfield School. The farm has expanded over recent years and there are today considerable new buildings for stock and crops. Mr Stan Thomas, John Thomas's nephew, now farms Copton.

Copton Farm from Stoke Lane 1998. *Howard Painter*

Birch Hall 1993. The property is now being renovated. *G. B. (Bob) Skipp*

Birch Hall

This was a brick and stone cottage with nine acres of land near the Greeve and approached today by a farm track. The cottage was built about 1820, then extended by a stable and outbuildings. The view from the site is quite outstanding. Betty Smith was the owner and Peter Pitt her tenant in 1840. George Osborne and his wife Ann, both agricultural labourers, were here in 1871, and by this date Birch Hall may have been part of the Greeve. The house has recently been sold by the Worcester Consolidated Municipal Charities, and is at present being renovated.

Wake House

The house stands further along the track that led to Birch Hall. The name suggests that it was near this site that the ancient church festivals or wakes were held. Ann Wilcox owned the two acre holding in 1840 and Henry Jenks of Avenbury Court rented it from her. James Mitchell an agricul-

The Wake House, Avenbury, March 31st 1956, Hilda and Jim James' Wedding Day.

The Wakehouse, Avenbury 1988, when Philip and Kay Skipp purchased the property.

tural labourer lived here with his family in 1851 and his son Joseph was occupying the cottage by 1871. The house has recently been rebuilt.

The Wakehouse, Avenbury 1990.

Thomas Haywood with eight acres and Mark Davis with ten acres had adjoining landholdings on the parish boundary with Stoke Lacy and they probably both lived in that parish.

Pavonine (was Lampacre Cottage) showing bake oven and altered roof level.
Howard Painter

Stoke Lane (Stokes Lane)

In 1840 a cluster of houses stood and still stand today to the south-west of the parish on the Avenbury-Stoke Lacy boundary with dwellings in both parishes; this appears to be the spot recorded in *Kelly's Directory* of 1885 'EDGELEY LANE is a small place 2 miles south-west, (of Avenbury) situate on an eminence'. There were eight dwellings here in Avenbury parish in 1840 of which three no longer stand; those remaining are today called: Homeland, Pavonine, Quarry Cottage, The Firs and Rose Cottage. Homeland and Pavonine were earlier called Lampacre Cottages and may have been built on the land given to the parish for the upkeep of a lamp in the parish church which was recorded in the chantry certificates of

Interior of Pavonine showing some of the family's collection of bygones.
Howard Painter

1547-1548 (see pages 51, 52). These two cottages were occupied by William Davies and John Brookes who were owner-occupiers. Quarry Cottage belonged to William Wight and was occupied by Richard Davies who later appears to have moved to Claypits. The Firs was occupied by two households, the owner James Gurney in one and his tenant Mary Evans in the other; Rose Cottage belonged to Richard Hills and was occupied by Ann Gardener or Garness. Of the three houses that no longer stand, one belonged to William Vernall the owner-occupier, one belonged to the Heath Farm and one to Munderfield Farm. Firtree and Stone House Cottages have been built since 1840 (Map 11).

The households and population during the last 140 years in Stoke Lane as shown in the census returns of 1851 and 1871, and enquiry in 1994 are as follows:

	households	occupants
1851	10	49
1871	8	42
1994	7	19

The present houses in Stoke Lane appear to date from approximately 1800-1850 and are basically stone-built, from local material, hence probably Quarry Cottage.

Munderfield Row

Row could indicate a row of cottages, alternatively it could mean 'rough' or 'overgrown'. There were some 20 dwellings here in 1840 adjacent to the Ledbury Road, stretching from the drive of Cusop to the Holly Bush near the parish boundary with Bishop's Frome. Munderfield Row also proved popular for later

The Mission Church, School and School house in 1999. *Howard Painter*

development and the school which was built in 1876 has been converted to a private dwelling, as has the mission hall which was built about the same time and is now known as Chapel Cottage; the village hall built in 1936 has disappeared during the last few years. In addition, several more houses have been erected, some quite recently, and most of the older houses have been extended and renovated. The earliest properties (Chestnuts, Tanglewood and Stocks Cottage) date from the late 17th century and are timber-framed, the Perns has later timber-framing in the structure and the remaining houses are principally of stone and brick. Avenholme and

Stone House at Munderfield 1970s.
Phyllis Williams

Growland 1999. *Howard Painter*

Chestnuts (Jasmine Cottage) 1999, front view. *Howard Painter*

Chestnuts (Jasmine Cottage) 1999, rear view. *Howard Painter*

Woodland View are modern houses which are approached from Munderfield Row, as is Claypits which was built on land hitherto part of Cusop and Munderfield farms; the present brick house dates from about 1860 but there was a cottage there earlier (Map 11).

A member of the Corbett family walking by Chestnuts (Jasmine Cottage).

In 1851, there were 81 people in 20 households (excluding Claypits) along the Munderfield Road and two empty houses; by 1871, 80 people were living in 23 households with one house empty. Four Copton and Growlands properties were listed in 1851 with 17 inhabitants, while in 1871 the same properties had 22 people. Over a quarter of the Avenbury population lived in this small part of the parish. The proportion is probably very similar today with 33 properties including Claypits near the Munderfield Road and three houses at Growland and Copton.

During recent years many of the smaller houses and cottages have been rebuilt, modernised and extended; until these improvements many families must have lived in desperately overcrowded and cramped conditions. Claypits was in 1871 called New House and divided into two dwellings with Susannah Davis and her extended family of son, daughter, son-in-law, grandson and nephew with Henry Passey a lodger in one part and Thomas Yarnold's family of three in the other part. A family of nine lived in Growland Cottage and the same number in the cottage next to the Holly Bush Inn. Several cottages had workshops near the house where the tradesmen worked and some of these still stand today.

MUNDERFIELD ROW AND STOKE LANE IN 1994.

Munderfield Row

1. Cusop Farm Cottage
2. Cusop Cottage
3. Cusop Cottage
4. The Willows
5. Avenholme
6. Woodland View
7. Claypits
8. The Orchards
9. The Old School House
10. Chapel Cottage
11. Stone Cottage (Hornsby)
12. Village Hall (1936-*c*1980)
13. Fairview now Tanglewood
14. Long Cottage
15. Rose Cottage
16. Lower House
17. The Hollies
18. Avendale
19. Chelston
20. Brambles
21. Post Office
22. Stocks Cottage (Gunsmiths)
23. Hawthorne Cottage
24. Chestnuts (Jasmine Cottage)
25. Perns
26. Briars (School House 1840)
27. Vine Tree Cottage
28. Stone House
29. Copton Farm
30. The Beeches
31. Frensham
32. Yew Tree
33. Yew Tree Cottage
34. Holly Bush
35. Copton Fields
36. Growland Farm

Stoke Lane

1. Homeland (Lamp Acre Cottage)
2. Pavonine (Lamp Acre Cottage)
3. Quarry Cottage
4. Stonehouse Cottage
5. Firtree Cottage
6. The Firs
7. Rose Cottage

Virtually all the small houses at Munderfield are close to the road and although some have encroached on the road verges, many more appear to stand on former strips or crofts of farming land. These dwellings would have been built by craftsmen and labourers who could augment the produce of their holdings by regular or seasonal work. Some cottages may have been built by the parish to

Long Cottage, Munderfield Row 1999. *Howard Painter*

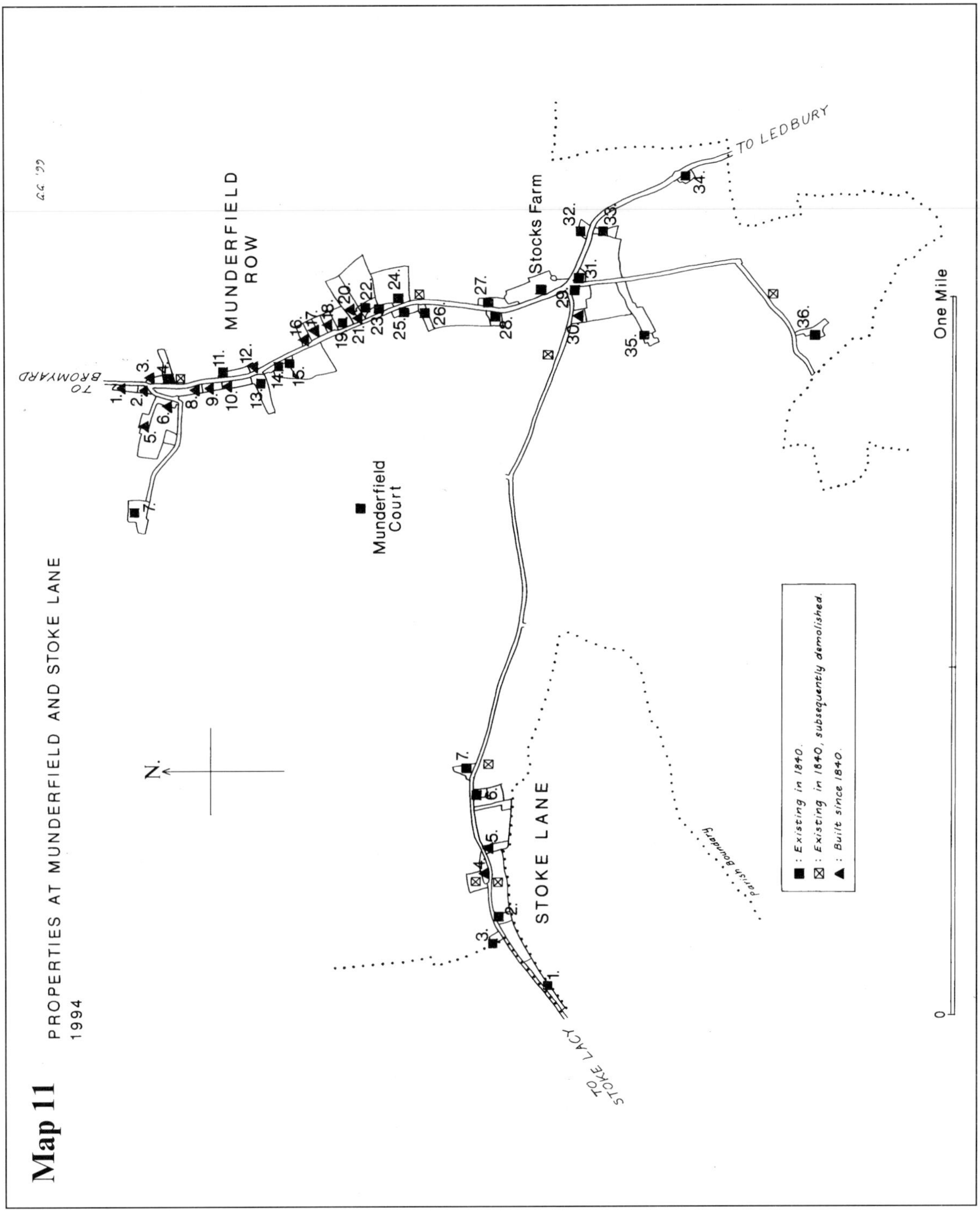

Map 11 PROPERTIES AT MUNDERFIELD AND STOKE LANE 1994

house the poor and homeless and were at a later date sold. The majority of the Munderfield properties date from the late 18th century to the present day, with most being 19th century. Some of today's houses would have been built on well established sites. For instance an indenture of 1802 describes one of these properties when Edward Long of Worcester was releasing to John Walker of Crusehill, Suckley:

> 'All that decayed messuage or tenement and yard formerly in the occupation of Richard Hodges and late in the occupation of John Edwards, blacksmith deceased but now void situate at Mundrefield in the parish of Avenbury alias Anbury in the county of Hereford. And also those five pieces of arable and grass land following also situate at Mundresfield aforesaid (that is to say) two small pieces of grass land planted with fruit trees containing by estimation two acres be it the same more or less lying together and bounded on one side thereof by the Turnpike Road leading from Bromyard to Ledbury and by a common field on the other side therof. A piece or parcel of arable land formerly used as a hopyard containing by estimation one acre and two roods....bounded on one side by land of William Cooke of Mundrefield aforesaid and on the other side by land of Mr Walker of Bromyard apothocary. A piece or parcel of enclosed arable land containing

Tanglewood, Munderfield Row 1999. This 17th-century cottage now has a renovated front. Formerly call Fairview, the cottage was in 1871 known as Weathercock House because it sported a weather-vane. It is said that at one time a bakery shop was kept on the premises, which afterwards removed to the Lower House, Munderfield. *Howard Painter*

by estimation two acres...having a field called Castle Field on the one side and land of Mr King and the said William Cooke on the other sides therof. A piece or parcel of arable land lying and being in a common field called Champles Field containing by estimation one acre...and bounded by land of John Freeman Esq. and Mr Wood of Wick near Worcester.' [4]

This property comprised six and a half acres of land and a decayed (ruined) house and certainly included strips in a common field. Many of the smallholdings at Munderfield probably developed in this way, acquiring small strips and parcels of scattered land that had belonged to larger farms and then building a house or cottage on the property.

Perns, Munderfield Row 1931.
Royal Commission on the Historical Monuments of England

The Perns at Munderfield illustrates a different origin. The unusual name could derive from *paren* which means 'growing with pears'. In 1779, John Smith who was a tailor of Munderfield, sold to Francis Tomkins, a wheelwright of Avenbury 'all that piece or parcel of orcharding commonly called or known by the name of the Perns' containing about half an acre. Before his death in 1800, Francis Tomkins had built a house on the land, which was later divided into two cottages. When John Jeffries Hyde of Instone Court in Bishop's Frome purchased the property in 1914, the description ran: 'all those two cottages...called Perns'. [5]

Perns, Munderfield Row 1999. *Howard Painter*

Bill Corbett with granddaughters outside the Perns 1946.

Mary Jane Corbett at the Perns.

Holly Bush, Munderfield, July 1999. *Howard Painter*

Developments such as Munderfield frequently attracted independent and free-thinkers and we find that in 1833 the houses of Samuel Brace and John Vernalls were licensed as places of religious worship for Protestant Dissenters.[6] In 1840, John Vernalls a farm labourer was living in Growlands Cottage which was reached by the lane running alongside Copton Farm. Samuel Brace, a blacksmith, was living in 1851 in a house close to the Stocks Farm.

Holly Bush, Munderfield during its days as an inn, Martin Cook on left.

Hubert Dean of the Holly Bush learning to thatch. 1933.
Bromyard Local History Society Collection

The Munderfield and Stoke Lane properties were not built as substantially as the larger farmhouses and would have had a much shorter life. There could well have been small cottages here at the time of the hearth taxes but they may not all have been charged and listed because their occupiers were exempt on the ground of poverty. In a hearth tax assessment duplicate made for Avenbury in 1664, 36 out of the 53 households listed had only one hearth. Of these, 23 householders appeared at the very end of the document. The assessors usually travelled from house to house by the shortest route which would indicate that these 23 one hearth houses lay together and most probably at Munderfield.[7] The hearth tax for 1671 lists 27 householders of which 13 had only one hearth, but the constable Edward Woodyatt reported another 15 persons not included presumably because in that year they were too poor to pay.[8]

Stocks Cottage (Gunsmiths), Munderfield. *Charles Grant*

Chapter 10

A Fleeting Glimpse

of the lives of some 17th-century Avenbury families from wills and inventories

'Consideringe and wayinge the disasters doubts and ambiguities that soe rise after the deathe and decease of those that dye intestate I doe ordain and make this my last will and testament in manor and forme following'

HRO Will of Margaret Pychard, widow, of the Venne, Avenbury. Proved 30th April 1591

Even today many people fail to make a will and thereby die intestate, and this can cause considerable problems for their next of kin, by whom an application has to be made to a probate court for letters of administration. Probate administration was a duty of the ecclesiastical courts until 1858 when England and Wales were divided into civil probate districts. From 1529 and up to 1858 the law required that, with or without a will, an inventory and valuation of the goods and chattels of all deceased persons should be made if their value exceeded £5. The inventory and valuation did not include houses and land, but did include wearing apparel, ready money, household goods, stock, harvested and growing crops, provisions and fodder, and money owing to the deceased. The ecclesiastical courts could charge a probate fee which was on a graduated scale according to the value of the estate. The valuers of the goods, cattle and chattels of a deceased person were called appraisers. These were usually two or three of the neighbours, friends or even a relative of the deceased, who were expected to be reliable and responsible people. Then, as now, probate inventories tended to avoid any over-estimate of the value of the property to the benefit of the dependants.

The majority of surviving wills, letters of administration and inventories for the parish of Avenbury and other parishes in the diocese of Hereford can be found in the Herefordshire Record Office. If the deceased had property in more than one diocese, administration was proved in the Prerogative Court of Canterbury and these records are now kept at the Public Record Office in London; there may be some local wills to be found there. Unfortunately the pre-1662 inventories for parishes within the diocese of Hereford have been lost. Nevertheless we are very fortunate to have those wills and inventories that have survived the intervening centuries, for they give a glimpse of the families, houses, furniture, stock and other aspects of life of the people we have met in the mid-17th-century taxation lists, in the parish registers and other parish records.

To modern eyes the valuations seem impossibly small, but it should be remembered that inflation has existed for longer than our own lifetime. In the late 17th century a Herefordshire farm bailiff could earn a yearly salary of £3 10s plus food, and a living-in farm servant £2 10s annually; living-in servant maids earned about £1 10s a year. Stonemasons and other skilled tradesmen would have been earning about a shilling a day.[1] It is thought that a multiple of at least 300 should be used to convert 17th-century money values to those of the present day.[2] The monetary system used was that of £(pounds) s(shillings) and d(pence). 12d = 1s and 20s = £1.

TABLE 12

AVENBURY INVENTORIES 1665-1705

A Total value of estate to nearest £
B Value of farm livestock
C Value of crops growing & harvested, including corn, grain, hay
D Value of farm implements
E Value of household goods, including provisions, hops, cider, flax, hemp etc.
F Money owing to deceased
G Number of oxen
H Number of cows
I Number of other cattle
J Number of sheep or if mentioned /
K Number of horses
L Number of pigs or if mentioned /
M Number of rooms mentioned in house

Name of deceased	date of will	A £	B £	C £	D £	E £	F £	G	H	I	J	K	L	M
John ffidoe of Little Froome	1692	414	152	107	23	132		6	8	30	10	5	9	11
Anthony Browne of Little Froome	1674 +	161	97		12	50		8	8	13	19	6	/	9
Sarah Charlott of Kewsopp	1696 +	298	116	45	9	75	51							
Thomas Hill of Hackley	1700	127	64	29	4	15	15	4	4	15	7	3	5	
Ann Gyles of Hopton Sollers	1705 *	220				20	200					1		
Roger Woodyate	1673	68	29	14	3	21		4	3	6	/	1	/	7
Richard Corbett of Birchyfield	1697	76	28	22	3	20		2	1	5	6	1	/	
William ffarley, gent (Burgess)	1676	110	61	18	4	26		4	5	11		5	9	
Henry Pitt of Noakes	1666 *	183	81	40	8	53			10	10	89	7	/	10
Anne Pitt of Noakes, widow of above	1670 +	136	77	33	3	23			10	17	85	5		
Nicholas Evans	1683	135	50	17	3	20	45	2	6	11	16	3	12	
John Morris	1684 +	193	54	24	4	25	87	4	6	10	15	1	/	
Nicholas Vaughan	1665	9		2			7						/	
John ffarley, gent	1675	13		1		12								
William Nott of Hackley	1679	12				1	11							
John Conny of Rough Mintridge	1689	70	41	10	3	16		4	4	7	8	2		
Roger Robinson	1688	94	17	10	1	6	60		3	2	13	1	/	
William Jones	1684	28	14	3	1	2	8		3	5	23	3	6	
Catherine Sely of Munderfield widow	1677	9		1		5	3						3	2
John Jones	1680	28	15	3	2	8			3	6		1		
John Lewis	1684 *	21	1			5	15				7	7&6 goats	/	
Thomas Coney	1667	11				11								

*Bibles and/or books
+Legacy to poor or church

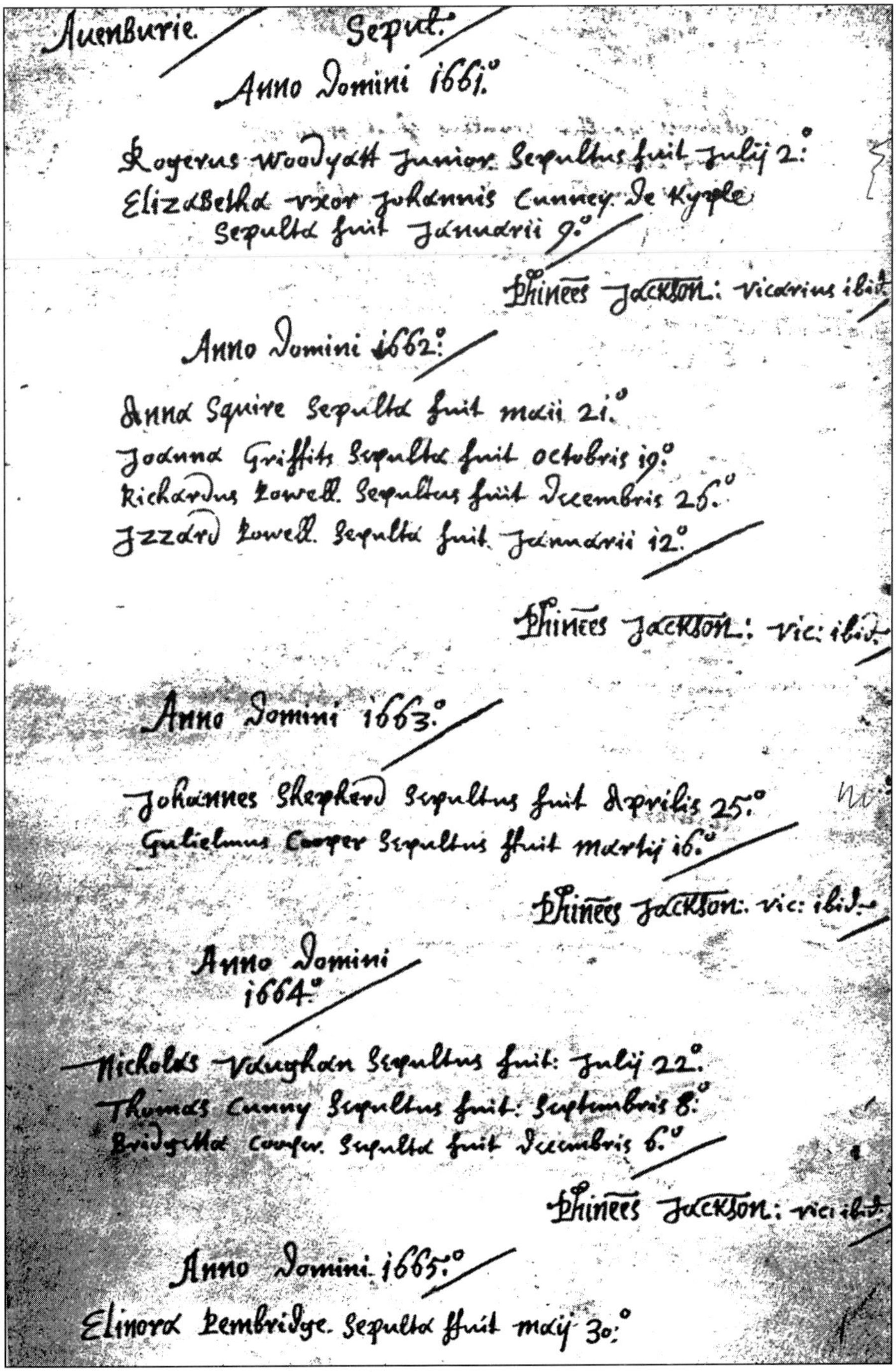
Avenburie Seput:

Anno Domini 1661°

Rogerus Woodyatt Junior Sepultus fuit Julij 2°

Elizabetha vxor Johannis Cunney de Kyple
Sepulta fuit Januarii 9°

Phinees Jackson: vicarius ibid

Anno Domini 1662°

Anna Squire Sepulta fuit maii 21°

Joanna Griffits Sepulta fuit octobris 19°

Richardus Lowell Sepultus fuit Decembris 26°

Izzard Lowell Sepulta fuit Januarii 12°

Phinees Jackson: vic: ibid

Anno Domini 1663°

Johannes Shepherd Sepultus fuit Aprilis 25°

Gulielmus Cooper Sepultus fuit martij 16°

Phinees Jackson: vic: ibid

Anno Domini
1664°

Nicholas Vaughan Sepultus fuit: Julij 22°

Thomas Cunny Sepultus fuit: Septembris 8°

Bridgetta Cooper Sepulta fuit Decembris 6°

Phinees Jackson: vic: ibid

Anno Domini 1665°

Elinora Pembridge Sepulta fuit maij 30°

HRO Avenbury Parish Registers.
Page of burials 1661-1665.

In Table 12 sums have been valued to the nearest £ and cannot be strictly accurate but rather show the relative value of household goods, livestock and arable crops. The numbers of livestock are as listed in the inventories, but for simplicity horses, mares and colts have been added together under horses; 'other cattle' include bovines of all types from aged bulls to calves, except for oxen and cows; sheep include lambs; and pigs include piglets; poultry has not been added to the list because surely every farm and probably most households would have kept poultry of some sort. The stocking rate seems incredibly low by modern British farming standards.

Livestock

Table 12 shows that in Avenbury, as in most of Herefordshire, mixed farming was the usual pattern and, in this district, the value of farm livestock was greater than the value of arable crops. Farm implements, 'implements of husbandry', appear of little value. They included hand tools, ploughs, harrows, carts, wains and 'tack of the team', which would have been the harness used for horses and oxen and, apparently, bridles and saddles used in order to ride the horse. The motive power for agriculture in the 18th century was draught animals, usually oxen, which were the most valuable animals on the farm. The Pitts at Noakes and Roger Robinson on his farm appear to have used heavy horses. In some cases where oxen were not kept the heavy hauling could have been done by neighbours and their teams as contract or exchange work. Many horses listed would have been used for both riding and work.

Horse-drawn binder working, possibly at the Burgess.

Horse-drawn binder, possibly at the Burgess.

Herds of cows were small. Only eight cows were kept at Little Froome in 1674 and 1692, Noakes had the largest herd at that time of ten cows, while Nicholas Evans and John Morris each kept six cows. These farms probably combined rearing calves with making cheese and butter to sell at Bromyard Market. Sheep appear to have been quite thin on the ground compared with the size of even small flocks today. Pigs were probably kept on most farms and by cottagers, but some farmers such as James Powell seem to have supplied local markets.

Crops

'Corn & grayne of all sorts' and 'pease & pulses' were common entries. John ffidoe of Little Froome had 'hard corne in the barne' worth £10, lent grain (spring corn) of all sorts worth £25, hay in the barns worth £22 and 40 acres of corn in the ground at £50. His inventory was taken in October, harvest was finished and 40 acres of winter corn had been planted. Sarah Charlott of Cusop, whom we have met in Chapter 8, died in June 1696 before harvest, and she left 'corn in the house & barn', corn in the field, and growing 'poulse & pease' valued at £45. Thomas Hill of Hackley who died in April 1700 also left corn in the house and barn valued at £3, winter corn growing on the ground at £16 and his spring planted corn 'lent corn growing on the ground' at £9, while his hay and straw were worth £1. Root crops were not included in inventories although they must at this time have been grown. Possibly their value was low as they would have been used for home consumption and were unlikely to be taken to markets.

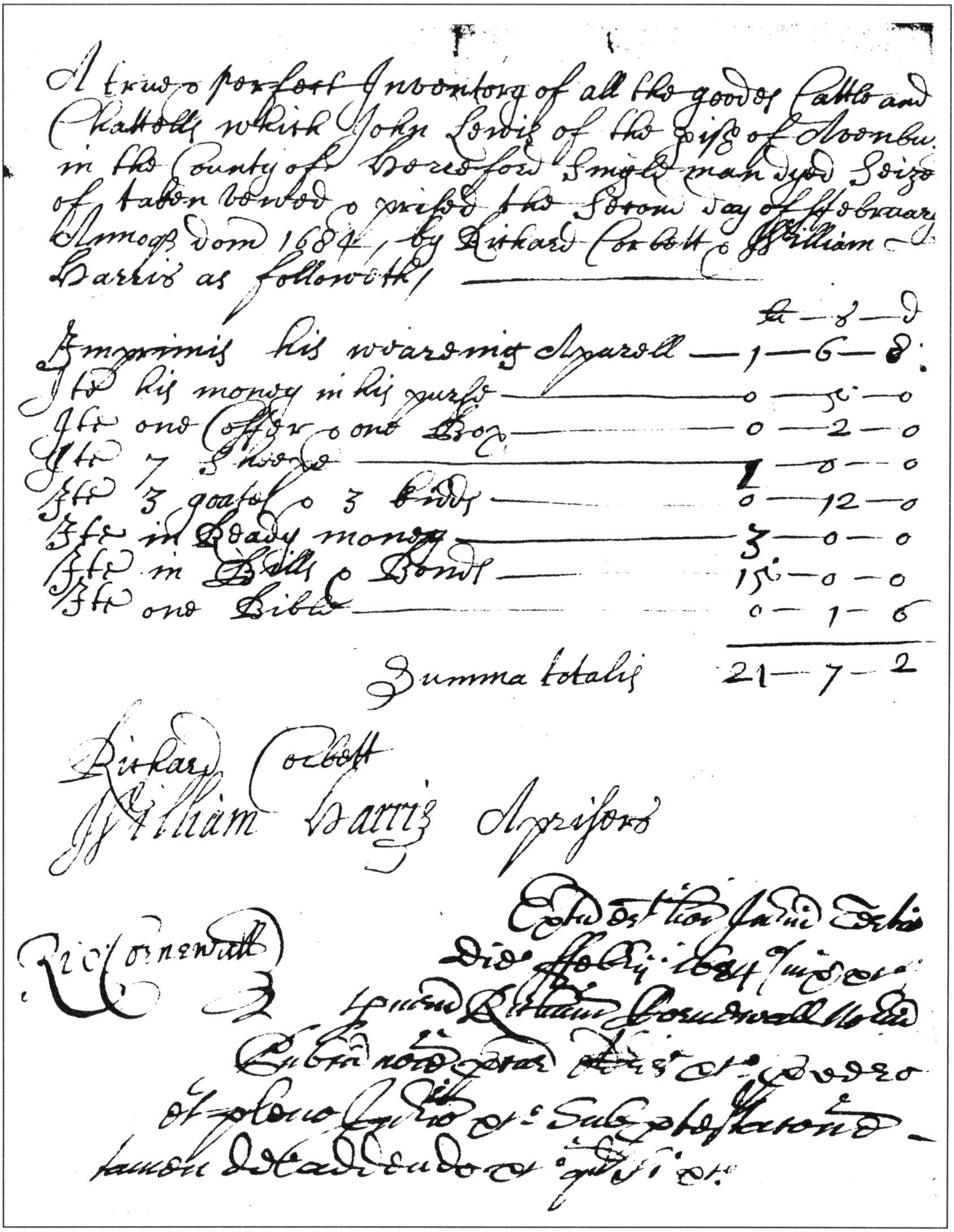

A true & perfect Inventory of all the goods Cattle and Chattells which John Lewis of the parish of Avenbury in the County of Hereford single man dyed seized of taken veiwed & prised the second day of February Anno Dom 1684, by Richard Corbett & William Harris as followeth/

	li	s	d
Imprimis his wearing Aparell	1	6	8
Item his mony in his purse	0	5	0
Item one Coffer & one Box	0	2	0
Item 7 sheep	1	0	0
Item 3 goates & 3 kids	0	12	0
Item in Ready mony	3	0	0
Item in Bills & Bonds	15	0	0
Item one Bible	0	1	6
Summa totalis	21	7	2

Richard Corbett
William Harris Apprisors

Ric Cornewall

[illegible]

HRO 1684 Inventory of the goods of John Lewis of Avenbury.

With their own crops and livestock, farmers in 17th century Avenbury were self-sufficient, and could maintain their larders, feed the living-in servants and provide such commodities as milk, flour and root vegetables to other workers. Flax and hemp were grown and processed at home to make up sheets, table linen and cloth, and wool could be saved from sheep and spun for woollen garments. Many inventories listed spinning wheels separately. Wood for building, repairs, heat and cooking was found on the farm. There would have been a bartering system whereby neighbours helped one another out with labour and implements at busy times of the year, for as they say, 'many hands make light work'.

Lending and Borrowing

For all this self-sufficiency, money was still an essential commodity and column F of the Table shows that lending and borrowing were an important part of the local economy. In 1705 Ann Gyles of Hopton Sollers had £200 out on loan, £100 to William Wall of Dymock in Gloucestershire and the other £100 to Benjamin Pember of Newport, Herefordshire. Nicholas Evans was owed £45 8s 'from several persons by bill and bond'. Roger Robinson, whose goods and stock totalled £94, had over half of that sum, £55, owing by bond and a further £5 owing on 'a lease of a hopyard'. Sarah Charlott, the widow of Robert Charlott, drew up an account of her late husband's estate in 1683. Robert left money, goods and probably farm stock and crops worth £134, and debts, from which the estate was exonerated, of £49 3s 6d. His funeral expenses came to £30 8s; Mr Haniball Williams, a mercer of Bromyard, was paid £7 8s 6d 'for goods out of his shopp'; Edward Houlder, a smith, was paid £2 6s 'for work done by him in his shopp'; servants' wages came to £7 18s; fees and other charges came to £1 3s. The servants and traders must have been pleased to receive their money at last if, as it seems, Robert Charlott had been ill for some time.

These were the days before reliable banking but these records show that money could be accumulated. For many people, especially farmers, surplus money would have been used to improve the house or buildings or buy more stock, but some we see were prepared to lend.

Leominster Fair 1556

Bromyard's markets and fairs were for Avenbury the most important, but farming families could go further afield and did. A rare account of the activities at Leominster Fair in 1556 has survived and been transcribed.[3] Buyers and sellers came from Herefordshire, Gloucestershire, Staffordshire, Warwickshire, Shropshire, Worcestershire, Wales and even further afield. 'Robert Hawley of Anbury (Avenbury) bysides Bromyard bought a grey mare, a grey nagg & a whyte nagg of John Addys of Cheryngton in Whushir (Wiltshire)'. Was Robert Hawley a cattle dealer? For later 'Robert Haly of Anbury pareshe sould a grey nagg to Thomas Valentyne of the pareshe of Hanley in Blackwell Park (Worcestershire)'. 'William Jones of Byshoppe Frome in com. (county) Heref bought ii black oxen of William

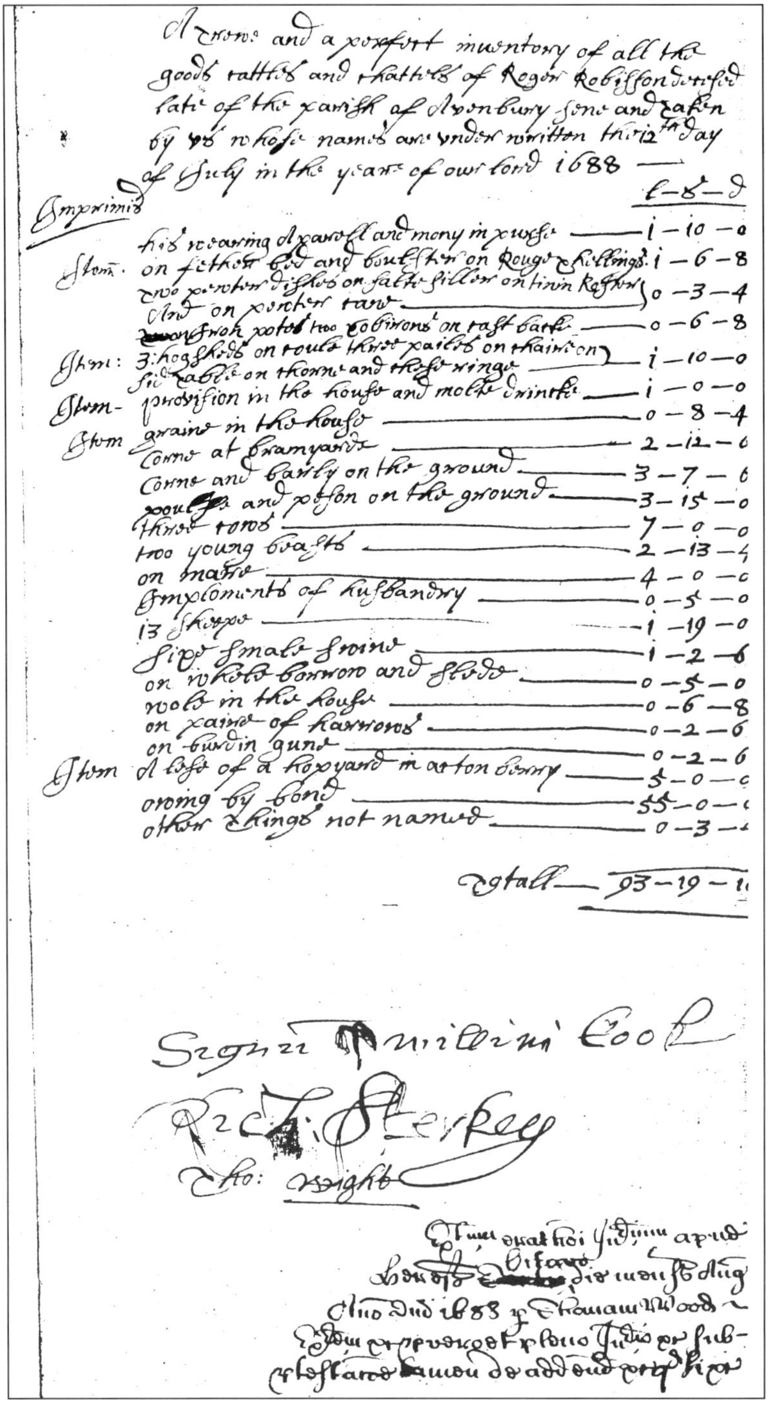
A trewe and a perfect inventory of all the goods cattles and chattles of Roger Robisson deceased late of the parish of Avenbury done and taken by us whose names are under written this 12th day of July in the year of our lord 1688 —

		£–s–d
Imprimis	his wearing apparell and mony in purse	1–10–0
Item.	one fether bed and boulster one rouge & billings	1–6–8
	two pewter dishes one salte siller one tinn kettle And one pewter tancard	0–3–4
	iron potts two cobirons one salt barke	0–6–8
Item:	3 hogsheds one coule three pailes one chaire one side table one thorne and these tinge	1–10–0
Item-	provision in the house and molte drinke	1–0–0
Item	graine in the house	0–8–4
	Corne at Bramyards	2–12–6
	Corne and barly on the ground	3–7–6
	poulse and peson on the ground	3–15–0
	three cowes	7–0–0
	two young beasts	2–13–4
	one mare	4–0–0
	Implements of husbandry	0–5–0
	13 sheepe	1–19–0
	sixe smale swine	1–2–6
	one whele barrow and slede	0–5–0
	wool in the house	0–6–8
	one paire of harrowes	0–2–6
	one birdin gune	0–2–6
Item	A lease of a hopyard in Aston berry	5–0–0
	owing by bond	55–0–0
	other things not named	0–3–0
	Totall	93–19–10

Signum Willimi Cook

Rich: Sterkey

Tho: wright

HRO Inventory of the goods of Roger Robinson 1688.

Cattle drinking in a pool at the Heath.

Dalow of Mylson in the County of Salope, for 6 pounds'. 'Roger Crompe of Pencombe bought a black oxe of James Hall of Almeley'. 'Edmund Russell of Suckley bought ii bullocks, one black & thother bryndyd of Evans ap Rice of the parshe of Bygildy'. 'George Cowper of Wackton in the Com of Heref bought one oxe blak of Thomas Sucker of Logaston in the said com for 46 shillings'. There were some 192 transactions entered at the fair on that day involving horses, oxen, beasts and sheep.

Household Furniture, Goods and Provisions

Household goods and furniture did not usually make up a large proportion of the deceased's estate. In the case of William Nott of Hackley who died in 1679, the bond owing to him by Thomas and William Spooner from Pencombe of £10 16s was virtually all he appeared to possess, for his other assets were only one brass pott 11s, a table board 1s, an old bedd 1s, a coffer & some boards 4s, and a barrel, which added up to 17s. His brothers Edward and Thomas Nott were granted administration of his estate and he may have been a dependant or servant at Hackley. Mrs Catherine Sely or Scilly of Munderfield died in 1677 and probate was granted to her son Richard Hancocks. The Hancocks or Hancox family were at Munderfield before 1600, for an earlier Richard Hancox of Munderfield made his will in 1598. Catherine Sely and Richard Hancocks were listed together in the Hearth Tax returns of 1665 with four hearths, '1 stopt up'. Munderfield may have been shared equally between them for they both had an estate valued at £6. The value of Catherine's inventory at her death was £8 18s 6d and she appeared to have for her own use two rooms in the farmhouse: 'In the deceased's Chamber' and 'In the Chamber at ye stairs head'. There was £2 18s owing to her for rent, her corn was worth 15s and the remainder of her goods were household apart from 'one old side saddle one pillin cloth' 1s 6d.

At the other end of the scale John ffidoe who died in 1692 and who rented Little Froome from Anthony Browne, had the most valuable inventory of all those found. His clothes and ready money came to £6. In the kitchen he had equipment worth £16 10s; in Mr Browne's chamber and in Mr Browne's little chamber were bedsteads, beds and furniture worth £11, and in the chamber over the parlour beds, bolsters, blankets and so forth worth £3. In the parlour there were three chairs and a little table board worth 10s, in the little coploft a flock bed and bedstead, a coffer and wool worth £1 7s, and in the coploft over the parlour chamber, beds and coverings worth £1 10s 6d. In the two chambers over the hall there were beds and furniture valued at £14 and these must have been where the family lived; in the chamber over the kitchen there were three bedsteads, one old cradle and a chest all worth £4; in the service rooms of backhouse and dairy there was £8 worth of equipment. There was £5 worth of cheese in the house, £13 worth of hogsheads for cider and beer and 20 pairs of sheets, three dozen napkins, seven tablecloths and other linen valued at £10 and spinning wheels worth £2. The value of hops and cider fruit was £36.

Avenbury Families

> 'And as for such goods and estate as the lord have bestowed upon (me) I give and bequeath as followeth'
>
> The will of Nicholas Evans of Avenbury, yeoman, 19th September 1693

Wills can be very useful in filling out family relationships. However there are complications. When a widow remarries she may bring a new surname into the family property. When daughters marry they too bring a different surname onto the scene, but the family can remain in the parish and, in the absence of sons, probably on the same farm which then passes by the female line. In the present case there is an added complication that the surviving church registers in Avenbury only date from 1661, which means that the families who lived in the parish before then are quite difficult to trace if the surname is not continued. The Boyce and Lane families are of particular interest, but also illustrate the difficulties.

Richard Boyce with other men signed the glebe terrier for Avenbury in 1589, and Richard Boyce and Edward Lane both appear as signatories to the 1619 glebe terrier, while Richard Boyce and Henry Boyce with others signed the 1628 terrier. Edward Lane of Hopton Sollers made his will in 1620 and left gifts of *munck corn* which was 'beer-corn or barley' to several people including Henrie Boyce of the Heath and 'his poore wiefe & children'; also to 'Henrie Boyce my sister's sonne, one of my oxen called Tagg, being a blacke tagged oxe' and to his cousin 'Henrie Boyce the bedd wheruppon he doth lye and the blankett & canvasse on the said bedd, and a paier of sheetes on the said bedd'. Edward left 12d to the church of Avenbury and bequests to three servants and the remainder of his estate to his wife Brigett who was his executrix. It would appear that Edward and Bridgett Lane, who died before the registers start, had no surviving children and the beneficiaries of their estate were relatives, servants and friends.

Richard Boyce made his will in 1637 leaving all his estate to his wife Alice except for bequests to his daughter Alice, the wife of Roger Woodiyate (Woodyate), and their son, Edward. Alice Boyce, Richard's widow, died the following year and made a lengthy will. She left a bequest to her son Richard Boyce and also to her son John Shepard and his children (probably from a previous marriage). Roger Woodyate and his children all received gifts of money, as did the children of her other son-in-law Thomas Conney. Alice, the daughter of Thomas Conney, had her grandmother's best feather bed, blanket and coverlet. The residue of her estate, after all debts, legacies and funeral expenses had been paid, went to Thomas Conney her son-in-law. It is not clear what happened to her son Richard Boyce. The only Boyces appearing in the burial registers are Margaret (1681) and Jane (1707). So the Boyce family, like the Lanes, disappear from the Avenbury scene, but the Shepards, Woodyates and Conneys are all met with in taxation lists, wills and inventories later in the century.

In 1663 Roger Woodyate had an estate valued at £6 and evidently was the owner-occupier of a moderately sized farm, paying tax on one hearth. Where did he live? Possibly at the Stocks or Copton Field Farm, but we cannot be sure. He died in 1673:

> 'whilst he lived and was of perfect mind and memory with serious intent to make his will and settle his estate after his death. Did on or about 20 January in the year of our lord God English style 1673; utter and declare these words following or words to the same effect viz: I give and bequeath all the estate whatsoever I shall die possessed of to my loving son Edward Woodyatt, whom I make my executor, he paying my debts and I wish it were more for him'.

The witnesses to this declaration were John, Sara and Maria Love. Maria Love was to marry Edward Woodyate in 1680. Edward Shepard (of Brookhouse) and Richard Wyne made the inventory of goods, cattle and chattels which amounted to £67 16s 10d. They also listed furniture and goods in the parlour, the chamber over the parlour, the hall, the chamber over the hall, the bolting house

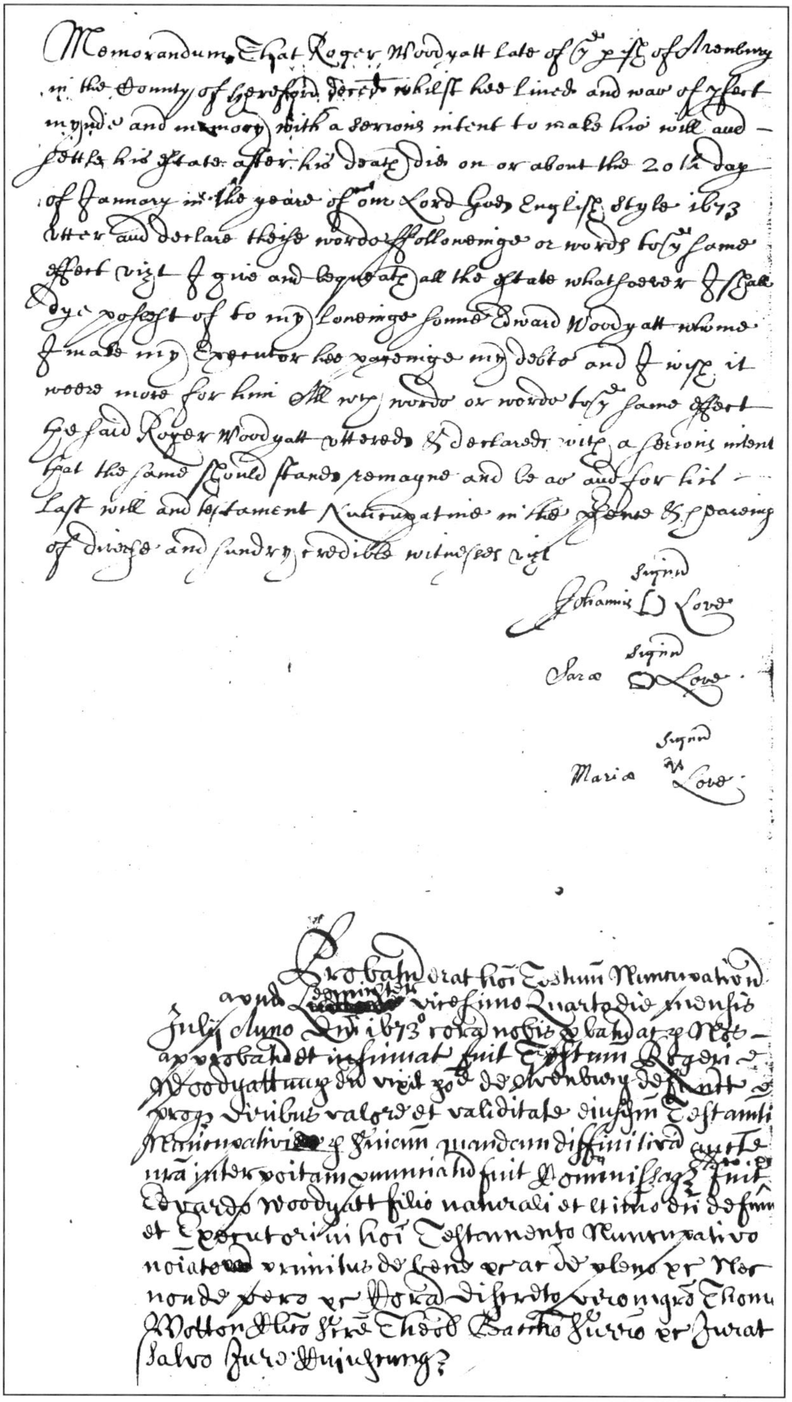

HRO Declaration regarding the last wishes of Roger Woodyatt 1673.

(which was a room where meal and flour was sifted to separate the bran from the flour), the servants' chamber and in the buttery: seven rooms, three of which appear to be upstairs. John Love appears to have been a fairly close neighbour and he too had one hearth. Another grandson of Alice Boyce also remained in the parish, for in 1694 John Conney of Rough Mintridge left goods and stock worth £70, principally to his wife Margaret; his estate in 1663 had been valued at £6, with one hearth.

Some wills were simple and well balanced as in the case of William ffarley, gent who appears to have lived at the Burgess:

> 'As for my estate both reall & prsonall I bequeath to my dear wife Marie Farley and do make her my sole executrix and I doe give unto my daughter Jane, my daughter Marie, my daughter Elizabeth, my daughter Berthya, my daughter Frances, my sonn Rowland, my sonn Edward twenty pounds a piece to be paid to them by my executrix at any time before her death. And this I publish to bee my last will and testament ye fourth day of February Anney Domn 1676 Will ffarley'

Anthony Browne of Little Froome who died in July 1674 left 20 shillings to the poor of Bromyard and 40 shillings to the poor of Avenbury and then:

> 'I nominate, constitute & appoint Mary Browne of Lydbury in ye county of Salop, spinster, my deare & only sister to be my sole executrix & ye executrix of this my will & testament. To whom I give & bequeath all my goodes, cattles & chattles, my debts, legacyes & funerall expenses being first satisfyedd & discharged.'

Many wills were quite long and complicated; the testator had obviously put a great deal of thought into making provision for as many dependants and relatives as was reasonable. Wills, inventories and the parish registers are perhaps the most poignant of the Avenbury records and they give an insight into the homes and families of some of our predecessors and one would wish that more such documents had survived.

Sick Bed Testaments

Many wills were made within a short time of the testator's death. To read what must, in many cases, have been the last wishes and concerns of dying parent, husband or wife, feels like an invasion of private grief. These documents have been stored away for centuries and few eyes can have seen them during that time.

> 'In the name of God Amen. I Richard Corbett of Birchenfield in the parish of Avenbury & county of Hereford yeoman being sick & weak in body but through Gods goodness of sound disposing mind & memory. Doe make this my last will & testament in manner following. And in the first place I comitt my soul unto the hands of God who gave it. Expecting to be saved only through the meritts of the Lord Jesus Christ. And for my body that it be decently buried at the discretion of my Executrix herein after named. And to my worldly goods, estate whatsoever & wheresoever (my just debts being

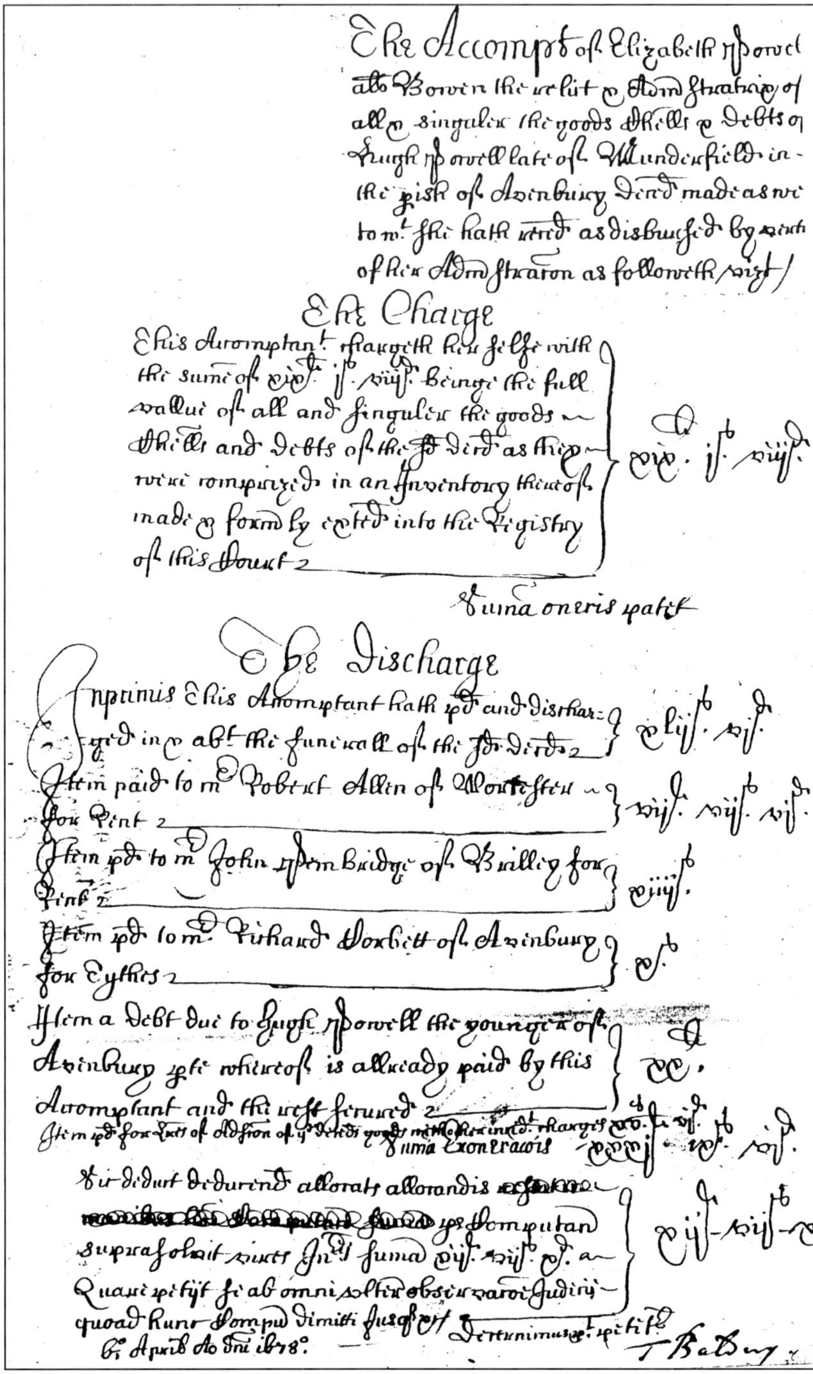

HRO The Account of Elizabeth Powell, alias Bowen regarding the goods and debts of Hugh Powell late of Munderfield in the parish of Avenbury 1678.

paid & funerall expenses discharged) I give bequeath & dispose of the same as followeth. I give bequeath & dispose of the sume of five shillings a peece to my five children James Corbett, Mathew Corbett, Richard Corbett, John Corbett & Rebecka Corbett to be paid to them by my executrix after named within two months next after my decease. And for all the rest & residue of my goods, stock & personall Estate whatsoever I give bequeath & dispose of the same unto Elizabeth my loving wife & her assigns for her naturall Life to have & to take the whole benefitt thereof to her own use & my will is & I hereby declare it soe to be that she dispose of what remaine of the stock & personall estate at her decease unto & amongst our said children above named according as she shall judge convenient. And I doe hereby nominate, constitute & appoint the said Elizabeth my loving wife to be the sole executrix of this my last will & testament.'

Richard Corbett signed this will on the 1st of June 1697, an inventory of his goods was taken on the 20th of July.

Nicholas Evans, yeoman made his will the 19th September 1683:

'being sick in body but of sound and perfect Memory, Thanks be given to Almighty God doe make this my last will and testament in manner and form following (vis) First and Principally I bequeath my soule unto the hands of Almighty God my Maker and Redeemer hoping through the Death and Passion of my Lord and Saviour Jesus Christ to inherit everlasting life. And my body I do commit to the earth to be decently buried by my executrix hereafter named. And for such goods and Estate as the Lord have bestowed I give; and bequeath as followeth (vis)....'

The inventory of Nicholas Evans was taken two weeks later on the 4th of October.

Occupation or Title

When a will or inventory was drawn up, the name of the testator was usually, although not always, qualified by the description of esquire, gentleman, widow, spinster, yeoman, servant, miller, tanner and so forth. 'The Valuation of the Raters' for 1663 makes a similar distinction for esquires, gentlemen and widows only. In 1663 of 34 people listed, 13 were of superior status: Gilbert Nicholett of Hopton Sollers, Alexander Gretton and John Hackett (for the glebe and tithes) bore the suffix esquire; John Browne of Little Froome, Anthony Rowden of Rowden, John Ball, John Broome, Richard Hancox, John Pembridge, John ffarley, Robert Charlott and John Browne of Hall Court, Bishop's Frome, all bore the title gentleman, and there was plain Mr Stitch at the Lower Venn. Mrs Katherine Selly and Anne Corbett were the only women on the list and were widows; the remainder of those named and the unnamed tenants would have been yeomen, while the smaller farmers could have referred to themselves as husbandmen. Thus thirteen landowners (of whom six lived outside the parish) were of superior status, two were widows and 19 would have been yeomen farmers. To the 19 should be added the tenants of the landowners living outside the parish. The ratio of superior status to farmers was about 7:25:2 widows.

A similar picture emerges from 30 wills and inventories with six esquires and gentlemen, sixteen yeomen, six widows, one tanner and one servant. The tanner was Thomas Dunn who made his will in 1600 and the servant was Thomas Mayfield who died in 1642, 'servant unto Mrs Joyce Jeffreys'. The ratio inferred from wills and inventories is 'rough and ready' and certainly inaccurate as these documents cover more than a century and relatively few people in the parish made a will in any one decade, let alone in the same year. Nevertheless this does reinforce the picture derived from the taxation list of 1663 in giving some idea of the class structure over 300 years ago amongst the landowners and yeomen farmers of Avenbury who had property, stock and chattels to dispose. There could well have been as many or more people and families without land, in rented houses, living at their work place, or with less than £5 worth of goods, who would not have felt the need to make a will.

Chapter 11

Parochial Care, Duty and Responsibility

'The parish is the territorial basis of community service'
W E Tait, *The Parish Chest* (1983), 10

The parish was a unit of local government, but answerable to higher authority. The manor applied to the value, ownership and management of the land and estates, whereas the parish reflected ecclesiastical authority and parochial responsibility. By the time when, from 1700 onwards, Avenbury records appear in any quantity, the importance of the manor had dwindled and the lord had not been resident for a considerable time. Nationally the powers of both manorial and hundredal courts had begun to decline in the 16th century. The power of the Avenbury inhabitants was invested in the vestry which had long been established for ecclesiastical affairs and was by the 17th century a management committee for the parish of which, by custom, the vicar was chairman. The parish officers were elected at the Easter vestry to serve for the ensuing year and were:

2 churchwardens or guardians
2 sidesmen
2 overseers of the poor
2 constables
2 waywardens or surveyors of the roads

These men (and very occasionally women) had to be chosen from substantial householders of a parish and in Avenbury, as in many parishes, they were chosen by rote, usually in turn, from the larger properties. They needed to be 'substantial' for their costs and expenses were not reimbursed until their accounts were presented to the vestry at the end of their year in office. They were invested with considerable authority as they needed the confidence to appear in court on behalf

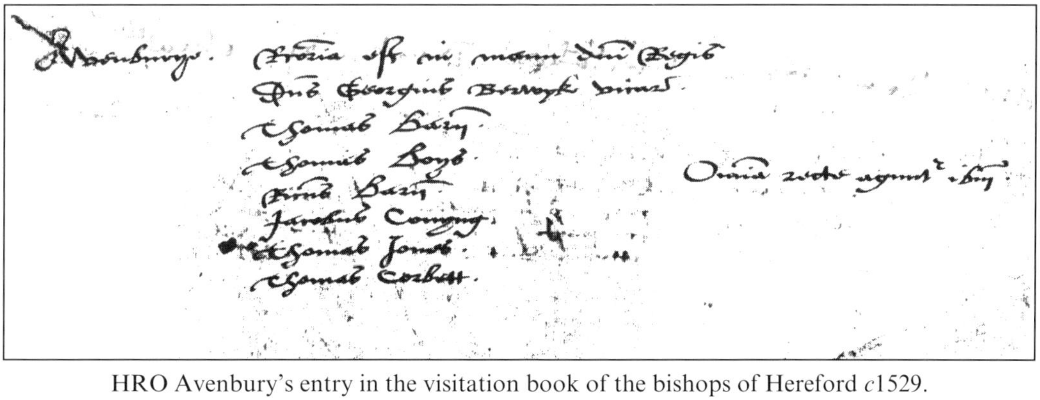

HRO Avenbury's entry in the visitation book of the bishops of Hereford *c*1529.

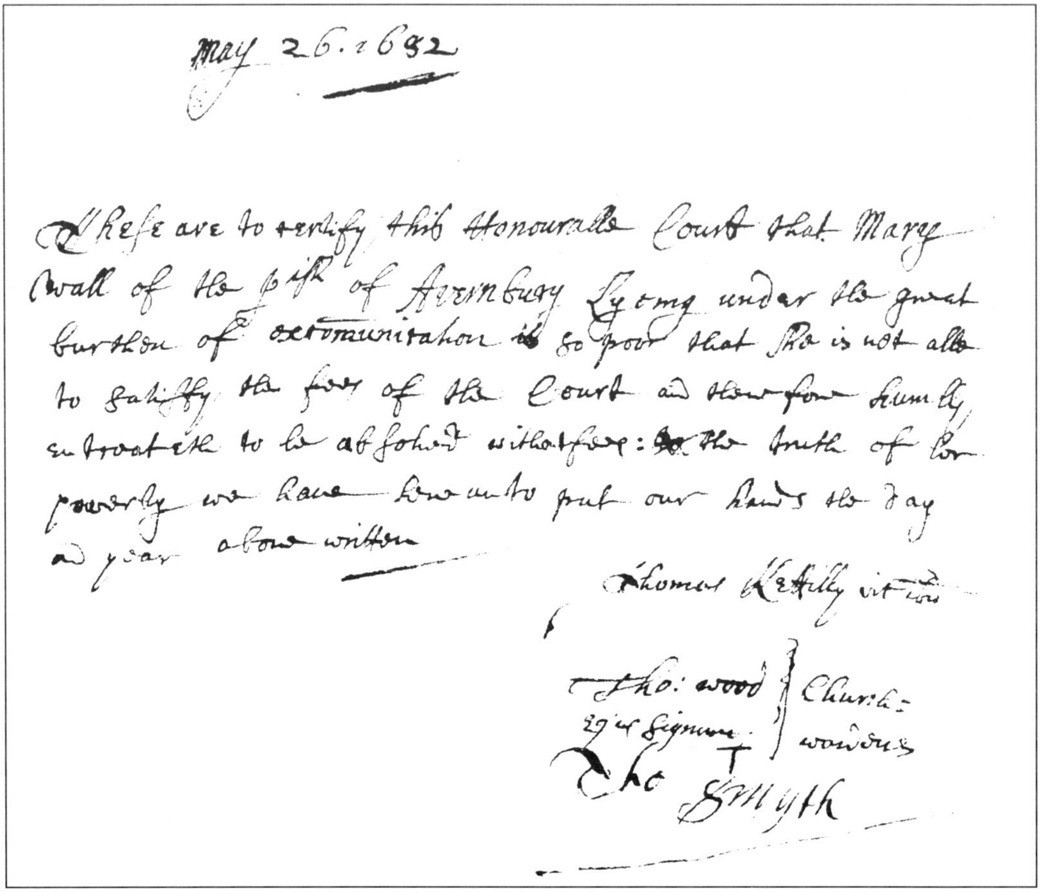

May 26. 1682

These are to certify this Honourable Court that Mary Wall of the p[ar]ish of Avenbury lying under the great burthen of excommunication is so poor that she is not able to satisfy the fees of the Court and therefore humbly entreateth to be absolved without fees: the truth of her poverty we have hereunto put our hands the day and year above written

Thomas Kettilly vicar

Tho: wood } Church-
his signum } wardens
Tho Smyth

HRO A plea to the ecclesiastical court from the vicar and churchwardens of Avenbury on behalf of Mary Wall in 1682.

of their parish. The vestry minutes, parish accounts and other records were kept in the church, in the parish chest which would have been especially purchased for that purpose. The Avenbury chest dated from the 14th century.

Churchwardens

The churchwardens were 'the proper guardians or keepers of the parish church' and they were also the channel by which the parish communicated with its bishop, diocesan officers and the ecclesiastical courts. In Avenbury the churchwardens of the 1589 and early 17th-century terriers called themselves 'guardians'[1] but by the early 18th century they had the better known title of churchwardens. Wardens are known to have been appointed as church officers as early as 1127 and by common usage there was the people's warden and the vicar's warden, although originally they were required to be chosen by joint consent of both the minister and the parish. The money expended by the parish officers was raised by a levy on property within the parish according to its value.

The earliest known churchwardens' accounts for Avenbury date from 1731 when Phillip Bennet 'Pd for comeing into my office Court Fees £1 0s 0d'. This was to cover travelling to Hereford to be sworn in as churchwarden. Phillip Bennet then paid the parish clerk's annual wage of £1 9s; bread and wine for communion during his term came to 14s and washing the minister's surplice 5s. He spent 18s 8d on documents and accounts, 7s 6d on bell ropes, 3s 6d on mending the windows, a total expenditure of £4 17s 8d. His income by levy was £5 18s 2d, although Mr Bennet wrote at the bottom of his account that his levy was short by 18s 1d. These accounts were fairly typical.

William Cooke's year as churchwarden in 1733 was more expensive because of the following repairs to the church:

'Paid Abraham Pulling for mending of the bell		2s	
Paid Francas Turner for iron worke		1s	8d
Paid Joseph Phelpots for repareing of the church and steple and cullers (gutters?)		18s	10d
Paid for nails, hare, lime, lath, tyle & hailing	£1	5s	4d
Paid to Mr. Stephans for mending the bell agin		3s	
Paid for beiropes, staples & nails		7s	5d
Paid to Mr. Stephens for mending the to bels		2s	6d
Paid for staples & nails		1s	11d'

The total expense on building work for the year was thus £3 2s 8d but Cooke's other expenses of £4 3s 3d were similar to those in 1731, except that in addition to 'washing the surplis twise 5s' he also had to have 'the surplis' mended for another 6d. However on a new page is written:

'Paid the Parritor with the presentment	4s
For working the lewn & accounts	2s'

which adds another 6s to his expenses. 'The parritor' was the apparitor, an officer of the ecclesiastical court and he appears again in 1735 when he was paid 1s 'for a prayer for ye Royale family'. 'The lewn' was the tax collected by the churchwardens from the parishioners.

'The Acct. of Charles Davis Church Warden, served for ye Noakes' in 1736 confirmed that the wardens served by rote based on property. He too spent a certain amount of the church income on the fabric: 'for bellropps 7s 1d; for making a gutter at the Chancel 1s; paid Mr Williams for glaicing ye Church 3s 1d; for mending ye Church and materiales 4s'. At this period unless extra items were needed the average church expenses were about £5 annually. Francis Smith, churchwarden in 1742, was meticulous in recording the communion wine and bread 'Oct ye 3rd for one botel of wine & 2 loves 2s 8d; Jan ye 3rd for one botel of wine & 2 loves 2s 8d; Apr ye 3rd for 3 pints of wine & 2 loves 3s 11d; Apr ye 10th for 1 qrt of wine & 2 loves 2s 8d; May 27 for 1 qrt of wine & 1 loafe 2s 7d.' The sum for the year was 14s 6d, very similar to the 14s spent in 1731 by Phillip Bennet.

Another year for repairs to the church was 1742, when 33s l0d was spent on stone, timber, nails and hauling of stone, also 'for 6 days worke 7s 6d'. A dial, dial post and putting it up came to 9s 6d and for a 'lader' 2s; was this a clock or a sundial? John Arden in 1743 paid 1s for 'a prayer for the sucksess of the kings armes' and 3s for 'a lock for the chest & a key for the church door'; mending the bells cost 11s and 'washing the sirpliss & scouring the plate' 8s. Although there were always two churchwardens, only one was responsible for the accounts. The churchwardens were supported by two sidesmen and the names of the four men for each year are recorded from 1733 and the same names regularly appear. Richard Corbett was elected in 1756 and a memo of 1757 said 'Mr Corbett continued in office of Ch. Warden on acct. of ye bell being broken'. The new bell dated 1757 was made by Abel Rudhall of Gloucester and inscribed 'Peace & Good Neighbourhood 1757' and was probably transported by water to Worcester and then by cart. When Avenbury Church closed, the three bells, including this one, were taken to St Andrew-by-the-Wardrobe, London. Subsequently they were blitzed but the two smaller bells by Rudhall and Taylor were recast.[2] We read that Mr Richard Corbett's disbursements for the years 1756 and 1757 amounted together to £25 17s fid and the money raised in the parish was £27 3s 1d. Apart from years with unusual items, the levy and disbursements were fairly steady and around £7 at this time.

Ten years later a note in the accounts reads 'June the 16th 1767. At a vestre meeting then held we do agre to seale the Church and at the same agred with John Milman to do all the sealling for four pound and we be to bring all materials to place as witness our hands this day and year first above written

the mark of Richard Baker
Francis Smith
the mark of John Coney
the mark of John Smith
John Miliman
William Cook'

Mr William Stephens who was churchwarden in 1810 came to grief after his year in office: '1811 May 23 At a Vestry Meeting then held it was agreed to regect the whole of Mr Wm Stephen's a/c other than what he can bring bills & vouchers to support. The a/c of Mr Edw West as CW for 1809 amounts to £12 5s was at this meeting produced & wholly approved' signed by Philip Bray, Thomas Jones, Rob Bray, R Smith, Fra Jenks, Hugh Jones, Edw West, Thos Perkins, Jn Walker, James

Jenks. Two months later Mr Stephens' accounts were allowed no doubt after much work on his part and supported by paperwork.

'1811 July 25 at a vestry meeting then held it was agreed to allow Mr W Stephens the following bills:

		£	s	d
1809	Prayer Book	1	6	0
1810	Transcript		3	0
	Chancellors fees at Bromyard		6	0
	Prayers & expenses		6	0
	Clerks fees	1	6	4
	Bread & wine for three feasts		16	9
	Bell wheel	1	17	4
	The masons bill	3	0	10
	Beards bill	1	18	11
	Visitation & for 3	4	0	0
	New cloth & towell		19	3
	Five briefs*		5	0
	Court fees		4	10
1811	Clerks fees	1	5	0
	Bread & wine for 3 feasts		16	9
	Washing surplis 6 times		15	0
	Transcript		3	0
	Presentments		6	0
	Visitation expenses	1	16	6
		21	**7**	**6**

signed Fra Jenks, Richard Smith, Edw West, Jn Walker, Thos Perkins'.

*Briefs were Royal Mandates for collections towards a good cause and were read from the pulpit.

There must have been many meetings to consider the church restorations, but neither these nor the accounts have been found with the parish papers. However on the 21st November 1871:

> 'At a meeting duly held this day to take into consideration the repairs of the Church and to bring before the Meeting the Arrangements of the Seats one objection to open Seats was taken by Mr Rd Allies on the part of his landlord'.

This referred to the removal of the old square enclosed box pews which were to be replaced by open pine pews. Vestry meetings would have continued until the church was finally closed and one would like to know what the feelings of the parishioners were at that time.

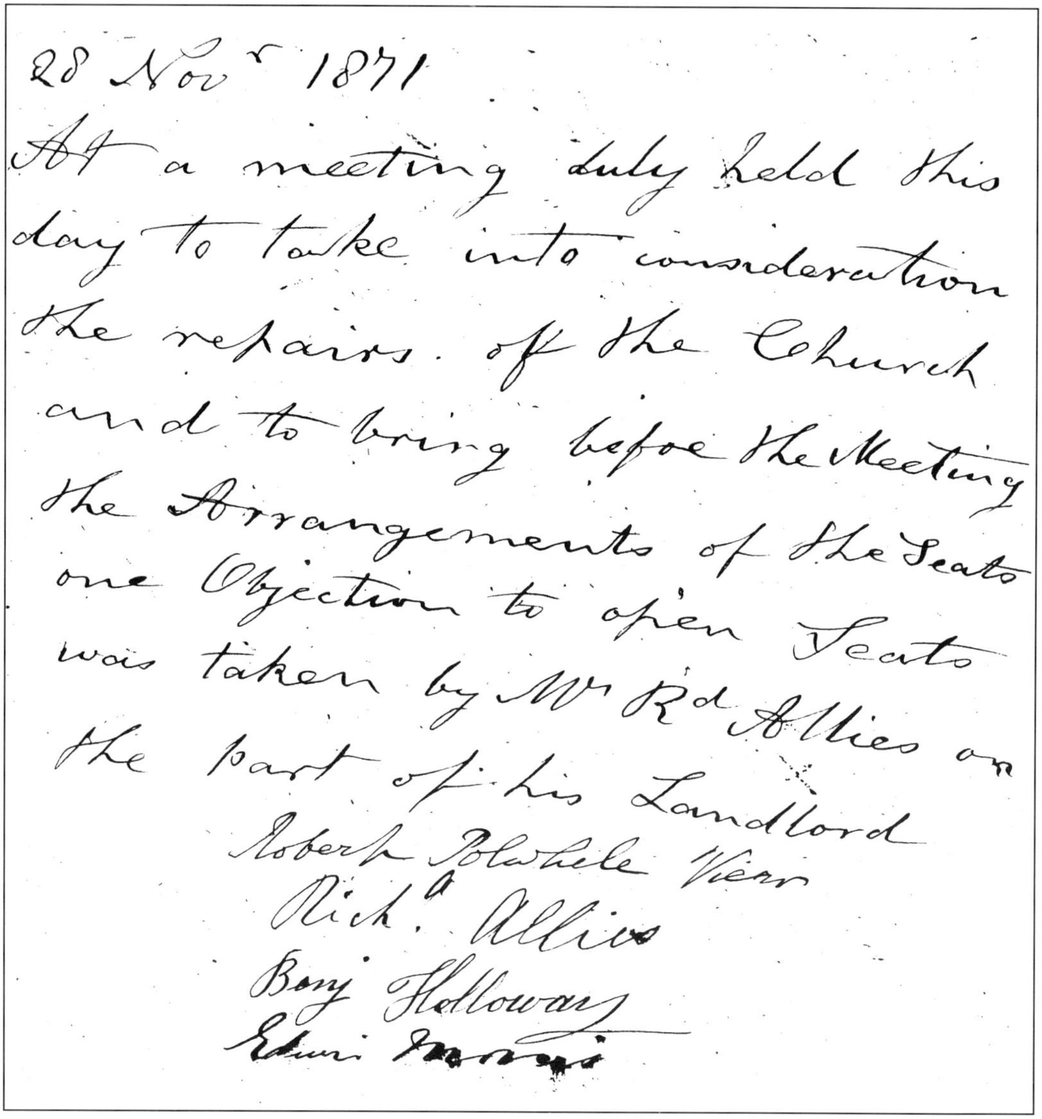

28 Novr 1871

At a meeting duly held this day to take into consideration the repairs. of the Church and to bring before the Meeting the Arrangements of the Seats one Objection to open Seats was taken by Mr Rd Allies on the part of his Landlord

Robert Polwhele Vicar
Richd. Allies
Benj Holloway
Edwin Morris

HRO Avenbury Parish Records.

Care of the Poor in the Community

In all communities there are people who, perhaps through no fault of their own, need help and support, for instance orphans, widows, the handicapped, sick and the unemployed. In early days the manor was expected to relieve the poor but morally the duty frequently fell upon the Church, and helping the deserving poor was regarded as a duty (albeit voluntary) of the more fortunate. There was an act as early as 1388 forbidding vagrancy and subsequent acts attempted to deal with the problem of beggars. An act of 1572 created the parochial office of overseer of the poor and an act of 1597 set down the rights and duties of the overseers and ordered that they were to be appointed by justices of the peace. The great Poor Law Act of 1601 really set the scene for the care of the parish poor and was the basis for community care until the 19th century. The 1601 act ordered that the churchwardens and two to four substantial householders were to be nominated each year as overseers to maintain and set to work the poor of the parish. The funds for this work were provided by taxation on every inhabitant and occupier of property in the parish.

The accounts for Avenbury date from 1730 as do the names of the overseers. There were two overseers nominated annually, by rote on the properties, each of whom dealt with a six month period.

'The widdow ffincher's accounts for the use of the poor in the first half year 1731

	£	s	d
pd for cloth for Mason	00	12	08
pd Burfoot	00	09	09
pd Burfoot	00	05	00
pd the widdow Brookes	00	07	00
pd widdow Shepard	00	00	11
pd for 2 coffins	00	14	00
pd for a coffin	00	05	00
Expence at meetings	00	03	00
pd for Aberlys child	01	05	02
pd for Masons funerrale	00	05	06
pd Edwd Powell	00	07	06
pd for shirts for Tho Walker	00	04	06
Expenses after James Harris	01	02	06
pd 20 weeks 8s per week	08	00	00
pd 6 weeks 6s 6d per week &	02	05	06
6s 6d more to Mary Harris			
for the presentment	00	01	00
pd the total	16	08	06
Recd of the Levy	17	11	08
Returned to Mr Smith	01	03	02'

It is rare to find a woman serving as a parish officer. Widow ffincher may have been the only person available to serve for her property and perhaps she was also an able businesswoman.

Francis Smith of Brookhouse kept the accounts for the second half of 1731.

'The a/c of the Disbursments of Fra Smith for the last half year in 1731

The repairing widow Perkins House	£	s	d
for 10 poles	00	03	06
pd the carpenter	00	02	00
pd the mason	00	02	04
pd for nailes	00	00	02
pd for straw	00	08	00
pd for thatching	00	07	00
	01	**03**	**00**
The charge of widow Walkers House			
for 3 load of stone	00	03	00
pd the mason	00	08	00
pd for the chimney	00	07	00
	00	**18**	**00**
The charge for widow Harris House			
for brick	00	01	09
pd the lime	00	01	--
pd the mason	00	02	08
pd the straw	00	06	00
pd the thatcher	00	01	06
pd the halling (hauling)	00	01	06
	00	**15**	**03**
The By Accounts			
pd the widdow Brookes at 2 payments	00	04	06
pd for Watkins funeral	00	12	00
pd the wid Perkins	00	00	06
pd for going to see Harris	00	03	00
pd for 3 bookes	00	03	09
pd for charge going after Harris	00	08	00
pd Mr Corbett	00	01	00
pd Mr Corbett for Expense	00	01	00
	01	**13**	**09**
The weekly pay			
pd Tho Walker	01	19	00
pd Dee	01	06	00
pd Wid Shepard	00	13	00
pd Wid Harris	01	06	00
Pd Mary Smith	00	12	00
pd Widow Baynham	01	03	03
pd Watkins	00	15	00
pd the A/Cs & levys	00	03	00
pd for 2 warrants	00	01	0
pd for other expenses	00	01	06
pd Cathy Walker	00	15	00
	08	**14**	**09**

The Bermingham Expense

Expense in the journey to Warwick	00	14	00
pd to the councile	00	10	00
pd the rule of court	00	04	00
pd to Sam Long	00	03	06
pd the councile more	01	11	00
pd the ffees of the court & rule	00	07	00
pd expense in journey	02	07	00
pd the taking the childe home	00	16	00
pd for the drawing the order	00	01	00
pd the journey to Bermingham	00	09	00
pd for the horse hier	02	07	00
	09	**09**	**06**
The whole A/Cs	22	14	03
The 2 levys	22	01	10
Recd of the Widdow ffincher	01	03	00
	23	**04**	**10**
Mr Smith to return to Mr Cave		10	7
Mr Corbett to return to Mr Cave	1	11	4
March ye 27 1733 Recd ye full overplus of Francis Smith	00	11	07
Edw Cave being overseer after him'			

The 'Bermingham Expense' appears to have related to the removal of a child from Avenbury back to Birmingham, which had the responsibility for the child's poor relief. This particular problem was not so acute in Avenbury as in some parishes. No parish wished to support, out of their limited resources, paupers who were the responsibility of another parish. Settlement criteria for poor relief in the event of hard times included:

- place of birth
- employment for a year and a day
- renting a house worth £10
- guaranteeing security to discharge the parish from all expenses it may incur on their behalf
- serving as a parish officer
- being bound apprentice to a parishioner; paying the parish rate.

Those unable to provide proof of settlement were removed from the parish, frequently at considerable expense. Of particular concern were unmarried mothers and the overseers were adept at arranging 'shot-gun marriages', for then the child would be the responsibility of the father.

Edward Cave and Phillip Bennett did not have such an expensive time the following year. Edward Cave expended £12 0s 3d and Phillip Benett £9 1s 4d. They were paying weekly sums to Edward Dee, Mary Harris, Widow Baynham, Widow Shepard, Cathy Walker, Frances Pooling, Widow Perkins and Thomas Walker.

They made repairs to the houses of Widow Baddham, Widow Harris and Widow Mason. For a frock and pair of shoes for Thomas Walker, which included making the frock, 5s 2d, and for a coat and two shirts for Edward Dee 11s. In 1735 there were 12 people in receipt of regular weekly relief of between 6d and 1s 6d; probably the sum varied with the number of dependants in the household. The overseers paid in 1742 'for cloaths for lame Jack' and 'pd for a frock for lame Jack'. Widow Aberly was in difficulties in 1746 for, between December and the end of February, £1 14s was spent by the overseer on medical expenses, a midwife and weekly payments.

Badges for the Poor

There was in 1736 an entry 'Pd for 6 Bages' 1s 6d; these '6 Bages' must have been badges issued by the parish to be worn by the poor and sometimes known as 'pees' as they bore the letter **P**. Needless to say they were most unpopular with those expected to wear them and do not appear again in Avenbury records, although some parishes maintained the custom into the 19th century.

Houses for the Homeless

The overseers regularly repaired houses for the poor and in many cases these appear to have been houses that belonged to the parish and were the forerunners of council houses. In 1677 John Watkins of Avenbury took a petition to the Hereford Quarter Sessions[3] that he and his wife being aged had lived in the parish for about 20 years paying rent and now his house had become ruinous and he could not repair it. The overseers of Avenbury were ordered 'to provide him forthwith with a house or pay him 12d a week until such provision'. The previous year a similar order had been made in favour of Mary Wall:

> 'for Avenbury parish to repair a house for Margaret Wall a poor woman there, in the place where it last stood with the consent of the lord of the manor or pay her 12d weekly until the house was repaired'.[4]

The fact that the consent of the lord of the manor was needed suggests that the house was on common wasteland of the manor. There is an 18th-century undated bill, 'Money laid out for the houses at the Pound'[5], which came to £28 12s 6d; these would have been cottages at the animal pound which lay between the church and Avenbury Court.

A complicated arrangement took place in 1748 when at a parish meeting it was agreed:

> 'to repair Hester Perkin's house and to remove Jone Walker to him(it) & put John Cayle in Jone Walker's house & alow Daniel Horish seaven shillings & sixpence to repair his house'.

Within 6 months at another parish meeting it was agreed that no more parish rents were to be paid and 'It is agreed at the same time a roome shall be put up for Moses Bickerton at the end of An Badham's house'.

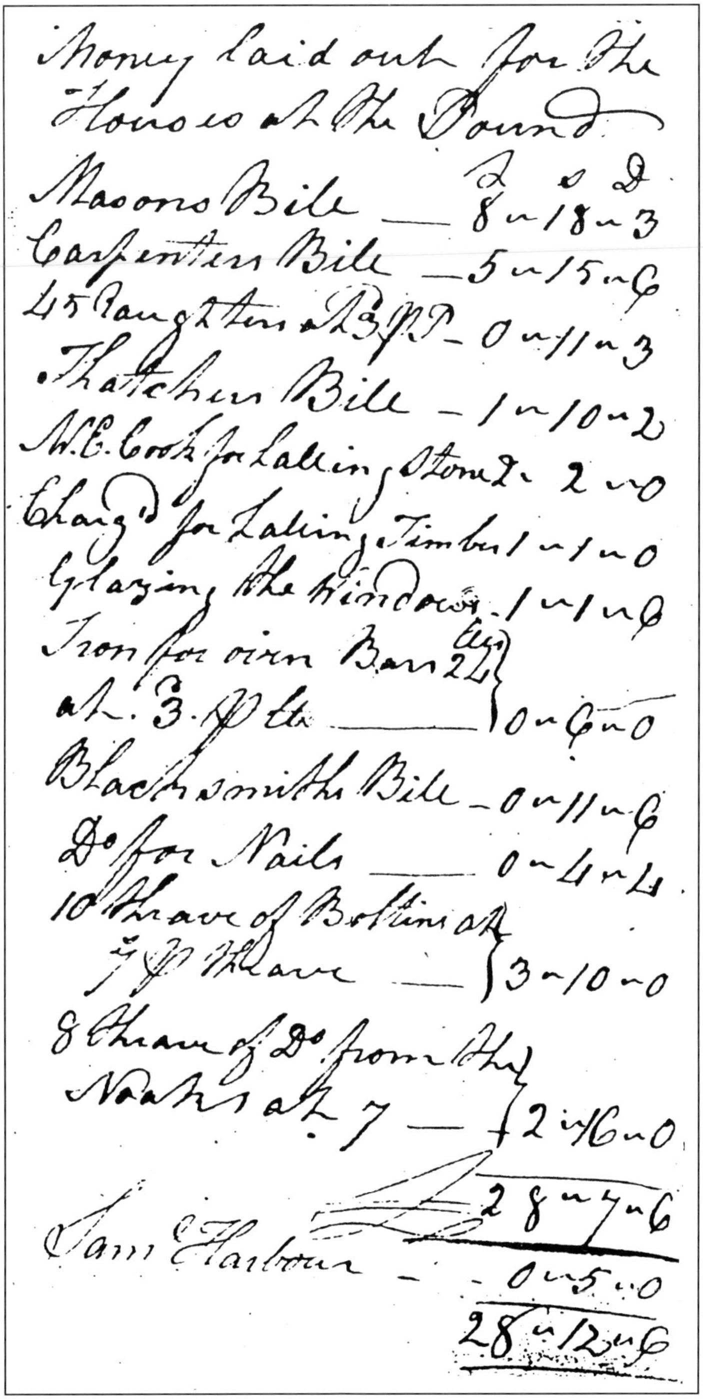

Money laid out for the
Houses at the Pound.

	£ s d
Masons Bill —	8 " 18 " 3
Carpenters Bill —	5 " 15 " 6
45 Laughters at 3 p. P. —	0 " 11 " 3
Thatchers Bill —	1 " 10 " 2
W. C. Cook for Haling Stone &c.	2 " 0
Charg'd for Haling Timber	1 " 1 " 0
Glazing the Windows —	1 " 1 " 6
Iron for oirn Bars 22 lb at 3 p lb —	0 " 6 " 0
Blacksmiths Bill —	0 " 11 " 6
Do for Nails —	0 " 4 " 4
10 Thrave of Bottins at 7 p Thrave —	3 " 10 " 0
8 Thrave of Do from the Naakes at 7 —	2 " 16 " 0
	28 " 7 " 6
Sam Harbour —	0 " 5 " 0
	28 " 12 " 6

HRO Avenbury Parish Records, Houses for the Poor.

On 28th February 1797:

> 'at a vestry meeting holden in the parish church of Avenbury this day properly & legally called on Sunday last past - we the inhabitants of the sd parish do covenant & agree on our part with Saml. Harbour, labourer on the other part, to build & erect a dwelling house free of all expenses, save & except the raising of sufficient wall stone free of all expenses to the inhabitants by the sd Saml. Harbour - and further the sd Saml. Harbour is to occupy the sd house only for the term of his natural life, then immediately to become the property of the parish as aforesd. signed Nathaniel Smith, William Cook, John Homes, Richard West, Richd Corbett, Edward Cook, James Cook'.

Coping with the poor and homeless in a sparsely populated parish like Avenbury must have put a great burden on the other inhabitants and in January 1749 it was:

> 'agreed at a parish meeting that all that be paupers & live in the parish shall be broght in to the next meeting except those that have setevecates (certificates)'.

Parish Apprentices

A perennial problem in the days of high mortality and poverty was the plight of the children. Frequently orphaned or with only one parent or too many in the family, an effort was made to provide them with a settled home. Some children were properly indentured to learn a trade, but many poor children were sent to houses and farms in the parish to serve for a period of seven years or longer to learn the art of husbandry for boys and housewifery for girls, which meant that in return for clothing, board and lodging, they were expected to help in the house, on the farm or in the workshop. Properties frequently took the apprentices by rote and on occasions the placing was not a success; nevertheless one hopes that most of the children had a better standard of living than they could otherwise have hoped for. In 1751 William Freeman agreed to take William Aberle, then aged seven years, as an apprentice without an indenture and he was excused from taking any other apprentice until young Aberle was 24 years old. Did the young man never earn any wages until then? In 1752 John ffidoe took John Hill apprentice for the Heath farm. There was a rush in 1757 when at a vestry meeting Messrs Wood, Cook, Bennet, Smith, ffincher and Corbett took between them Richard Smith, John Bickerton, James Hill, Elizabeth Bickerton and John Powell and 'all the above men are not to take any other prentice till these children comes to their proper age'. Their proper age was frequently 24 for boys and 21 for girls.

At a vestry meeting held in 1775 it was agreed 'to place prentisis in turn & to be bound according to law, Elizabeth Purlin is to go to Thomas Tayler of the Noakes'. At about this time the people who took parish apprentices began to receive money to help out with the expenses. 'Mr Holmes to have William Preese & was paid with him 3s 4d.' 'It is agreed that Thomas Cook is to have William Bayles as an apprentice & is to have 1s per weack for halef a year'; this last in 1781

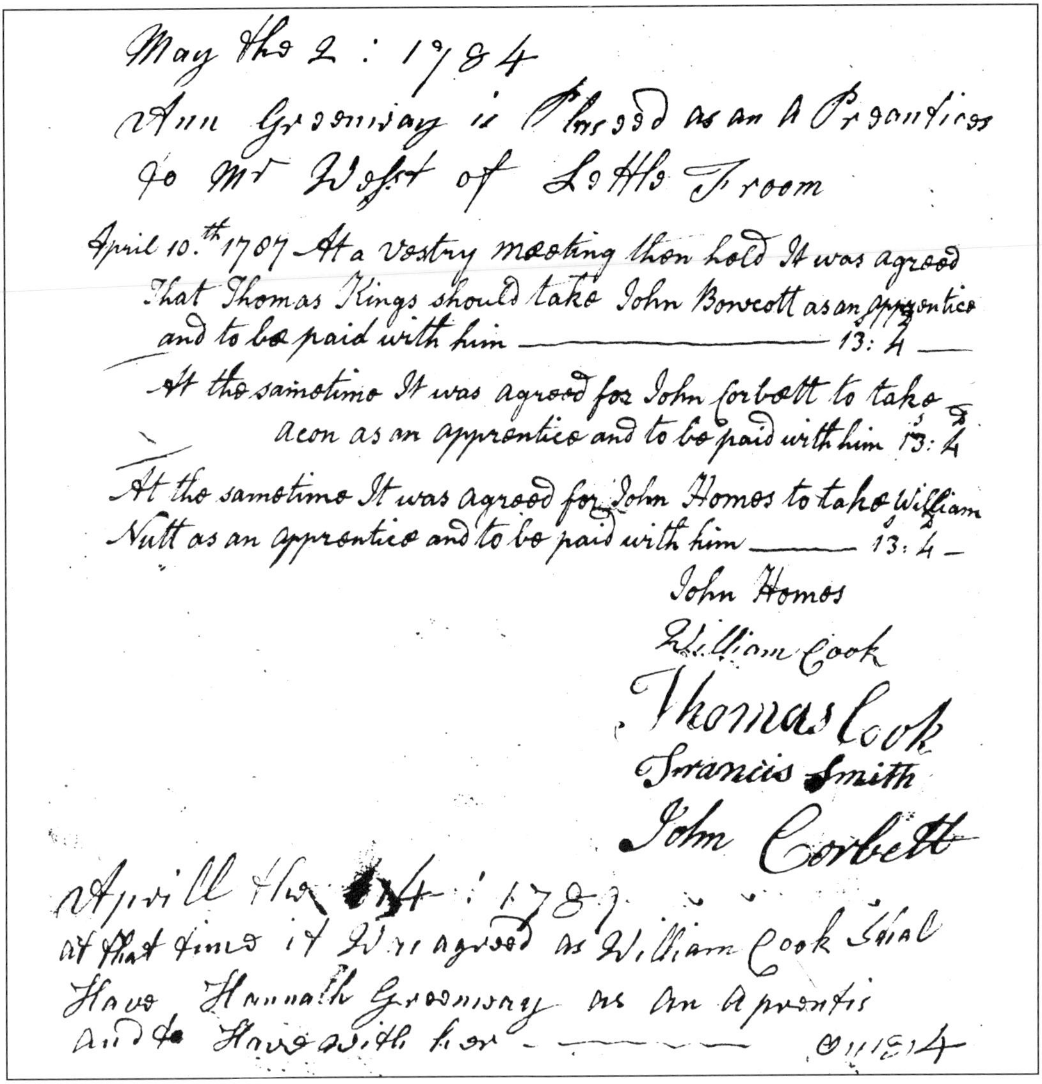

May the 2 : 1784
Ann Greenway is Placed as an Apprentice to Mr West of Little Froom

April 10.th 1787 At a Vestry meeting then held It was agreed That Thomas Kings should take John Bowcott as an apprentice and to be paid with him —— 13: 4 —
At the same time It was agreed for John Corbett to take Aeon as an apprentice and to be paid with him 13: 4
At the same time It was agreed for John Homes to take William Nutt as an apprentice and to be paid with him —— 13: 4 —

John Homes
William Cook
Thomas Cook
Francis Smith
John Corbett

Aprill the [illegible] : 1789
at that time it Wr agreed as William Cook Shal Have Hannah Greenway as An Apprentis And to Have with her —— 0:13:4

HRO Avenbury Parish Records apportioning to Apprentices.

and written by a happy speller. The passage of time and inflation increased the sum of money for in 1789 we read 'William Cooke shall have Hannah Greenway as an apprentis & to have with her 13s 4d.' There were several other placements although not all were accompanied by this sum, as the prosperous households could probably manage without the extra inducements.

In the 60 years between 1747 and 1807 some 62 children of the parish were sent as apprentices to different properties in Avenbury including the Greeve, the Glebe, Goodships, the Venn, Birchyfield, Sawbury Hill, Brookhouse, the Burgess,

Munderfield, Hopton, Little Froome, Noakes, Cusop and the Heath. In most cases the property was not mentioned, but it would appear that every farm including the Mill took children.

The care of the deserving poor within the parish was only part of the overseers' duties. It was incumbent upon them that they did not support the undeserving poor nor the poor from other parishes. The able-bodied poor of their own parish they were expected to put to work, whilst they had to remove, if necessary with a court order, paupers from elsewhere. Travelling soldiers, sailors and other wanderers could be helped along their way by sundry payments. The workhouse was also a possibility and in 1763 the overseers, Phillip Benett and Francis Smith, 'shall go to Hereford to agree with the workhouse by the head & agreed at the same time that Samuel Moss shall take one shilling a week or go from house to house', which means that parishioners would take it in turns to accommodate him. The churchwardens with the overseers were responsible for paying out of the poor levy a proportion towards the General County Rate. This helped to pay for bridges, gaols, the Shire Hall, the house of correction, the relief

GRAPH 1

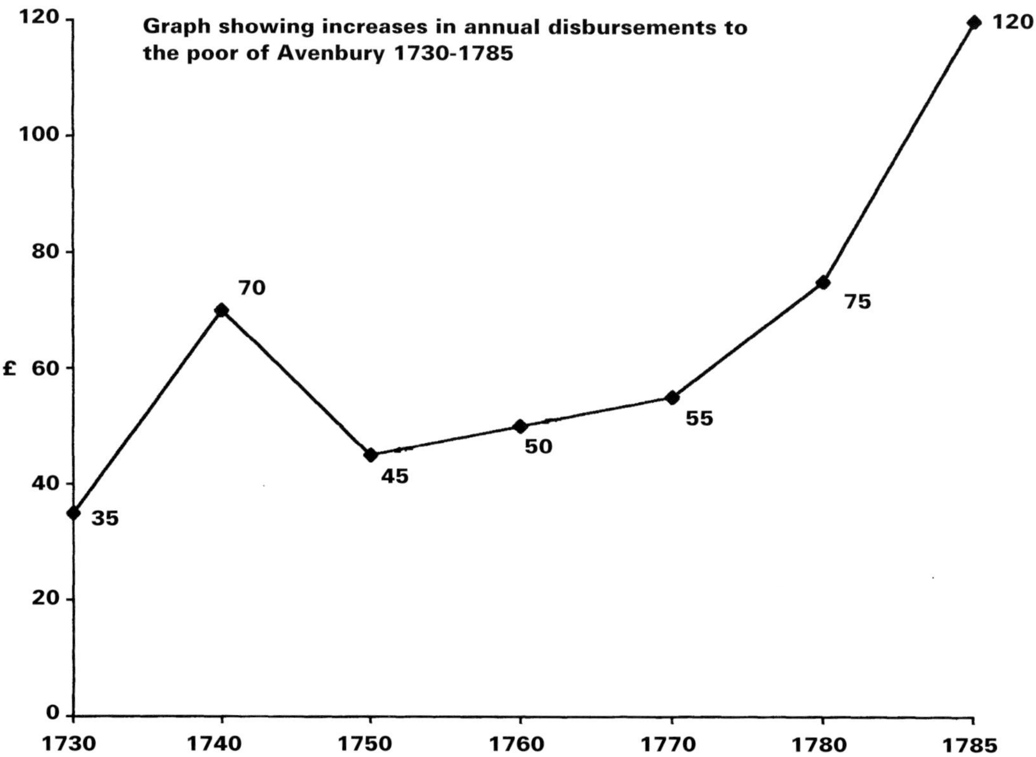

J Weale

of prisoners both in Hereford and London, coroner's fees and other salaries, and various charges relating to vagrants, felons and soldiers.

Collecting the levy and drawing up their accounts, which needed to be supported by vouchers and bills, must have been an onerous task for busy men. Furthermore they were only reimbursed at the end of their period in office and, apart from travelling and other expenses, they received nothing for their time; no wonder they needed to be 'substantial householders'. As early as 1753 it was agreed to allow the vicar, Mr Joseph Taylor, £1 for keeping and settling the accounts, and it was also agreed that the overseers at each monthly meeting should be allowed 2s 6d for their expenses and no more.

Over the years the overseer's annual costs escalated, through inflation, bad harvests, bitter winters, wars and other hardships. An entry in the Pencombe parish registers for 1795 reads:

> 'Memorandum. This year corn was exessive dear. In January a subscription was entered into by the inhabitants of this parish to supply the poor with flour at six shillings a bushel which was continued till June; when the price of wheat advancing to one guinea a bushel it was agreed, at a vestry meeting, to supply the poor with mixed flour at nine shillings a bushel viz one peck of Bean flour in three pecks of wheaten flour which was continued till harvest which providentially was very productive throughout the Kingdom.'

An entry signed by the vicar,[6] from the parish registers for Inkberrow in Worcestershire reads:

> 'For some months before the end of this year the Poor's levies of this parish amounted to nearly the enormous sum of one hundred pounds a week, owing to the extraordinary high price of every article of provision, which was on average during the winter 1800-1801 as follows

Beef	6d per pound
Veal & Pork	8d per pound
Bacon	14d per pound
Potatoes	5s the bushel
Wheat	£1 4s the bushel
Barley	15s the bushel
Oats	8d the bushel
Beans etc	13d the bushel

> At this time too every article which contributes to the support and comfort of the human body was proportionally high, it was indeed a time of universal suffering both public & private.'

Francis Smith disbursed £148 3s 9d for the poor for the last half of 1804, and he received £142 10s 9d by 12 levies and £5 13s from other payments. William Rogers for his half year of 1805 disbursed £119 18s 2d, and Mr Smith serving for the Mill disbursed £209 8s 2d in the same year.

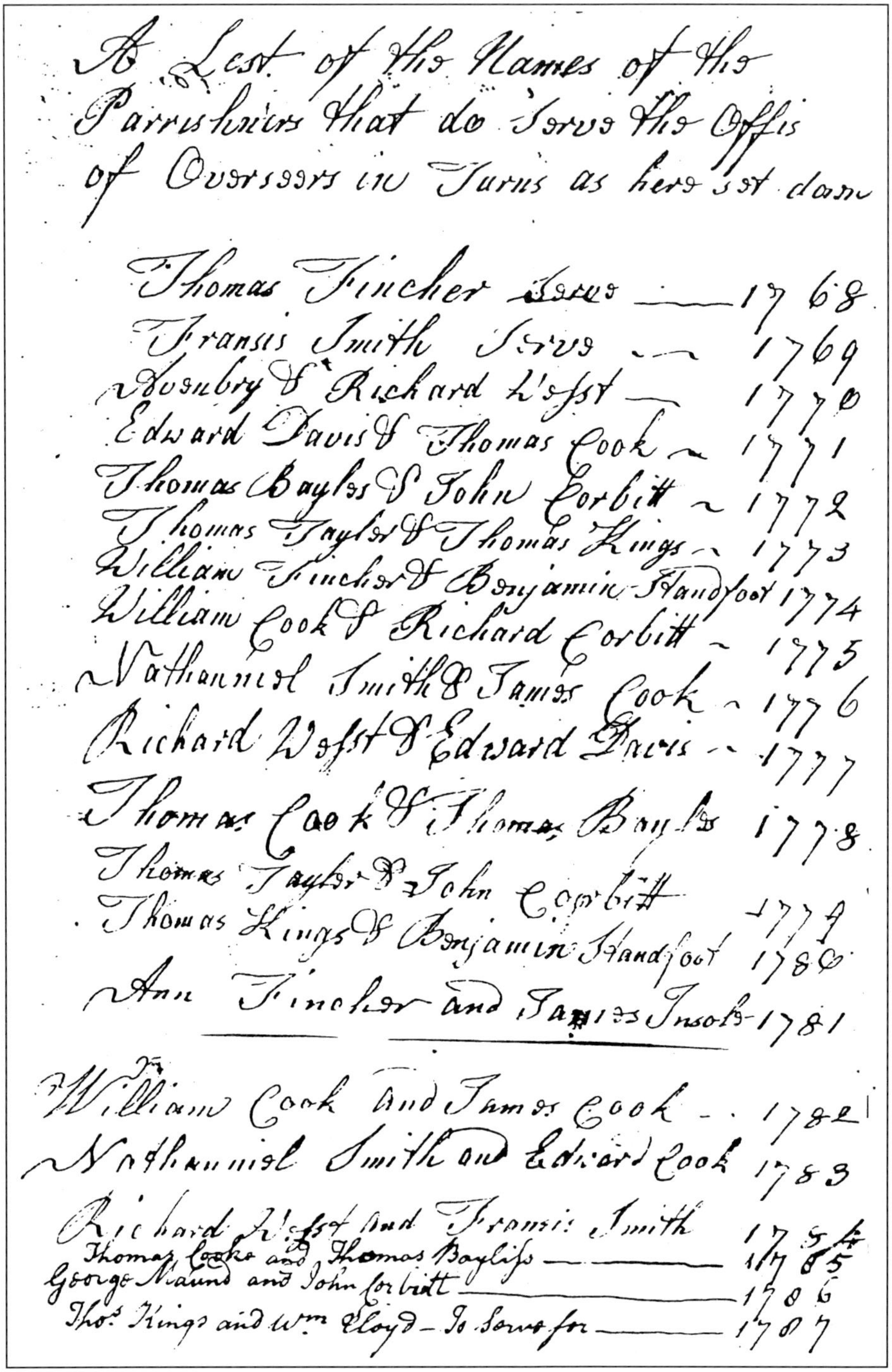

A List of the Names of the Parrishners that do Serve the Offis of Overseers in Turns as here set down

Thomas Fincher Serve — 1768
Fransis Smith Serve — 1769
Avenbry & Richard Weſt — 1770
Edward Davis & Thomas Cook — 1771
Thomas Bayles & John Corbitt — 1772
Thomas Tayler & Thomas Kings — 1773
William Fincher & Benjamin Handfoot 1774
William Cook & Richard Corbitt — 1775
Nathanniel Smith & James Cook — 1776
Richard Weſt & Edward Davis — 1777
Thomas Cook & Thomas Bayles 1778
Thomas Tayler & John Corbitt 1779
Thomas Kings & Benjamin Handfoot 1780
Ann Fincher and James Insole — 1781

William Cook and James Cook — 1782
Nathanniel Smith and Edward Cook 1783
Richard Weſt and Fransis Smith 1784
Thomas Cooke and Thomas Bayliss — 1785
George Maund and John Corbitt — 1786
Thos Kings and Wm Lloyd — To Serve for — 1787

HRO Avenbury Parish Records.

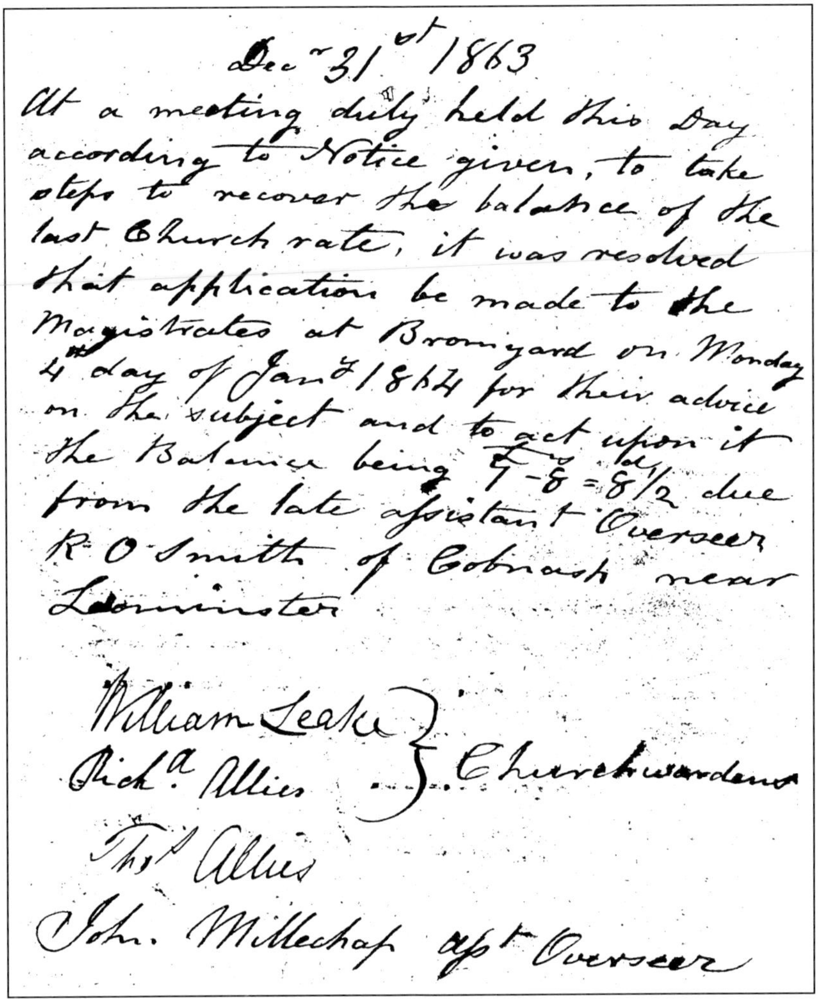

Decr 31st 1863
At a meeting duly held this Day according to Notice given, to take steps to recover the balance of the last Church rate, it was resolved that application be made to the Magistrates at Bromyard on Monday 4th day of Jany 1864 for their advice on the subject and to act upon it the Balance being £7-8-8½ due from the late assistant Overseer R O Smith of Cobnash near Leominster

William Leake
Richd Allies } Churchwardens
Thos Allies
John Millechap Asst Overseer

HRO Avenbury Parish Records Dec 31st 1863.

By 1811 the parish had decided to hire an overseer and pay him a salary for the duty and

> 'at a Vestry......for the purpose of choosing a standing overseer for the parish, we on behalf of ourselves & the rest of the inhabitants not present, agree to pay unto Thos Jones of Bromyard, baker a yearly salery of 10 guineas for the term of 5 years or so long or such time he shall do the office for this parish & to allow him a levy of 1s in the pd.'

In 1854, Mr Richard Oseman Smith was appointed deputy overseer for Avenbury at a salary of £8 10s a year. Mr Oseman Smith was probably a professional overseer employed by the parish to take some of the load off the parish officer and he needed to prove his credentials by 'his giving sufficient security in the sum of £200 for the due performance of his office.' However this appointment was not a success and on December 31st 1863

> 'At a meeting duly held this day according to notice given to take steps to recover the balance of the last church rate, it was resolved that application be made to the Magistrates at Bromyard on Monday 4th day of Jany 1864 for their advice on the subject and to act upon it. The balance being £7 8s 8½d due from the late assistant Overseer R O Smith of Cobnash near Leominster.'

This was signed by the churchwardens, William Leake and Richard Allies, Thomas Allies the overseer and John Millechap the then assistant overseer.

The problems arising in Avenbury were mirrored nationally. For the poor rate for the whole of England that in 1785 was just £1,912,000 leapt by 1803 to £4,077,891. The old poor law system was abolished in 1834 and parishes were united into unions, but retained their parish overseer, an office that was not dispensed with until 1925. Avenbury became part of the Bromyard Poor Law Union and the 33 united parishes decided to build a Union House with accommodation for some 160 people on the common land of the Downs adjacent to the A44, the road from Worcester to Bromyard. Each parish raised part of the cost, in some cases by selling their parish houses, and thereafter paid a proportion of the maintenance and charges according to use.[7] The Union, or Workhouse as it was also known, became in time a hospital and remained in use until 1989 when a new community hospital was built in Bromyard. The old Workhouse is now converted into flats.

Constables

The parish constable was, like the churchwarden and overseer, an authoritative man in the parish. He was responsible for law and order and had power of arrest. In early days the constable was appointed at the manorial court but from the 1530s, as the power of the manor dwindled, this duty was transferred to the vestry, the transfer finally being established in law in 1842. In Avenbury and in other parishes where the manorial influence had declined, this changeover probably took place comparatively early in the period. The constables worked closely with the other parish officers and also with the local magistrates, the - justices of the peace or JPs. Whilst the churchwardens were answerable to and supported by the ecclesiastical courts, the other parish officers responded to the royal courts which dealt with justice, finance and administration. In Saxon and medieval days the manorial court held by the lord of the manor was the most local jurisdiction, followed by the hundred court which dealt with the district, and the shire court administered by the shire reeve or sheriff. The cases were dealt with by the appropriate court according to the gravity of the offence. The appointment of JPs in the 14th century led to the creation of regular petty sessions under the local magistrates, which for this district met in Bromyard, and to quarter sessions which were attended by the JPs of the county in Hereford, and to which the constables had to report regularly.

Richard Hancox was constable of Avenbury in 1679 and he apparently was forced to pay considerables sums to the sheriff's bailiffs because the parish had failed to appear at several assizes; subsequently the parish was ordered to reimburse him the sums of £3 and 44s 9d. At another quarter session Avenbury parish was ordered to reimburse Richard Hancox the 20s he had been forced to pay 'by distress for issues lost by the parish and 2s for this order.' The money was raised by rates within the parish and it fell to Richard's fellow constable to assess the parishioners and collect the money for him. This led to complaints that were again taken to the quarter sessions. Robert Charlott complained that John Yates and James Callowhill who were the next constables had not made a fair assessment. They were alleged not to have assessed all the glebe and tithe of Richard Corbett junior, and to have neglected to collect the money from Mr Gilbert Nicholett for his estate. The court adjudged that both these matters should be rectified and the constables of Avenbury were required to appear at the next sessions to answer their contempt. The court also ordered 'the present constable to disburse by assessment the £5 4s 9d and also 2s 6d expended this session on the promises of Richard Hancox.'[8]

It would appear that some of this money was due for repairs to the roads. Gilbert Nicholett of Hopton appealed against his assessment and

> 'on full debate between him and the parishioners of Avenbury...and on proof made by several witnesses and also by a former verdict now produced in court that he ought not now assist in mending all the ways in the parish but has always at his own expense repaired the ways in the township of Hopton without assistance from the parish',

the court declared he should not be charged on his premises at Hopton. It is interesting to note that the Avenbury raters and assessors for the 'valuation of estates' recorded in 1663 were Richard Corbett, Robert Charlott and Richard Hancock;[9] and that in 1668 Gilbert Nicholett was sheriff of Herefordshire. Travelling to Hereford on both court and ecclesiastical business must have been a regular occurrence for the parish officers.

Avenbury seems at this time to have been a somewhat careless parish. In 1681 Richard Sheriff and Thomas Hill, both of Avenbury and probably serving or past constables, petitioned at the quarter sessions to be reimbursed fines that they had been forced to pay to the court by distress for issues lost and for the parish's non-appearance at several assizes. It was agreed that their disbursements should be examined and such money that they had spent on the parish should be paid to them. It then transpired that Richard Sheriff and Thomas Hill had spent £23 0s 4d for taking several indictments on the parish for not repairing highways and for their expenses regarding the same. Perhaps the parish was not solely to blame for at quarter sessions in 1674 the inhabitants of Avenbury had several times been presented by the grand jury for not repairing Hackley Lane. On examination two years later, it was judged that Avenbury was to repair

> 'so much of Hackley Lane as went to Hackley Bridge' Stoke Lacy 'so much as led from the house of John Morris to a certain prill of water leading to the

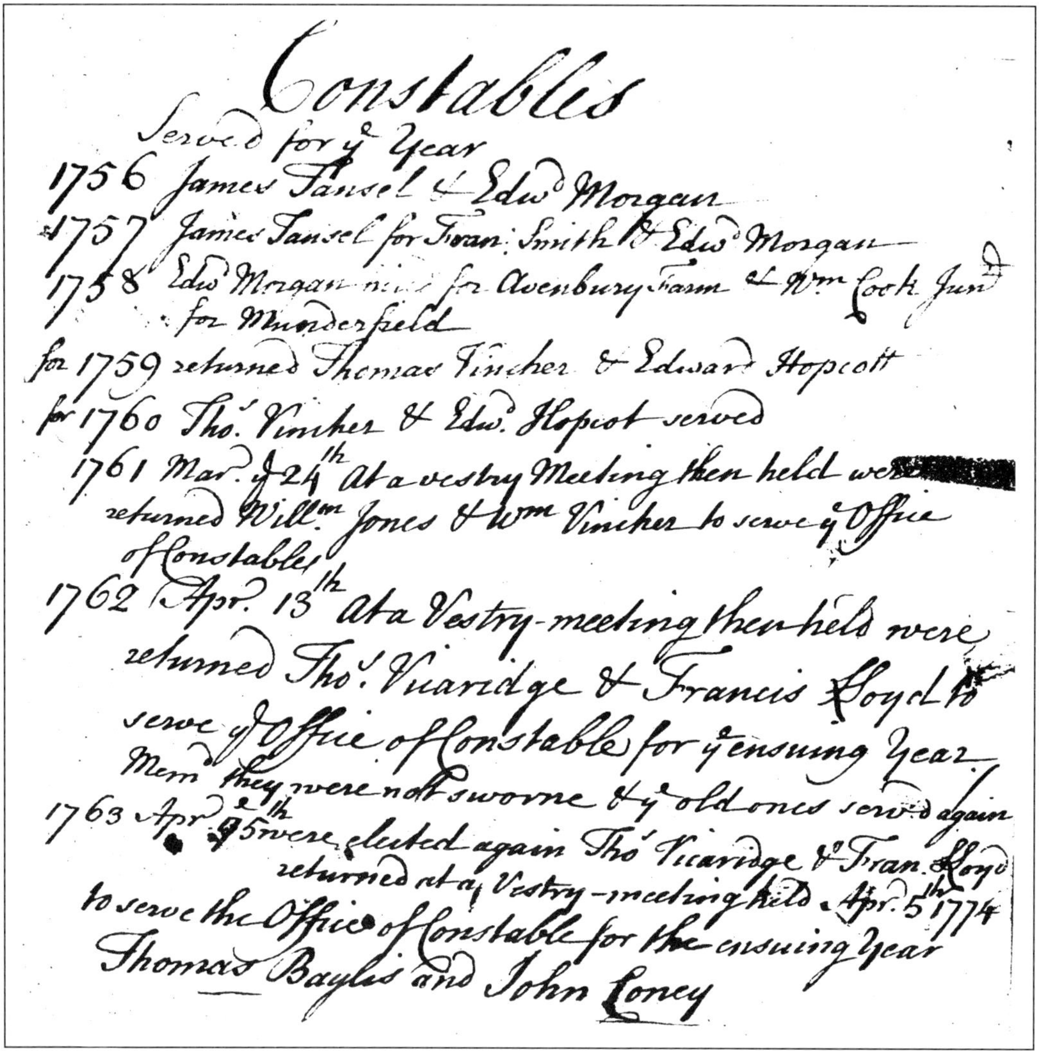

Constables
Served for ye Year
1756 James Tansel & Edwd Morgan
1757 James Tansel for Fran: Smith & Edwd Morgan
1758 Edwd Morgan ... for Avenbury Farm & Wm Cook Junr for Munderfield
for 1759 returned Thomas Vincher & Edward Hopcott
for 1760 Thos: Vincher & Edw: Hopcot served
1761 Mar: ye 24th At a vestry Meeting then held we[redacted] returned Willm Jones & Wm Vincher to serve ye Office of Constables
1762 Apr: 13th At a Vestry-meeting then held were returned Thos: Vicaridge & Francis Lloyd to serve ye Office of Constable for ye ensuing Year.
Mem they were not sworne & ye old ones serv'd again
1763 Apr: 25th were elected again Thos Vicaridge & Fran. Lloyd
returned at a Vestry-meeting held. Apr: 5th 1774 to serve the Office of Constable for the ensuing Year Thomas Baylis and John Coney

HRO Avenbury Parish Records.

> way towards Bromyard and Winslow to repair from the said prill of water to a place called Wash Wiere, and that from the Wash Wiere to the aforesaid was always repaired by the inhabitants of Hackley House'.

The report was given in at the next sessions 'and lost by the Clerk of the Peace'.[10]

In the parish records the lists of the constables start in 1756 when James Tansel and Edward Morgan were appointed to serve for a year. The following year James Tansel served 'for Francis Smith' and Edward Morgan was again his partner. In 1758 Edward Morgan was 'hired for Avenbury Farm & Wm Cook jun for Munderfield'. Four years later

> 'At a vestry meeting then held were returned Thos. Vicaridge & Francis Lloyd to serve ye office of Constable for ye ensueing year. Memd. they were not sworne & ye old ones served again'.

However they did get sworn in for the following year.

Waywardens, the Surveyors of the Roads

The responsibility for maintaining roads and highways had devolved on landholders and householders since early times. The great Highway Act of 1555 transferred this duty from the manor to the parish. The work was to be supervised by unpaid 'surveyors of the highways' nominated by the parishioners who also were to provide labour or horses and carts for eight hours on four days of the year. After 1691 the surveyors were appointed by the justices at special highway sessions from a list supplied by the parishioners and this system continued until the Highway Act of 1835. No waywardens' or surveyors' accounts have been found for Avenbury. However those for Whitbourne have survived for the period December 1792 to October 1794. These show that men were regularly paid for work on the roads and stone and gravel was purchased from various local quarries. Some £61 was spent during those two years and the money was raised by 'composition money' paid by landowners and householders in lieu of direct labour and the provision of horses and carts and also by a levy on the inhabitants of the parish.[11] Waywardens or surveyors continued to be elected in some parishes until towards the end of the 19th century. We find in Avenbury as late as 1870 'Mr James Hill be Waywarden' and in 1876 'Mr Richard Allies be Waywarden'. The surveyors were more responsible to the magistrates than they were to the parish which must have made their duties unpopular.

Turnpikes

The turnpike or toll roads came into being after the Turnpike Act of 1663. By this act it was possible to improve roads, usually roads that were part of the national network rather than local, and charge the users a toll. Turnpike trusts of responsible local men were established to manage the work, and minutes were kept of decisions made. An 'act for repairing several roads leading from the town of Bromyard' was made in 1751:

> 'These roads by reason of the soil therof and the heavy carriages passing through the same are become so ruinous and bad that in the winter season many parts thereof are impassable for waggons and carriages and also for horses laden and other parts are dangerous for travellers'.[12]

The trustees needed an annual income of £30 or an estate over £300 and were responsible for paying the debts and expenses of the trust. For their part of course they expected eventually to see an annual financial return for their investment.

The meetings of the trustees were held regularly in Bromyard, either at the Falcon Inn or the Kings Arms, and their minute books are in the Herefordshire Record Office.[13]

In 1775 the now well-established turnpike road from Bromyard, through Avenbury, towards Ledbury (that is the Munderfield Road) needed repair. The trust paid £100 to the Rev Ralph Cope Hopton, then rector of Bishop's Frome, and £100 to William Cooke who probably farmed at Munderfield (in 1767 William Cooke junior was at Munderfield Farm) to undertake the work, and £10 12s 4d to Samuel Page for hauling stone. These were considerable sums of money at that time. Piccadilly Toll Gate at West Hill, Bromyard, served both the Hereford and Ledbury roads out of Bromyard and the collection of the tolls was let out to local bidders. In 1787 the Rev John Walker contracted to collect there for £76 a year for three years. In 1792 an order was made to put up 'directional' posts on the road near Cooper's Green to show the direction to Hereford and Ledbury and at Flaggoner's Green to point the road to Leominster, as well as to erect milestones on the road to Bishop's Frome and Stoke Lacy. A gate at Munderfield near the Burgess Farm appears to have marked the end of the Bromyard toll road.

The Avenbury Lane leaves the Bromyard to Worcester road opposite the Petty Bridge Toll House. This early photograph also shows the toll gate.
Bromyard Local History Society Collection

Roadmen repairing the Avenbury Lane about 1910.
Bromyard Local History Society Collection

The Rev Ralph Cope Hopton was in receipt of the tolls on the Ledbury road in 1793:

the tolls of Munderfield Gate were	£32 10s 0d
the gatekeeper received	£6 19s 6d,
and repairs to the road came to	£26 1s 4d,

which meant that there was not a great deal left over for the Rev R Cope Hopton.

The toll charges then were:

for a coach or similar	drawn by six horses	1s 6d
	drawn by four horses	1s 0d
	drawn by two horses	6d
	drawn by one horse	3d
for a waggon, wain or cart or similar drawn by draught horses, oxen or beasts (which meant they were carrying a greater weight)	drawn by 6 horses or oxen	2s
	drawn by 5 horses or oxen	1s 6d
an unladen horse not drawing a cart		1d
a drove of oxen, cows or calves per score		10d
a drove of hogs, sheep and lambs per score		5d

In 1797 there was a proposal to put a gate at the entrance to the road to Little Froome near the present community hospital, but this apparently never came to fruition.

Charities

Some parishes had numerous charities and a board was placed in the church recording the gifts. Avenbury had very few and this probably reflects the fact that the lord and later the owners of the larger properties did not reside there. The earliest known gift was for a lamp in the church. The chantry certificates of 1547 described 'Two acres of arable land in the tenure of Thomas Boyse and Thomas Burne in the field of Avenbury, given to a lamp in the church'; the gift was worth 15s 8d.[14]

Nicholetts' Charity appears to have been established by a Nicholett of Hopton who directed that the rent of a five acre field at Lower Hopton in Much Cowarne should be used to buy bread for the poor of Bishop's Frome, Much Cowarne, Little Cowarne, Stoke Lacy and Avenbury. At the time of the *Charity Commissioners' Report* in 1836 the annual value was about £5 and Avenbury poor received 84 loaves worth 3d each annually from the occupier of the land.[15]

St Katherine's Hospital, Ledbury, at what appears to have been an early date, was granted just under an acre of land in two parcels in a field called Ox Leasow at Munderfield; in 1840 the land was in the hands of the tenant of Munderfield Farm, Robert Dent, as trustee. This may have been the same charity of which the Charity Commissioners said:

> 'that money had been given to the poor, donor unknown, but then in the hands of William Cook, and producing £1 per annum. Neither the minister nor churchwardens know anything of this charity. The parish books have been examined from 1733 to 1811, but no mention is made of it'.[16]

The charities that are recorded were gifts in perpetuity based on the annual income of rents from land. Other money would have been given for the use of the poor and needy in the parish by gift and bequest but it would have been used at the time. For instance, George Dowgyn of Hopton Sollers by his will of 1607 left a considerable sum for the poor and Alice Boyce by her will of 1638 left l0s for the poor of Avenbury.[17]

Avenbury Schools

The school at Munderfield was built for Avenbury children as a result of the Education Act of 1870, but there were schools for children of the parish before that.

In early days the local incumbents were frequently also schoolteachers and earned extra money by tuition. The *Puritan Survey* of *c*1642 reported of Avenbury:

'Impropriate to Richard Letchmere worth per annum £100. Mr Barber curate serveth for £8 per annum & seldom preacheth a careless Schoole Master of the Free Schoole of Bromyard and serveth the One also at Brockhampton and a very dissolute man in life'.[18]

Education would have been available for the better off families at schools in Bromyard and Worcester or even further afield where they could board either in school or in private houses.

A school, now called Romney Building, was built beside the Avenbury Lane in the Common Hayfield of Stanford Bishop in 1731 and as it lies to the extreme west of Stanford Bishop it was surely built to serve the children of nearby parishes too. Little is known of the school which was rebuilt again as a school in 1826, then used as a farm building and is now derelict as the result of a storm.[19] In 1834 William Vernall of the Vicarage House described himself in the church registers as

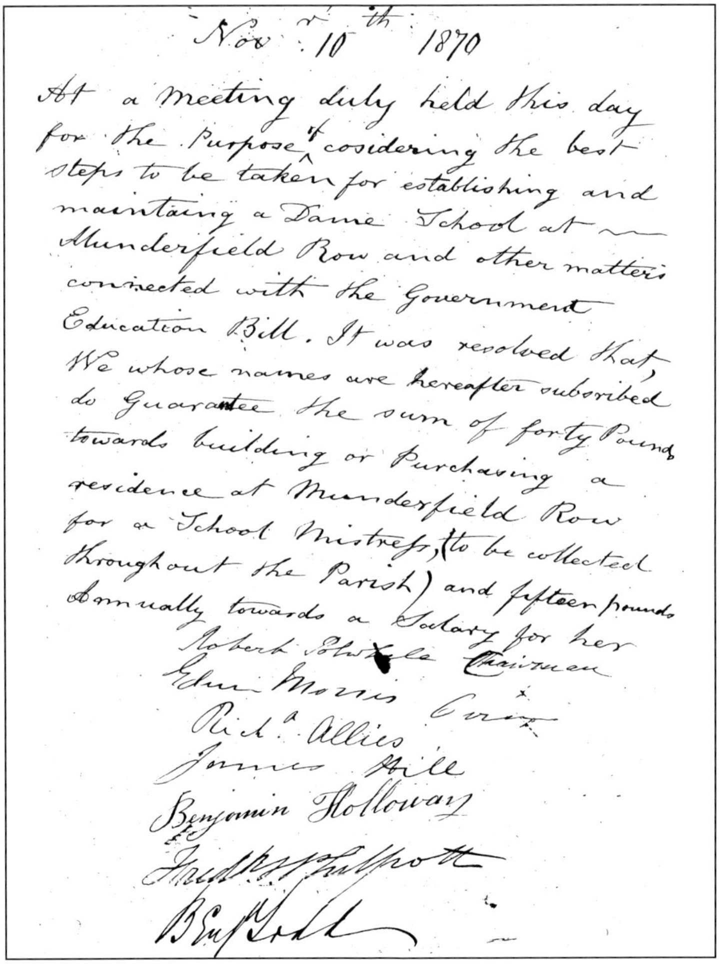
Novr. 10th 1870

At a meeting duly held this day for the Purpose of considering the best steps to be taken for establishing and maintaining a Dame School at Munderfield Row and other matters connected with the Government Education Bill. It was resolved that We whose names are hereafter subscribed do Guarantee the sum of forty Pounds towards building or Purchasing a residence at Munderfield Row for a School Mistress, (to be collected throughout the Parish) and fifteen pounds Annually towards a Salary for her

Robert [illegible] Chairman
Edwin Morris
Richd. Allies
James Hill
Benjamin Holloway
Fredk. Philpott
Benj. [illegible]

HRO Avenbury Parish Records 1870.

a schoolmaster. The tithe schedule of 1840 shows John Griffiths living in the School House at Munderfield Row (this is now a private house called the Briars).

Finally there was an announcement in *Littlebury's Directory and Gazetteer of Herefordshire* for 1867 that, 'a school has lately been erected in this parish' though no record of that school has been found.

However, in 1870 the Education Act was passed and on

> 'Novr 10th 1870
>
> At a Meeting duly held this day for the purpose of considering the best steps to be taken for establishing and maintaining a Dame School at Munderfield Row and other matters connected with the Government Education Bill. It was resolved that, we whose names are hereafter subscribed do Guarantee the sum of forty pounds towards building or purchasing a residence at Munderfield Row for a School Mistress, (to be collected throughout the Parish) and fifteen pounds Annually towards a Salary for her.
>
> Robert Polewhele Chairman'.

Avenbury School 1928. *Bromyard Local History Collection*

Back row:- ___ Hadwell, Trevor Collins, George Andrews, Bill Corbett.

2nd Row:- Gordon White, Rose Woodhouse, May Woodhouse, Winnie Hughes, Gwen Hughes, Peggy Mason, Ernie Andrews.

3rd Row:- ___ Woodhouse, Mary Corbett, Sybil White, Edith Andrews, Edna Hughes, ? Hadwell.

Front:- Jack Woodhouse, ___ ___, Jack Corbett.

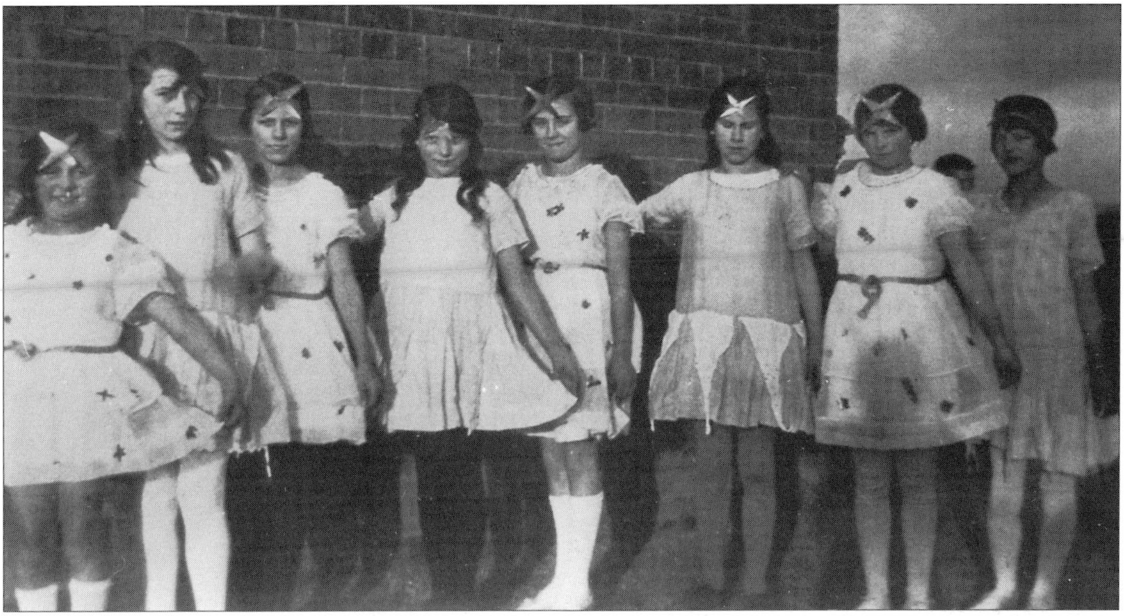

Avenbury School, Munderfield, Concert 1927. *Norma Linton*

Avenbury School, Munderfield *c*1932. D *F Hadley*

Back row:- George Baynham, Betty Dutson, Reg Harris, --- ---, Ralph Harris, Betty Harris, John Harris, --- ---, Teddy Carwood, Freda Hornsby, Reg Walker

Front:- Kenny Carwood, --- Smith, Norma Morgan, Marjory Smith, Vera Williams, --- Minett, --- ---, --- Minett, Olive Baynham, Don Hadley.

Avenbury (Munderfield) School outing 1933. *Norma Linton*
Miss Kathleen Walker (teacher) Miss Marian Grundy (teacher)

Munderfield School outing, Aberystwyth. *Norma Linton*
Norma Morgan, Mervyn Rees (smallest), Marian Grundy in front.

*c*1935, Avenbury School yard, Munderfield. *Norma Linton*
Audrey Williams, Margaret Hadley, Baynham, Norma Morgan, Vera Williams, Vera Neville, Rene Corbett, Freda Hornesby, Lily Bufton, with milk bottles.

The school and school house now converted to one dwelling, 1999. *Howard Painter*

Matters did not progress rapidly although the £40 was certainly raised for we find:

> 'At a meeting held on the 24th day of May 1875 after due notice given it was unanimously resolved on the proposition of Mr Richd Allies and seconded by Mr B Holloway that the Board of Guardians be respectfully requested to apply to the Local Government Board for their sanction to the Sale of the money invested in 3 per cent Consols belonging to this Parish and the payment therof to the School Board to be applied by them towards the cost of School buildings to be erected in the Parish £48 7. 10.
>
> Mr Benjamin Holloway chairman'.

Littlebury's Directory for Herefordshire of 1876-77 reported that 'A school board has been recently formed for this parish, and a new school is about to be erected at Munderfield Row, to accommodate 50 children.' In 1890 the average attendance at the school was 22 and the population of Avenbury in 1881 was 371 people in 83 inhabited houses.[20] An entry in the school logbook for 1st April 1924 reported 'Today we have begun a new School Year. No. on Books 41. No. present 39. I have rearranged the classes promoting several children.' A report on the school in 1944 shows that oil lamps were used for lighting, heating was by a combination of hot water pipes from a back boiler and an open fire. Well water was pumped, presumably by hand, for drinking, and rain water was used for washing; chemical toilets were used and there was a cesspit in the garden. The teacher's house was quite spacious with a kitchen, scullery, two living rooms and three bedrooms, but no bathroom. This was not so unusual at that time, for many farmhouses did not have bathrooms until mains water and electricity arrived in rural districts in the 1950s.

Mary Jane Corbett and Mrs. Eckley at Avenbury School Fete (?) about 1950.

Avenbury School which was established in 1877, closed in July 1960. It was decreed that the last date for admissions of under 5 year olds was 29th September 1958 and no over fives were admitted to the school after 28th April 1960.[21] The number of children at Avenbury School had dwindled and with greater facilities available in Bromyard schools, such closures were taking place all over the country. The old school is now a private residence called Old School House.

Old pupils of Avenbury School have happy memories of their schooldays there. They remember walking to school from all parts of the parish; those furthest away starting off in ones and twos, joining up with other children on their way. John Hodges of the Heath often waited for the local postman to accompany him. Mrs Norma Linton, the daughter of the last headmistress, Mrs Morgan, who lived in the School House, remembers finishing breakfast early so that she could run to meet some of the children and feel that she too walked to school of a morning.

Mrs Morgan was born in 1896 and held the post from about 1926 until 1960. Two teachers are well remembered. Miss Sadie Abell from the White House, Little Cowarne was for many years the infant teacher and cycled to school each day; if the weather was very bad, she stayed overnight with the Morgan Family. Miss Sadie Abell became Mrs Sadie Wall when she married a local farmer Tom Wall and they lived at Acton Cross in Acton Beauchamp. Miss Kathleen Walker was the other teacher; she lived at the Church House, Acton Beauchamp which is just over the border in Worcestershire and also cycled daily to Avenbury School.

Apart from school work the pupils enjoyed annual outings to sea-side resorts, music festivals in Bromyard, sports days and in particular one past pupil remembers the Coronation Day Sports when all the children received a mug. Each year the school performed a play or concert in Avenbury Parish Hall. Children from

Avenbury Parish Hall which was built in 1929 by William Jones of Bromyard. The final cost was £305 collected by fund raising events including an annual fete at Birchyfield and also by donations. The site was given by Mr. R. A. Eckley of Munderfield Court.

Stan Thomas

the school continued, if they passed the entrance examination, to Bromyard Grammar School or they went to St Peter's School, Bromyard.

> 'The school dentist came to Munderfield School with a mobile, hand turned drill.' Personal and painful recollection by an old pupil.

Avenbury Parish Hall 1936-1980

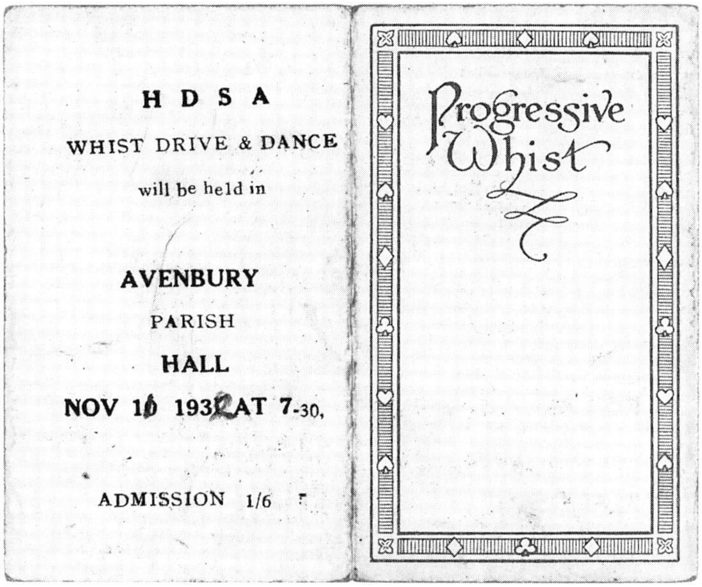

The advent of a parish hall for Avenbury was greeted with enthusiasm and community fund-raising as it presented a meeting place for local activities. Mr Eckley of Munderfield Court gave the piece of ground on which the hall was to be built. Donations and subscriptions were invited and fund-raising events organised. Whist drives formerly held at the school now took place in the hall. Avenbury had a flourishing Women's Institute which could now meet in the hall and during the Second World War it was the headquarters for the local Home Guard. Unfortunately in later years the expense of maintaining and running the building proved too difficult and around 1980 the sad decision was made to close this hard earned amenity of the parish.

Avenbury Women's Institute on a coach outing to the sea.
Driver Lionel Spreadborough of Bromyard.
Left to right- Miss Eckley, --- ---, Mrs. Godding, Mrs. Dent, Miss Turner, Mrs. Pearce, --- ---, Miss Dodds, Blanch Jones.
Inside Coach:- Rita Dean of the Holly Bush, Kathleen Godding.
Bromyard Local History Society Collection

Avenbury Women's Institute on an outing in the popular Bromyard char-a-banc 'Nuff Said'. The driver is Lionel Spreadborough.
Bromyard Local History Society Collection

Chapter 12

The People, their Occupations and their Homes

> 'In such homes as these, when the long cold night of winter drove the household within doors, when all were gathered round the ample ingle-nook, fairy tales were told and readily believed, and old ballads telling of love and courage - ever favourite themes - were sung to sympathetic hearers, and grey-headed elders told the customs and traditions of the district, handing them on from father to son though generations.'
>
> James Johnston, *The finding of St Augustine's Chair* (1898), 5

The People of Avenbury

The history of Avenbury is a history of the people of the parish, who for centuries have farmed and utilised the resources of the land to provide a living for their families. The crops, stock and produce paid and, in many cases, still pay the rent, rates and taxes; until recently a tenth of the profits made within the parish supported the church and priest. Money also had to be raised to provide for the poor, orphaned and destitute within the parish. Furthermore the inhabitants policed and kept order within their boundaries and maintained the local roads and ways. It was the people living here who built and planned the houses and buildings that stand today and many more properties that have now disappeared. The process continues and will continue, for buildings need constant maintenance and adaptation to serve different needs, with eventual rebuilding or abandonment. Hedges, trees, field boundaries, orchards, gardens and other man-made features are all the work of our predecessors and this generation too is making its mark.

This chapter will therefore start by considering the population and people living in the parish in the 19th century. The official census has been taken every ten years since 1801 up to 1991, with one exception in 1941 during the last war. Enumerators' reports for the census provide detailed information relating to households, names, ages, occupations and places of birth. To preserve confidentiality for a century, these are only publicly available until 1891; the next enumerators' report for 1901 will be released in 2001. The years 1851 and 1871 have been chosen for a detailed look at the inhabitants of Avenbury and these figures could serve as a template for anyone wishing to extend the picture. Finally an attempt is made to estimate the possible population of the parish between 1086 and 1991, using the figures given in the *Domesday Book* of 1086, subsequent taxes, surveys and census returns to the most recent return of 1991.

The population of Avenbury in 1991 was 199 men, women and children, living in 74 houses with an average household size of 2.6 people. In 1801 there were 316 people living in the parish in 53 houses, giving an average household size,

Members of Avenbury Women's Institute and others dressed as gypsies.

The 'Meals on Wheels' crib at Little Froome.
Mrs. Molly Littlehales, Mr. Barlow, Miss Gladys Smith, Mrs. Hill.
Bromyard Local History Society Collection

North Ledbury Hounds. Fox gone to ground. Probably at Bythan.

Avenbury residents in period costume for a play or pageant.

nearly two centuries ago, of 6 people. Table 13 and Graph 2 show that the population peaked in 1871 to 395 people in 78 houses; in 70 years the population had increased by nearly a third and the houses by a half. The largest increase in houses was at the beginning of the 19th century from 53 in 1801 to 83 twenty years later, although during the next ten years, the parish lost almost a quarter of its houses and by 1831 was down to 64. This was followed by the building of 16 houses in the next 10 years.

TABLE 13

Population of Avenbury 1801-1991 from the Census Returns

date	population	male	female	occupied houses	families/ households	unoccupied houses	mean household size
statute acres 3,233							
1801	316			53			5.9
1811	342			69	70		4.88
1821	333			83	86		3.87
1831	344			64	69		5
1841	382			80		9	4.77
1851	354			73		8	4.84
1861	371			74		4	5
1871	395			78			5
1881	371			83			4.46
statute acres 2,912 (detached part of Avenbury transferred to Bredenbury in 1882)							
1891*	306	158	148	71		5	4.3
1901	334	170	164	68		7	4.9
1911	335	175	160	76	76		4.4
1921	303	162	141	68	74		4.4
1931	318	156	162	77	77		4.1
1941	no census taken during wartime						
1951	300	151	149	82	85		3.6
1961	230	125	105	76	76		3
hectares 1178							
1971	234	127	107	80			2.9
1981	218	117	101	75			2.9
1991	199			74			2.6

*Note that following the transfer from Avenbury to Bredenbury of Noakes, Sawbury Hill and Wiggall, the 1891 census for Bredenbury included 24 persons formerly in Avenbury.

GRAPH 2 - Population, number of houses and average household size in Avenbury from the Census Returns 1801-1991

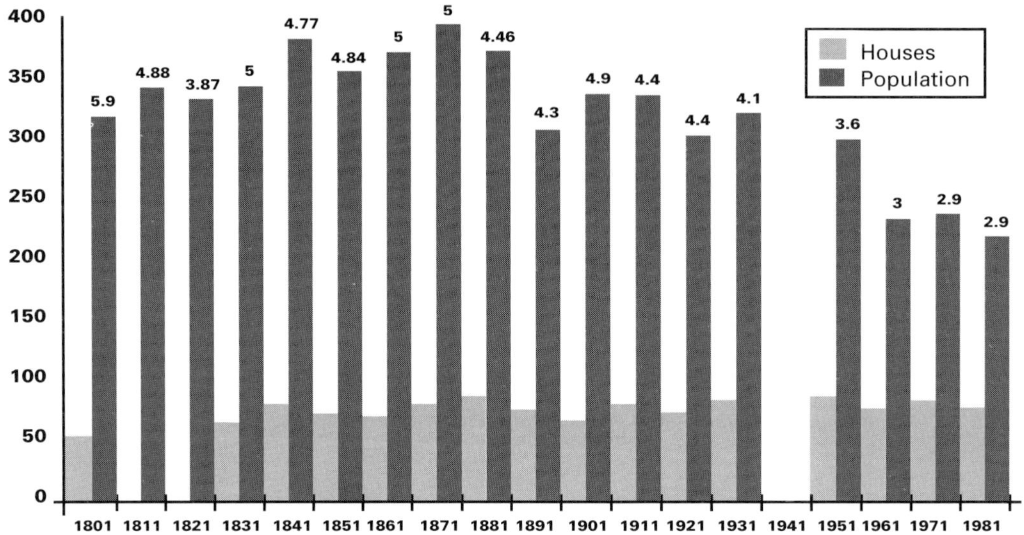

It is frequently said that in the past people were born, lived and died in the same place. The following figures show that this is a misconception for Avenbury in 1851 and 1871 and probably also at other times.

GRAPH 3 - Place of birth of Avenbury inhabitants 1851 and 1871

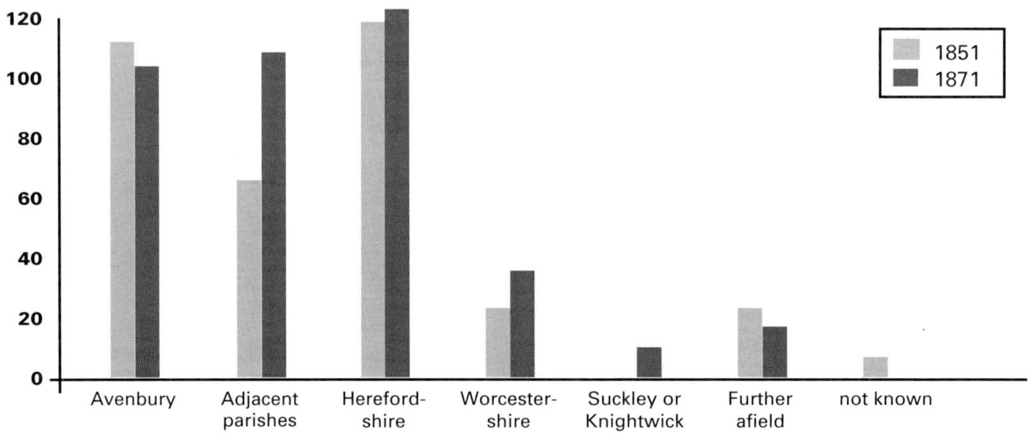

Further afield included:
1851 Salop; Warwickshire; Gloucestershire; London; Staffordshire; Ireland; Leicester; Yorkshire; Durham; Cumberland; Middlesex; Scotland; Radnor.
1871 London; Warwickshire; Oxford; Cornwall; Yorkshire; Gloucestershire; Birmingham.

Graph 3 shows that in 1851 and 1871 more than a quarter of the population had been born in this parish and most of the remaining inhabitants had been born in Herefordshire. Nevertheless it is surprising to find that 26 people in 1851 and 17 in 1871 were born beyond the boundaries of Herefordshire and Worcestershire. James Pearson at the Heath came from Yorkshire and Mary his wife from Gloucestershire; Patrick Gilmour of Hackley, Janet his wife and their eldest son at home were all born in Scotland, while their three younger children were born locally. John Kempson of Birchyfield was born in London and his wife Jane in Cumberland (now Cumbria). In 1871 William Berriman, bailiff at Brookhouse, was born in Yorkshire and the vicar Robert Polwhele, as his name indicates, came from Cornwall.

TABLE 14

Age and sex of Avenbury Inhabitants 1851 and 1871

	1851				**1871**			
Age	Male	*	Female	*	Male	*	Female	*
75+	3	2	9	5	7	6	6	6
65-74	9	7	9	9	8	7	6	6
55-64	11	8	11	9	12	8	11	9
45-54	17	15	16	13	25	20	15	13
35-44	25	16	19	16	20	18	19	16
25-34	18	8	24	13	28	13	21	17
15-24	42		29		25	2	37	7
5-14	47		37		50		51	
1-4	13		15		30		24	
Totals	**185**	**56**	**169**	**65**	**205**	**74**	**190**	**74**
	354				395			
Married below the age of 34 years								
	8		16		15		24	
Married below the age of 29 years								
	3		8		8		15	

* married, widow or widower

Table 14 shows the sex differential and the age range in the parish and how in 1851 no one under the age of 25 years was married; 20 years later just two men and seven women below that age were married. These small numbers probably reflect that couples, in the past, needed to work for many years in order to save sufficient money to set up a home together.

The People of Avenbury, their Occupations and their Houses from the Census Returns of 1851 and 1871

Until recent times nearly everyone who lived within the parish depended on farming for their livelihood. Today still, Avenbury is a rural parish and virtually everyone who earns their living within its boundaries does so from agriculture. It was the land and the stock that needed the labour and the farmhouses were the centres for this industry. There were, in 1851 and in 1871, nineteen farms employing labour of which Birchyfield, Northfields and Wiggall had only domestic servants; the remaining farms were the employers of both agricultural and domestic labour (see Table 17) and in many cases these overlapped. Women usually looked after the poultry and dairy as part of the household chores, whilst men would be responsible for providing wood for fires and some of the heavier work; both sexes were involved in field work.

Table 15 shows that 120 people in 1851 and 141 people in 1871 were employed as farm servants. In addition there were the farmers and their families who earned their living from the land and its produce and they are not listed as employees although in a sense some of them were. For instance at the Burgess in 1851, William Leake's three sons aged 14-19 were each described as 'Farmer's son at home' and his 12 year old daughter Hannah was 'a daughter at home' and no doubt they all worked. At Hopton, William and his wife Ann had a son and daughter 'at home', Benjamin aged 27 (who was farming Hopton 20 years later) and Margaret aged 25.

By 1871 there were similar variations. At Lower Venn, Jane Davenport, the widow of Henry Davenport who was farming there in 1851, had in her household: Thomas her son aged 19 , two daughters Mary and Caroline, and Caroline's husband, 45 year old George Yeates, who described himself as a farmer and who was probably the brother of William Yeates then farming at the Heath. At Upper Venn, William Leake, who appears to be the son of William Leake who had farmed the Burgess 20 years earlier, was the unmarried head of the household and his two sisters Jane and Mary lived with him. Birchyfield was a large household, and although described as a farm in 1851, its head of household, John Kempson, entered himself as 'Esquire Justice of the Peace for Herefordshire'. He lived at Birchyfield with his wife Jane and 29 year old son John, together with two nieces and a nephew; their staff comprised: a governess, cook-housekeeper, two housemaids and a groom. Definitely a 'gentleman's residence' and it was for this role that the house was designed and not as a working farmhouse. Francis Pike 'Formerly Captain 86th Regt.' lived here 20 years later with his wife Annie and two young children; their staff comprised four 'domestic servants'.

TABLE 15

Occupations in Avenbury from the 1851 and 1871 Census Returns

	1851			1871		
Occupation	**Male**	**Female**	**Total**	**Male**	**Female**	**Total**
Agricultural labourers	58	20	78	52	32	84
Farm servants	5		5	17		17
Pauper agricultural labourers	3	11	14			
General servants	7	3	10	1	11	12
House servants	1	8	9	4	19	23
Farm labourers				1	1	2
Labourers	3	1	4	1	2	3
Total			**120**	**Total**		**141**
Boot and shoe makers			3			3
Blacksmiths			3			2
Carpenters			1			5
Wheelwrights			2			
Bricklayers			1			1
Masons						3
Turnpike gatekeeper (Burgess Gate)			1			1
Innkeepers			2			
Miller at Little Froome Mill			1			1
Market woman			1			
Needlewoman, dressmaker, seamstress			2			3
Laundress						2
Saddler						1
Shopkeeper						1
Errand boy			1			
Retired medical man			1			
Cattle dealer			1			
Gardener						1
Scholars	under 5					6
	5-10 years		5			39
	over 10 years		3			31
Governess	Birchyfield		1	Hopton		1
Vicar						1

The following occupations were used on occasions to describe what a member of the family or staff did: housemaid, dairymaid, cook, housekeeper, groom, stableboy, farmboy, waggoner and waggoner's boy, farmer's son or daughter at home.

Table 15 shows that only 21 people in 1851 and 26 people in 1871 were involved in other occupations and the greater number of these were ancillary to and supported farming and farming families. Our 'retired medical man' was 76 year old William Plumtre Grape, who lodged at Wiggall with Thomas and Martha Purser. The 1840 tithe schedule shows William Grape to have owned 11 acres here which could have been the same property. William Hall who was a gardener, lived in one of the Hackley Cottages; these were built around 1860 probably by John Kempson as estate cottages for his Birchyfield Estate which included Hackley Farm. Robert Polwhele the vicar, was living in the then new vicarage, which is now called the Old Vicarage, built in 1854 between the church and Avenbury Court.

It is interesting to find that a 'School House' in Munderfield Row, now called the Briars, was recorded in the tithe schedule, but no schoolteacher appears in either the 1851 or 1871 census; the school at Munderfield was not built until 1875-6, so where did the 'scholars' go for their education? There was a governess employed at Birchyfield in 1851, but no children of that household listed with the eight scholars in Avenbury. The three scholars from Hopton which employed a governess in 1871 are included in the 76 total for the parish at that date, but where did the other 73 go? Probably to the schools at Bromyard, Stoke Lacy or the school in Rumney building at Stanford Bishop.

Where did the people of Avenbury live ?

To a large extent they lived in the houses that are still standing today. In 1840, 72 dwellings were listed, although the census return for 1841 shows 80 occupied houses and this probably reflects more than one household in some dwellings, most likely in the redundant farmhouses. In 1851 there were 74 separate households and in 1871 there were 79 households (see Table 16).

Most of the houses standing before 1801 would have been timber-framed with wattle and daub infill, and whilst substantial black and white houses can stand for many centuries, some of the poorer cottages could have been fragile. In the years after 1801 a great deal of building, rebuilding and renovation took place in the district. Birchyfield was completely rebuilt as a gentleman's residence around 1810; Cusop which is a timber-framed house of about 1600 had a new brick front about 1800; the Burgess was extended in stone and at Avenbury Court the roof was raised and the upper storey replaced in brick. Goodships was rebuilt in the early 1800s, when several new properties were built, for instance Northfields about 1790, the New Vicarage in 1854 and Hackley Cottages about the same time.

Building has always taken place, but just at this time, 1801-1860, there did appear to be quite a flurry of construction work and many new cottages appeared. They were built in stone which was quarried locally or brick which again would have been produced near at hand. The 1886 Ordnance Survey map shows a brick-yard on the Ledbury Road opposite the Burgess. The majority of these new cottages were for farm workers and craftsmen, and were erected along Munderfield Row and Stoke Lane, in some cases on plots of land purchased for the purpose, but on occasion space was taken from the roadside verges. Graph 2 shows that the population has dropped since the peak of 1871, although the number of houses has remained fairly constant since 1841; however the number of people in each household has declined from 5.9 in 1801 to 2.6 in 1991.

Avenbury Women's Institute members preparing for a fancy dress parade in Church Lane, Bromyard.

Dressed up for an Avenbury pageant.
Back row:- Tom Jones, Mrs. Lewis, --- ---, Polly Jones, Blanch Jones, Maud Cook, --- ---, --- ---, Mr. Lewis.
Front row:- --- ---, Adam Jones, Mrs. John Hodges (Heath Farm), --- ---.
Bromyard Local History Society Collection

Hop picking children at Brookhouse, 1920s.

Coach outing from Bob Hartwright's Rose & Lion.
Back row 4th along:- Frank Turner of Avenbury
5th along:- Jack Corbett of Avenbury.

TABLE 16

Size of households in Avenbury 1851 and 1871

	1851		1871	
Number of people in household	Number of households in that category	Total number of people living in such households in parish	Number of households in that category	Total number of people living in such households in parish
1	7	7	7	7
2	6	12	8	16
3	13	39	13	39
4	12	48	9	36
5	10	50	9	45
6	7	42	9	54
7	9	63	11	77
8	4	32	5	40
9	2	18	3	27
10	2	20	2	20
11	1	11	2	22
12	1	12	1	12
Totals	**74**	**354**	**79**	**395**
Averages	4.78		5	
Total houses	82		83	
Unoccupied houses	8		4	

However the final lines of Table 17 show that the 19 larger farms which had living-in staff in 1851 had 133 occupants and an average household size of seven. The remaining cottages and houses in the parish numbered 55 and housed the remaining 221 population and averaged four per household. Of these the head of 38 households were agricultural workers, four households were smallholdings and the remaining 13 had a head of household with a different occupation. In 1871, with Northfields uninhabited, there were 18 larger farms with 125 occupants averaging 6.99 per household and the remaining 61 households had 270 occupants averaging 4.4 per household.

The Houses

The tithe schedule shows that in 1840 there were in the parish :

30	farm homesteads, which included smallholdings
30	houses and gardens
12	cottages and gardens
72	Total dwellings

All the cottages and gardens in 1840 belonged to farms and had probably been built for married farm workers. At the same time, of the 30 houses and gardens, Pound House belonged to Avenbury Court and Henry Jenks the farmer had the tenancy of another two houses; three houses belonged to Munderfield Court; 15 others were tenanted and nine owner-occupied.

The census returns show:

	1851		1871
	19	farmhouses	18
	4	smallholdings	5
	38	farmworkers houses	42
	13	other dwellings	14
Total	74		79

Some of the houses occupied by farm workers' families were redundant farmhouses or smallholdings and included the Greeve, Nurbury's, Bythan, Cooper's Green, Wake House, Birch Hall and the Kilns. Others appear to have been built as farm cottages, and a proportion could have originated as houses built by the parish for the poor and homeless and these may have been occupied in 1851 by the 'pauper agricultural labourers'. Some properties would have been built by independent individuals who had sufficient resources to erect a house for either their own families or to rent out, and these would have been inherited or sold. For instance, some of the Growland and Copton properties appear to be the result of John Vernall's occupation; for he at around 1826, divided his 40 acre farm into six fairly equal smallholdings presumably for his children.

What is obvious from the development along Munderfield Row and Stoke Lane is that at some time road side space had to be utilised for house building. There was no other common land in Avenbury; whereas in the nearby parishes of Bromyard, Whitbourne and Stanford Bishop there was ample space on Bringsty, Badley Wood and Wofferwood Commons and the unenclosed area of Bromyard Downs. Munderfield Row was an obvious development site, for it lay on a principal road out of Bromyard and there would have been steady traffic by coach and cart to Bishop's Frome and Ledbury. Blacksmiths and wheelwrights would have picked up more than local business and so would the innkeepers of Avenbury at the Holly Bush and New House Inns (both near the Stocks). Stoke Lane was not such a busy route but it did lead to Stoke Lacy and the Hereford Road.

A possible estimate of the Population of Avenbury 1086-1991

Is it possible, starting from the census returns 1801-1991, to estimate the approximate population of Avenbury in previous centuries? Various returns were demanded over the years, based on different national needs and criteria. Some returns were based on persons, not always the whole population but in some cases those over 14, and sometimes those who were communicants; other returns were made on estates and property, hearths and windows.

Roadmen repairing the Bromyard to Bredenbury road at Sawbury Hill.
Bromyard Local History Society Collection

The Holly Bush, Avenbury on the road to Bishop's Frome.
Bromyard Local History Society Collection

Road work gang in Bromyard area. *D F Hadley*
Fred Hadley of Avenbury *3rd from left,* Tom Turner of Avenbury *3rd from right.*

Mr. Fred Hadley at Munderfield, Avenbury with his Round Tank BSA 250 cc Au 9703, *c*1933.
D F Hadley

William Corbett taking his lunch break. He lived at Perns and worked at Instone.

Domesday Book

The Domesday return of 1086, which supplied the Norman king with the value of the manors of his new kingdom, is the earliest known return for Avenbury. The parish of Avenbury comprised the manors of Avenbury, Little Froome, Hopton Sollers, Noakes and Sawbury; and as the value of the manors was very similar then as in 1066, the population had probably little changed over the 20 years. In 1086 there were four to five manor houses (Sawbury was described as waste in so much that it paid no tax, but there surely were people living there). There are still farmhouses standing on these five sites today. There were 30 village farms spread across the parish, three smallholdings, two mills, and the parsonage and glebe of the two priests. These represented a total of at least 40-42 land holding households. There were in addition ten slaves who could have had families and surely there were other workers such as carpenters, masons and agricultural workers not recorded because they held no land in the manors.

The Avenbury household sizes from the official census returns 1801-1991, range from 5.9 down to 2.6 and average over the 190 years 4.2 persons per household, however this may be on the low side because until 1951 the average size of households was 4.7 and has dropped considerably since that year. If a household size of 4.5 is used as a multiplier of the possible Domesday population for a minimum of 42 families, we find an estimated population of 189 plus ten slaves. This gives nearly 200 people spread across the parish. However suppose the slaves also had families and there were perhaps another ten workers without land, we then multiply 62 families by 4.5 and have perhaps 279 people living in the parish.

Poll Taxes

In 1377, 1379 and 1381 a poll tax was levied upon people in the country over certain ages; young people, usually under 14 or 15, together with the very poor were exempt. The 1377 return for Avenbury appears to show 41 people over the age of 14 liable for tax and for Hopton Sollers 20. In 1851 out of a total population for Avenbury with Hopton Sollers of 354, 112 were under 14 years old and in 1871 out of 395 people, 155 were 14 and younger. Did the same situation exist 500 years earlier that a third or more of the parish inhabitants were under 14 years? If so then the population of the parish had dropped to about 100 and by adding the very poor and indigent who may have numbered another ten families of some 40-50 people, we can see a possible total population in Avenbury in 1377 of 150. This could have happened, for during 1348-9 a series of plagues known as the Black Death assailed England and it is thought that in some places half of the population perished. The hitherto thriving town of Bromyard could only return 84 persons for this poll tax, although the number returned is always likely to be an under estimate as taxes were as unpopular then as now.

The Survey made for Henry VIII of Chantries and other Religious Foundations in Herefordshire 1547-8

These returns are preserved in the Public Record Office in London, but a copy of the Herefordshire returns can be seen in the Hereford Dean and Chapter Archives at the Cathedral Library. Avenbury is recorded as having a lamplight in the church which was paid for by the rent of two acres of arable land in 'the field of Avenbury' which had been donated for that purpose. There were 100 'Housling' people, that is communicants and therefore parishioners above the age of 16 years. In this case it seems unlikely that the poor would be left out of the survey so the possible population of Avenbury in 1547-8 was around 150 men, women and children.

The Compton Census 1676

'16 was the age at which men and women were by law in a capacity to receive Holy Communion'. Anne Whiteman, *The Compton Census of 1676* (1986), xxxiii.

This return was made to ascertain parishioners who worshipped in the parish church or practised other means of worship. In Avenbury 141 people were Church of England, there were no 'Papists' (that is Roman Catholics) and six people were Nonconformists. Whether this number of 147 referred to the whole population of the parish or to those over 14 or 16 is not clear; if inhabitants of the parish under the age of 16 were excluded from the census, they could have numbered 50 more souls and it shows that the population at this time was between 147 and 200.

The Valuation of Estates for the Militia Assessments 1663

As the name indicates the purpose was to raise money for military operations embarked on by the crown. In Herefordshire, properties were charged on the yearly value of the property at the rate at which the premises could 'honestly be leased' and in this county this appears to have averaged about 3s an acre. Raters were chosen from the more substantial farmers of the parish and in the case of Avenbury they were Richard Corbett, Robert Charlott and Richard Hancock. The raters began their list at Little Froome and finished at Hopton and 33 property owners were charged. The most valuable estate in the parish was the glebe and tithes then in the hands of John Hackett, Gilbert Nicholett of Hopton was next, followed by Edward Shepard of Brookhouse and Mr Stitch for Lower Venn who were all assessed at £27 or more; at the other end of the scale two men were assessed at £1 and probably had about 10 acres of land. The total charge on the parish was £383. In this case it is obvious that the poorer families did not pay any tax, neither did servants and their families. There could have been another 20 families over and above the 33 charged property owners, possibly 50 households averaging 4.5 or 5 per household and a possible population of 225-250 (see page 67).

The Hearth Tax Returns 1664, 1665 and 1671

This was a tax on hearths and has been desribed on pages 68 and 69. It was based upon 2s a hearth of every ratepayer worth more than £1 a year. In 1664 the year after the Militia Assessments, 84 hearths in 31 houses were charged but 21 houses were not charged on account of poverty. So the estimate of 50 households in 1663 is borne out by 51 houses in the parish the following year. The Hearth Tax Returns for 1665 can be seen on micro film in the Herefordshire Record Office and show that Gilbert Nicholett of Hopton had nine hearths, John Brown of Little Froome had eight hearths and ten people had just one; in all 25 people were liable to Hearth Tax in that year.

Conclusions

To try to assess the population of Avenbury during the past 900 years may appear an ambitious exercise, nevertheless from the existing records an interesting picture does emerge. Graph 4 is accurate as to recorded estates and houses and shows a probable minimum of around 30 properties in the parish pre-1700 with sufficient income to support their households and a surplus to pay national taxes. Table 17 shows that the average farm household in 1851 was seven. Hopton housed ten people in 1851 and 12 in 1871; Lower Venn also had a household of 12 in 1851 and Hackley, Birchyfield, Rough Mintridge and the Heath all exceeded the average household. It would seem that for the manors and larger farm households

GRAPH 4 Recorded Estates and Houses 1086-1991

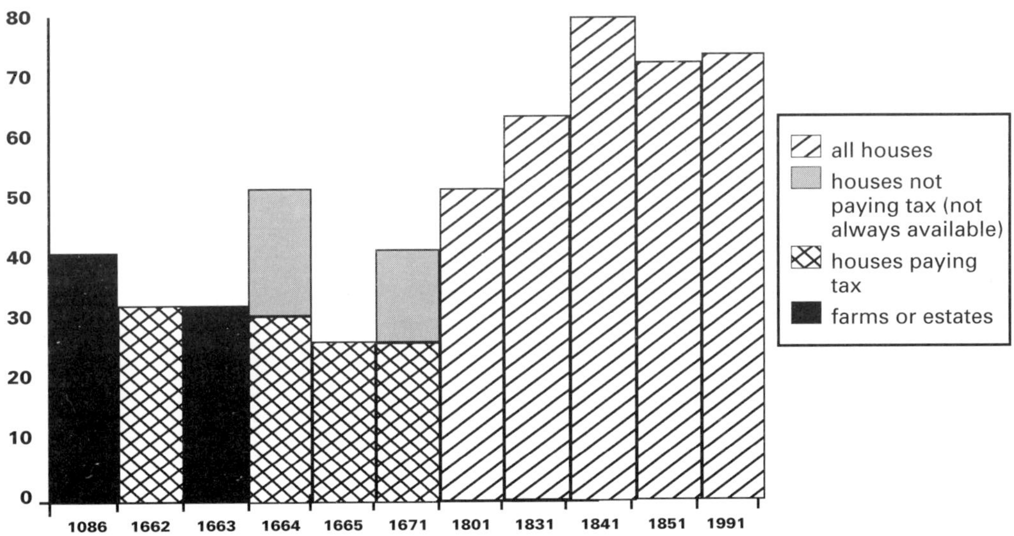

Avenbury with Hopton Sollers, Noakes, Little Froome and Sawbury.
Domesday Survey 1086 and Militia Assessments 1663.
Hearth Tax Returns 1662, 1664, 1665, 1671.
Census Returns 1801, 1831, 1841, 1851, 1991.

4.5 is a low multiplier and the size of the pre-1700 houses would confirm this. Cottages for landless families are recorded; for instance the terrier for Avenbury parish dated 1589 describes 'one little cottage house new erected' and 'one other cottage house newly erected' upon parts of the glebe. There are also orders in the Herefordshire Quarter Sessions records of 1676 and 1677 for the parish 'to repair a house for Margaret Wall a poor women there' and the following year to rebuild a 'ruinous' house for John Watkins of Avenbury.

The population of Avenbury in the 20th century appears to be similar to that of the 17th century. The inhabitants at that time would have been more evenly spread across the parish and the majority were involved directly with agriculture, producing food and products to serve their own community, travellers passing though the parish and the larger population in the market town of Bromyard. Because of modern machinery and developments there are fewer people involved with agriculture. Today the focus for the population is on the Ledbury Road at Munderfield. These cottages, that were built as homes for tradespeople, smallholders and farm workers, are now occupied by people working in diverse occupations who have moved here because they enjoy life in a rural parish. Avenbury's history has been shaped by the inhabitants who have lived here, from the lords, villagers and priests of the manors that were recorded in 1086 to the people of the large fertile agricultural parish that it is today.

GRAPH 5

An estimate of the population of Avenbury 1086-1991 using 4.5 as the average household size.

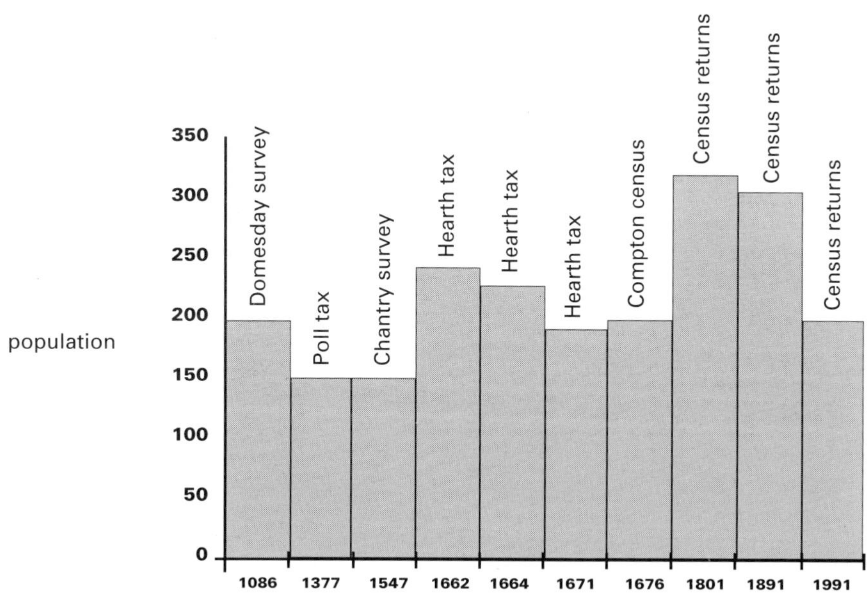

Bromyard Local History Society Collection

No 11 Platoon (Bromyard)
2nd Battalion Herefordshire Home Guard.

Frank Turner (Burgess), Stanley Parker, _____, --- ---, --- ---, Ron Bernard, Arty Webb (Sweetshop), Rob Bateman (Baker), Fred Orgee (Rough Mintridge).

Bert Calder, Tom Bloomfield, Jim Dallow, Jack Perkins, Sid Davies, Percy Taylor, Sid Taylor, George Williams, Norman Paske (Little Froome).

Ewart Newbold, Frank Wall, Charlie Lock, Bomber Jones, D.C. McKie, Horace Preece, Tipper Bedford, George Aldridge.

Bromyard Gala 1998. *Raymond Denton*

Bromyard Gala.

TABLE 17

Avenbury properties with acreage and household size 1840, 1851 and 1871*

	1840	1851	1871
HOPTON	319 acres	300 acres	350 acres
	1 dwelling	5 labourers	4 labourers 2 boys
head of household	**William Holloway**	**William Holloway**	**Benjamin Holloway**
household size		10	12
family		4	6
staff: male		5	2
female		1	4
BROOKHOUSE	303 acres	330 acres	356 acres
	3 dwellings	7 labourers	7 labourers, 1 boy, 5 women
head	**Thomas Berriman**	**Stephen Phelpotts**	**Stephen Philpotts**
size		8	6
family		5	5
staff: male		3	1
female			
LITTLE FROOME	294 acres	340 acres	340 acres
	4 dwellings	8 labourers	8 labourers, 1 boy, 3 women
head	**Edward West**	**John Nott**	**Richard Allies**
size		4	6
family		3	3
staff: male		1	1
female			2
MUNDERFIELD COURT	386 acres	285 acres	287 acres
	4 dwellings	7 labourers	3 men
head	**Robert Dent**	**Robert Dent**	**Frederick Philpott**
size		7	9
family		4	6
staff: male		2	2
female		1	1
LOWER VENN	172 acres	180 acres	165 acres
	1 dwelling		2 men, 1 boy
head	**Mary Payne**	**Henry Davenport**	**Jane Davenport**
size		12	8
family		10	7
staff: male		2	1
female			
STOCKS	86 acres		85 acres
	1 dwelling		2 labourers, 1 boy
head	**Mary Fidoe**	**Mary Fidoe**	**Richard Hayling**
size		5	5
family		4	2
staff: male		1	2
female			1

BURGESS with	132 acres 1 dwelling	247 acres	247 acres
GREEVE	113 acres	2 labourers	6 labourers, 2 boy
head	**Sarah Derry**	**William Leake**	**Ben Todd**
size		7	4
family		5	3
staff: male		1	
female		1	1
UPPER VENN	179 acres	200 acres	220 acres
			2 labourers
head	**James Edwards**	**James Edwards**	**William Leake**
size		9	8
family		5	4
staff: male		3	3
female		1	1
HACKLEY	80 acres	171 acres	170 acres
		8 labourers	4 labourers, 1 boy
head	**James Evans**	**Patrick Gilmour**	**William Holloway**
size		9	10
family		6	6
staff: male		2	2
female		1	2
BIRCHYFIELD	66 acres		
head	**Thomas P Payne Wight?**	**John Kempson**	**Francis Pike**
size		11	8
family		6	4
staff: male		2	1
female		3	3
ROUGH MINTRIDGE	41 acres		70 acres
head		**William Morris, bailiff**	**Richard Corbett**
size		10	10
family		9	8
staff: male		1	1
female			1
THE HEATH	198 acres	199 acres	198 acres
	1 dwelling	3 labourers	2 labourers
head	**Robert Hancock**	**James Pearsom**	**William Yeates**
size		8	11
family		4	10
staff: male		2	1
female		2	
AVENBURY COURT	191 acres		150 acres
	2 dwellings		2 labourers, 1 boy
head	**Henry Jenks**	**Henry Jenks**	**Edwin Morris**
size		7	4
family		4	2
staff: male		2	1
female		1	1

THE NOAKES	189 acres plus Redhill Cottage	195 acres 7 labourers, 1 boy	100 acres 4 labourers, 1 boy
head	**William Green**	**William Green**	**Joseph Corbett**
size		6	6
family		1	4
staff: male		3	2
female		2	
CUSOP	141 acres	140 acres 1 labourer	150 acres 4 men, 1 boy
head	**William Hill**	**William Norman**	**James Hill**
size		3	4
family		2	1
staff: male		1	1
female			2
SAWBURY HILL	78 acres	140 acres 1 boy, 2 labourers	131 acres 3 labourers
head	**William Gillam**	**Martin Gillam**	**Thomas Parlour**
size		6	7
family		2	6
staff: male		2	1
female		2	
GOODSHIPS	35 acres	30 acres 1 labourer	33 acres 1 labourer
head	**Ann Williams**	**Ann Williams**	**Jane Williams**
size		4	4
family		3	3
staff: male		1	1
female			
NORTHFIELDS	15 acres		uninhabited
head	**John Williams**	**Mary Ann Maund**	
size		2	
family		1	
staff: male			
female		1	
WIGGALL		17 acres	19 acres
head		**Thomas Purser?**	**Thomas Tarbath**
size		5	3
family		4	3
staff: male			
female		1	

*Notes:
19 farms employing labour.
1851 - farmers claim a workforce of 51 men and 2 boys.
1871 - farmers claim a workforce of 54 men, 12 boys and 8 women. This particular return appears incomplete as not every farmer completed the section and the actual workforce must have been larger.
1851 - male employees living in 34, female employees living in 17, total employees living in 51: 19 farmhouses total occupants 131 = 6.9 per household.
1871 - male employees living in 23, female employees living in 19, total employees living in 42: 19 farmhouses total occupants 125 = 6.57 per household.

Smallholdings not employing labour but occupier listed as farmer

	1840	1851	1871
OVERDINE		8 acres	8 acres
head of household		**Samuel**?	**Thomas Amyes**
size of household		3	2
HOLLY BUSH	6 acres	6 acres	7 acres
head of household	**Peter Pitt**	**Peter Pitt**	**Peter Pitt**
size of household		2	2
GROWLAND GROVE,	5 acres	13 acres	11 acres
GROWLAND DINGLE	5 acre		
head of household	**Mary Vernall** **John Vernall**	**Edward Vernall**	**William Jenks**
size of household s		2	3
NEW HOUSE (now Claypits)	4 acres		7 acres
head of household	**John Taylor**		**Susannah Davies**
size of household			7
COPTON FIELD FARM, COPTON COTTAGE (COPTON FARM)	7 acres	6 acres	6 acres
head of household	**James Vernall**	**James Vernall**	**James Vernall**
size of household			

Town Crier at Bromyard Gala, Birchyfield 1998. *Howard Painter.*

Chapter 13

The Church of St Mary, Final Days

'Avenbury Church had three beautiful bells, one of which bore a Latin inscription meaning. 'I am Gabriel, messenger from heaven.' As the church was dedicated to St Mary the name of the bell doubtless commemorated the archangel's annunciation to the Virgin. The other bells were named, if I remember rightly, Paul and Andrew, but Gabriel was the master. He was the passing bell and his tolling aided the departing soul and accompanied the body on its last journey to the grave. He was said to toll of his own accord when a vicar died or when tragedy affected the parish.'

Letter written to *Bromyard News and Record* by Mrs Marian Holbourn and printed February 20th 1958

Now begins the last and perhaps most remarkable phase in the eventful life of Avenbury Church. It essentially embraces the 90 odd years from the late 1840s to the late 1930s, but we need to begin a little earlier.

The medieval tenor bell from the Worcester foundry now preserved in the Church of St. Andrew-by-the-Wardrobe, in the City of London.
F Sharpe, *The Church Bells of Herefordshire* (1969), 53, plate XVI

When John le Rous granted the church to Abbey Dore it was complete and relatively new and would have needed little more than maintenance work for several centuries. By custom the rector was responsible for repairs to the chancel and the parish for work on the nave. So thereafter the chancel became the responsibility of Abbey Dore, and later a lay impropriator. Decisions regarding repairs and improvements would have been made by the vestry, which represented the inhabitants of the parish under the chairmanship of the vicar. The churchwardens would then have arranged for the work to be done and raised the money by subscription, fund raising and church rates. The surviving churchwardens' accounts for Avenbury

Avenbury Church Herefordshire *c*1840-1850. Watercolour initialed R S H, belonging to Mr. and Mrs. Peter Stokes. *Photographed by Richard Percy*

date from 1731. The north aisle must have been removed by this date as no record can be found in the accounts for such a large undertaking. For over a hundred years only minor repairs are recorded and there is no inference of serious trouble. Indeed John Duncumb, not usually averse from frank description, writing about the church in 1812 had only detailed observations to record. (He did however interestingly mention that there was a descent of five steps from the south porch into the church - usually evidence of the ground outside having risen due to burials.)[1] However, there must have been a marked deterioration over the next 30 years or so, for in 1849 the accounts record:

> 'The Parish Church of Avenbury was under repair from April 1849 to the following July - during which time the late vicar R. H. Williams was suffering under mental infirmity, which terminated in his death June 20th.'
>
> William Cooke vicar of Bromyard 22nd August 1849.

'The Church is a small plain old building' was the description given in 1851.[2] The story 25 years later was very different:

> 'This church which a few years ago seemed to be sinking into a state of utmost hopeless decay and ruin has undergone considerable repairs and improvements within and without, under the superintendence of the vicar' (Rev Robert Polwhele). 'The tower, "a splendid specimen of those massive square buildings with deeply splayed windows, which date from about the thirteenth century," has been cleaned and pointed, the roof carefully repaired, and the heavy stone tiles removed, and replaced by the best brown

Avenbury Church from the south east 1931.
The Royal Commission on the Historical Monuments of England

Broseley tiles. The walls of the church have been divested of the mortar and whitewash with which they had been disfigured, and pointed throughout. The roof of the nave on the north side has been stripped, repaired and covered with new Broseley tiles hung on cleft oak laths, and the whole of the roof surmounted with ornamental cresting. Seven new lancet windows have been inserted in the north and south walls of the church, and one in the tower. Various improvements have also been made in the interior of the church, the chief of them being the removal of the gallery, and the throwing open of the fine tower arch and window beyond. The rood screen (which had been whitewashed) has been cleaned and repaired, a new altar-cloth, fittings for desk and pulpit etc. supplied also a good stove. The old pews have been carefully restored, and the other pews lowered and repaired'[3].

Jakeman and Carver's *Directory & Gazetteer of Herefordshire* for 1890 continues the story:

'A complete and thorough restoration of the church has been accomplished under the present vicar, the Rev J.Wilson M. A. The restoration consisted of a new three-light window filled in with cathedral glass, placed in the east end of chancel, the gable being raised with new stone coping, and a cross fixed thereon. The old lath and plaster ceiling has been removed and the oak timber roof displayed. The old square box pews, pulpit, and reading desk have been taken away, and replaced with new oak pulpit, desk, and lectern; the chancel has been furnished with two altar or chancel chairs of oak, provided by E.B.Luxmore, Esq., a full set of communion plate (given by the same donor), four stalls of pitch pine, and a sweet-toned American organ.

The old oak pews in the nave have been removed, and new open pitch pine seats of comfortable and pleasant construction substituted. The oak screen has been renovated and improved, with neatly carved gates affixed. A new Musgrove stove has also been placed in the chancel, so that now there are two stoves for heating purposes. The stone flagging has been removed, and the whole church throughout floored with Godwin's tessellated tiles. The remainder of the roof the north side of the chancel - has had the heavy stone tiles taken off, and, through the kindness of E.B.Luxmore, Esq., has been covered with the best Broseley tiles. The walls internally have been much improved by being finished in a granite stained distemper. The improvements and restoration were carried out from designs, and under the superintendence of Mr. Haddon, of Hereford. The re-opening of the church took place August 18th. 1881'.

Further confirmation of this transformation is happily given by Dr James Johnston the author of a book about Stanford Bishop called *The Finding of Saint Augustine's Chair* printed in 1898, who visited Avenbury Church in about 1840 and again about 40 years later. Writing of his first visit he said that the interior then was small

'with an old oak screen to separate the chancel from the nave, and overhead a remnant of old panelling originally painted blue with a few silver stars added. Decay had marked this with its tooth, and lines of weather-stains gave colour to the walls'.[4]

Avenbury Church from the north east 1931.
The Royal Commission on the Historical Monuments of England

But of his second visit after the restoration he recalls that he had

> 'quietly walked round the outside to see what changes had been made. The broken, leaking roof had been replaced by a new one, the walls had been restored, crumbling stones removed and all their joints freshly pointed. In fact it had been well restored and made fit for its purpose...I went into the church. How changed was the interior from what it was when I last saw it. Light, clean and comfortable, with modern pews inserted in the nave. A few strong ancient forms of old black oak, with folded napkin-pattern carved on their upright ends, telling of near four centuries' wear, were still placed there to do duty for the rustic labourers, and the old oak screen dividing nave from chancel, bright with fresh varnishing, still remained. The ceiling was well whitewashed and showed no sign of damp or weather-stain..... I walked into the chancel to see the tomb of the Crusader. I must own that I was sorely vexed to find how it was treated: the lower part of his chain-mailed legs and the tip of his sword were all that could be seen: all else was hidden from view, for over his head, his arms, and his body was placed a spick-span new harmonium! .....Another little matter caused me some irritation. An old piscina in the S wall of the chancel had carefully been filled with plaster, so that its place was seen no more'.[5]

So much work and enthusiasm, this was surely a Victorian restoration that would today have earned approval and yet within 60 years the church was to be closed and deserted, and less than a century later was in ruins.

Early 17th-century panels, probably from a former pulpit, incorporated into the 15th-century screen between the chancel and the nave. 1931.
The Royal Commission on the Historical Monuments of England

Memorials

John Duncumb left a very full account of these. The inscribed figure of the knight in armour (argued in Chapter 3 as probably one of the last of the Avenbury family) was under the north wall of the chancel; also on the north wall here there was a memorial to Thomas King late of Cusop who died in 1802, at the age of 37; on the south wall a marble tablet was inscribed to the memory of Nathaniel Smith late of Brookhouse who died in 1804 at the age of 25 years. On flat stones within the church the following people were commemorated: Richard Barnes who died 1623, the daughter of Thomas Corbett of Bromyard who died in 1637, Richard Corbett who died 1689 and his widow Jane who died in 1698, Richard the son of John Corbett who died in 1701 and John Corbett probably his father who died the following year. Of the Charlott family, William aged 66 died in 1658, another Charlott died in 1660 and another William Charlott died in 1671, his wife Mary the following January, Elizabeth their daughter died the same year as her father, Mary another daughter died in 1678 and Rebecca the last daughter to be recorded in the church, in 1691. Mr Charlott, gent was buried in 1682 and his widow Sarah in 1696. From Little Froome we find Anthony Browne, gent died 1716 and John Browne, gent in 1724. John the son of Richard West also of Little Froome died in 1801 aged only six years. Dorothy Somers was buried near the font in 1632 and Penelope Whitehead the daughter of Richard and Elizabeth Whitehead of Stanford Bishop died in 1676.[6]

The Bells

The largest and oldest of the bells, the Gabriel bell inscribed *missi de celis habeo nomen Gabrieli* 'I have the name of Gabriel who was sent down from heaven', dated from about 1410-1420 and was probably cast at Worcester. This was for Avenbury parishioners the passing bell whose tolling aided the departing soul and accompanied a body on its last journey to the grave. There were two smaller bells in the church, one made by Abel Rudhall of Gloucester in 1757 and the other by Ward J Taylor of Oxford.[7]

The Church Fittings and Furniture

The parish chest was even older than the Gabriel bell and was made in the 14th century to house the church treasures and documents and was kept in the chancel; it was seven feet long, iron-bound with carrying rings and the front feet were carved with large four-petal flowers. When the church closed in 1936 the chest was removed to the Old House in Hereford. There was a beautiful carved screen between the chancel and nave made in the late 15th century with 11 closed lower panels and above 11 open panels with a central doorway. The communion table with turned legs, moulded top rails and shaped brackets dated from about 1630. There was a silver communion cup of 1571, cover-paten of about the same date and a pewter flagon. For whom were the recesses made, one in the south wall of the chancel and one of the 14th century in the outer south wall of the nave? Also in the nave, there were early 16th-century benches with moulded rails and ends carved with linen-fold design.[8] Before 1548 two acres of land worth apparently 15s 8d, had been given to provide for a light in the church. Despite its now ruinous state, in its time Avenbury has been a well cared for and loved parish church.

Avenbury's 12th-century font during its final days in the Parish Church.
Peter Corbett

The Norman font repositioned in Munderfield Mission Church.

The Font

George Marshall FSA, in *Fonts in Herefordshire* described how

> 'This interesting church ceased to be used for divine service about 1923, (this must be a printer's error for it was nearer 1933) and its valuable fittings dispersed to the four quarters of the compass, or suffered to fall into decay, or left to the mercy of the plunderer. An Elizabethan chalice has luckily found a home in the Hereford Museum, but a fine 13th-century chest, a pre-Reformation bell, an almost unique 13th century stone coffin lid with the figure of a knight, linenfold and other panelling, Jacobean carving and sundry valuable objects, including the architectural features of the building from the Norman period onwards, have been either sold or abandoned to a precarious fate. But to come to the font. This has now found a resting place in the chapel at Munderfield in the parish. It has a circular sandstone bowl mounted on an octagonal stem, part of which is modern, the upper part most likely so trimmed when the lower new part was supplied. The diameter of the basin is 22 inches, with sloping sides and a flat bottom, the depth is 12 inches. The rim is 3 inches wide with lock marks, there is a lead lining and a one inch drain hole but there are indications of a larger one. The total height is 43 inches. The date of the font is probably late 12th century.' [9]

The chapel at Munderfield had been built at the end of the 19th century, by the Rev John Shepherd who was appointed vicar of Avenbury in 1859, as a mission room for the parish.[10] With the closing of the parish church, the mission hall was improved and adapted to serve as a religious focus for Avenbury. The building is now converted to a house. Considering the improvements and work to Avenbury Church during the second half of the 19th century it is quite amazing that the authorities decided to abandon the centuries old structure and only maintained services in the parish with the aid of the elderly rector of Stoke Lacy, as we shall see in the next section. For despite the new vicarage built in 1854 the endowment was now insufficient to support a minister.

The End

The Rev E H Archer-Shepherd, who died at Avenbury Vicarage in 1931, was the last vicar of the parish; he had served there for 34 years (1897-1931) and had followed the Rev John Wilson who died in April 1897 after 19 years as vicar. In 1882 part of Avenbury parish had been transferred to Bredenbury under the Divided Parishes Act, and now the remainder was divided between Stoke Lacy and Bromyard. The parishioners of Munderfield Row would have had a long walk if they did not possess transport and they were to be accommodated at the end of the 19th century with a mission church. The occupants of property at the Venn were as close, if not closer to Stanford Bishop Church. The remainder of the population lived in scattered farmhouses and cottages, which were still, for some, a fair distance from Avenbury Church. When the church did close it was decided that Hackley, the Goodships, Cusop, the Burgess, Avenbury Court, Brookhouse and all houses to the north of them should be joined with the united benefices of Bromyard. The rest of the parish was to be joined with the united benefices of Stoke Lacy. The Mission Room or chapel of ease at Munderfield remained to serve those who wished to attend there.

A letter from the Rev George Morgan, rector of Stoke Lacy, to the bishop of Hereford and written 29th March 1932, begins:

> 'The Vicarage at Avenbury is, I believe to be sold next month. I fear it will not fetch much - possibly £500. The old church at Avenbury was condemned by the Commission and was to be pulled down. There was considerable feeling about this and it remains - one service is given there a month. But it was considered important that a service should be held every Sunday in the centre of the late parish'.[11]

During the next few months the Rev George Morgan explored several ways of maintaining church services in Avenbury and, as he pointed out, being 80 years old himself

> 'I don't feel that I can take so many services and I cannot reduce the number of services here' (at Stoke Lacy). 'Some people from Avenbury have gone to Stoke Lacy and a few to Bromyard. They will probably continue to do so, but the bulk of the population lives in a road called Munderfield Row in the centre of which is the old Mission Hall and the Parish Hall which we are now using temporarily. I am afraid most of these have gone no where, but we are beginning to get some of them to the services in the Parish Hall - on the average about 30 or 40'.

Munderfield Mission Church.

The former Mission Church at Munderfield in 1999. *Howard Painter*

Munderfield Mission Church, Easter Festival 1970.

D F Hadley

Apparently the one service a month continued to take place in the old parish church at Avenbury, but Mr Morgan managed to raise money to rebuild and enlarge the Mission Room, where he had built a chancel and sanctuary which was divided from the remainder of the hall by the old screen from St Mary's. Here with the help of a lay reader or a Church Army representative he proposed to continue his ministry in Avenbury and asked the bishop of Hereford if part of the 'Mission Church' should be consecrated for this purpose. The population of Avenbury at this time was about 300 people. The Mission Church remained in use and the old church became completely disused. Although attendance at church services was not high, there was a thriving Sunday School held in the Mission Church with about 20 children attending regularly. This church finally closed in about 1975 and has since been converted to a private dwelling.

To return to St Mary's, the bells were sold to the church of St Andrew-by-the-Wardrobe in London, and the church furniture was also dispersed in part to Stoke Lacy and Bromyard Churches. The church was left empty, and for many years fresh flowers were placed at the south doorway at Easter. Bromyard had responsibility for the building and in 1940 the diocesan registrar suggested to the parochial church council that the roof should be removed to make the building safe. Correspondence took place over the next two years.[12] The PCC replied that

Avenbury Church Bells after their removal from the bell tower. Here they are being put into crates for their journey to St. Andrew-by-the-Wardrobe in London, in 1933.
Bromyard Local History Society Collection

in their opinion they had no responsibility for the structure of the church but wished to authorise the Hereford Diocesan Board of Finance to take any necessary steps to demolish or dispose of the structure. In reply the Diocesan Board of Finance declined to accept that resolution. They stated the legal position that Avenbury Church was a chapel of ease attached to Bromyard parish, which was solely responsible for it.

A letter from the Ecclesiastical Commissioners in 1942 stated that there was no possibility of the church being used for divine service. The church had no architectural merit and no repairs had been done for 15-20 years and part of the roof of the nave had collapsed. Apparently Mr George Cadbury had offered £100 to repair the church some time ago but he now wished to use the church as a parish hall or library and would be prepared to pay for the renovation. The bishop of Hereford was in favour but would like the chancel kept for prayers. Time passed and in March 1970 Mr L J Slzuriat applied to purchase the church and churchyard, with the intention of tidying it up and making the building safe. The church then was formally declared redundant and the sale to Mr Slzuriat was completed before August 1972.[13]

The disused church with no roof on the nave. *Peter Corbett*

Avenbury: a Haunted Church

There is an early legend of the Avenbury ghost as remembered by Miss Alice Smith. Miss Smith, whose father was churchwarden and bell-ringer at Avenbury Church in the early part of the 19th century, has lived at Burley for most of her life. In her younger days she was in service at Avenbury Vicarage. The story runs that in the 1600s the ghost of Nicholas Vaughan was said to haunt the churchyard, so much so that his body was reburied in the brook next to the church. It was covered with a very large stone which can sometimes be seen sticking up above the water level. It was believed that if his body was covered by running water he would no longer haunt the churchyard. The church registers show that a Nicholas Vaughan was buried at Avenbury in July 1664.

After the death of the last vicar, the Rev E H Archer-Shepherd, stories began to abound that Avenbury Church was haunted. A letter was printed in the *Bromyard News and Record* of 20th February 1958, written by Mrs Marian Holbourn, the late vicar's daughter. Mrs Holbourn claimed that in September 1896 music being played in the empty church had been heard by Mrs Wilson the then vicar's wife and by the three grown-up children of Colonel Purser of Bird's

Avenbury Church Tower February 1955.
Ethel Paske

Avenbury Church Tower *c*1970.
Eric Binyon

Eye, Bromyard. Music was heard again by a man and his son walking up the road in 1919. Her father 'not a man to let his imagination run away with him' also heard what he thought was the organ playing when no one was in the church. Mr Archer-Shepherd thought it was probably music originating in Bromyard which is only a mile up the Frome valley. Mrs Holbourn favoured the theory that 'the cause of the music is to be found in the mentality of those (including myself) who hear it.'

Mrs Holbourn continued her story of church haunting by apparition as well as music. 'Mrs Smith, who lived in a cottage on a rise overlooking the church, said that one evening she saw a funeral attended by a crowd of people, all without heads. When this came to the ears of one of the churchwardens, he also related that many years earlier he had had a similar vision but recognised the congregation as a company of monks with their cowls over their heads...it would have been easy to mistake them for a headless company'. Another event concerned the experience of a couple who had since moved to Leamington Spa, but were living in Bromyard in about 1880. In a letter written by them to the Rev Mr Archer-Shepherd in 1919 they described a Christmas afternoon visit to the wife's parents who lived between Avenbury Church and Bishop's Frome. The couple returned home about midnight in a snowstorm and sheltered in Avenbury Church porch and 'we heard what at first were many human voices conversing. The church seemed full of extremely happy, joyous human sounds. Although we distinctly heard so many voices in the church, we could not distinguish a word they said....The wonderful sounds came distinctly from the inside of the church'.

The Rev. E. H. Archer-Shepherd, the vicar of Avenbury, Herefordshire, which boasts of a musical ghost. It has been frequently heard playing on the church organ. The vicar himself has heard the ghostly music, but has never seen the ghost. Village children, on the other hand, have heard groans in the church. —(*Daily Sketch.*)

The organ in Avenbury church on which the ghostly player indulges his musical abilities. It usually performs when the church is deserted.—(*Daily Sketch.*)

HRO. Final Register of Baptisms before amalgamation 1920-1930, newspaper cutting pasted in last pages of register.

A similar letter was written by Mrs Holbourn in December 1970 to *The Churches' Fellowship for Psychical and Spiritual Studies*, with an interesting paragraph confirming Dr Johnston's complaint that a new organ was installed over the tomb of the knight in the chancel:

> 'At one time the pedal-organ stood on top of this tomb. One evening when the organist was practising, a loud groan came from under the organ. This was interpreted as a protest regarding the position of the instrument upon the crusader's tomb rather than a comment on the performance of the organist. The organ was removed and the groans were not repeated'.

In this letter Mrs Holbourn also says that the foundations of a pre-Reformation monastery could still be traced under the turf of Church Meadow. The foundations are still there although less pronounced but this was the site of the old parsonage not a monastery. It seems likely that stories of Avenbury's haunted church were encouraged by Mrs Marian Holbourn for these stories have not yet been found in any other literature. Music and bells can still be heard that seem to come from the vicinity of the ruined church but the cause appears to be its position in the valley which funnels sounds from Bromyard down the course of the river Frome. Needless to say few people are happy to visit this romantic site at midnight, or even after sunset.

The history of the church at Avenbury is perhaps the most unusual of any in this part of Herefordshire. With Bromyard, this was the only manor with priests recorded at Domesday in Plegelgate Hundred. We know that Bromyard was an important Anglo-Saxon minster and mother church and Avenbury too could have been an early and significant church, a fact that may be confirmed by its position in a meander of the river Frome. It served the spiritual and pastoral needs of a large manor and larger parish, and the extension of the fabric with a north aisle at an early date could indicate a large congregation at the time. The early village between the church and manor house moved to Munderfield leaving the church well away from the bulk of the Avenbury people and, despite all the 19th-century efforts to maintain and improve the old church, it finally was deserted and left to the mercy of nature rather than man. Today despite the size of the parish there is no place for religious worship nor even a parish hall.

A large part of the history of Avenbury hinges on the fate of the abandoned and ruined church. An aspect enhanced by tales of hauntings by cowled monks and ghostly music emanating from within. How could the ecclesiastical authorities and the parishioners consent not only to the closing of the church, but to the subsequent sale of a religious site to a lay person who lived in Birmingham? Now neither the church nor the parish have any control over the fate of this ancient sacred enclosure.

Today the landscape of the parish is much as it has been for a thousand years and longer, a prosperous and fertile farming area. There are farms, houses and cottages and a population in the region of 200. Modern transport enables the inhabitants to work, shop and relax within a large area rarely more than an hour's travel from home. Close proximity to the town of Bromyard with its active churches, good schools, associations, clubs, sports and leisure centre, shops, and other opportunities, has inevitably contributed to the decline of such amenities in Avenbury. The parishioners here have always looked to Bromyard for a wider and fuller life than could be enjoyed in a rural setting and the final move of closing their parish church was perhaps inevitable.

Avenbury Church and churchyard wall in 1999.

Howard Painter

ABBREVIATIONS

Bromyard LHS Bromyard and District Local History Society
HRO Herefordshire Record Office
HS High Sheriff
IPM Inquisitions Post Mortem
JPs Justices of the Peace
PRO Public Record Office
TWNFC Transactions of the Woolhope Naturalists Field Club
VCH Victoria County History

NOTES AND REFERENCES

Introduction

1. John Blair, 'Secular Minster Churches in Domesday Book', *Domesday Book a Reassessment* (1985), 104-142
2. H P R Finberg, *The Early Charters of the West Midlands* (1961), 141, 214

Chapter 1 Past Times

1. Philippa J Bradley, *The Flint Collection from Keep Hill, Herefordshire* (1989). A copy can be seen in the Bromyard Local History Society Archives; Ivan Turner, *Riding on a Plough* (1994)
2. Ronald Hutton, *The Pagan Religions of the Ancient British Isles* (1991); Peter Berresford Ellis, *The Celtic Empire* (1990); Anne Ross, *The Pagan Celts* (1986); Graham Webster, *The British Celts and their Gods under Rome* (1986)
3. S C Stanford, *The Welsh Marches* (1980); Martin Millett, *The Romanization of Britain* (1990); H P R Finberg, *The Gloucestershire Landscape* (1975)
4. Finberg (1961), 217
5. J Hillaby, 'The Origins of the Diocese of Hereford', *TWNFC* (1976), 16-52; J Hillaby, 'Early Christian and Pre-Conquest Leominster', *TWNFC* (1987), 557-685; Finberg (1961), 218; J Hillaby, 'Leominster and Hereford. The Origins of the Diocese', *Hereford Medieval Art, Architecture and Archaeology* (1995), 5, 13
6. L and J Laing, *Anglo-Saxon England* (1979); Henry Mayr-Harting, *The Coming of Christianity to Anglo-Saxon England* (1991); Bede, *A History of the English Church and People* (1968)
7. Ed W W Capes, *Charters and Records of Hereford Cathedral* (1908), 1
8. Hereford Cathedral Dean and Chapter Archives, 2342
9. HRO Bromyard Terriers 1589 and 1637
10. Ed Steve Bassett, *The Origins of the Anglo-Saxon Kingdoms* (1989); Blair (1985), 104-142; Della Hooke, *The Anglo-Saxon Landscape, the Kingdom of the Hwicce* (1985); David Dumville, 'Essex, Middle Anglia, and the expansion of Mercia in the South-East Midlands', *The Origins of Anglo-Saxon Kingdoms* (1989), 132-3; F M Stenton, *Anglo-Saxon England* (1971), 297-302; David Hill, *An Atlas of Anglo-Saxon England* (1981)
11. Phyllis Williams, *Bromyard, Minster, Manor and Town* (1987), 10, 202
12. Finberg (1961), 141
13. Ed Frank and Caroline Thorn, *Domesday Book, Herefordshire* (1983), 2, 49; 7, 9

Chapter 2 Military and Manorial Tenure
1. Bruce Coplestone-Crow, *Herefordshire Place-Names* (1989)
2. Jean Hopkinson, *Little Cowarne A Herefordshire Village* (1983), 2-3
3. J Amplett, *The Kyre Park Charters* (1905), 100
4. HRO *The Red Book of the Bishops of Hereford*; Swithun Butterfield, *Survey of the Bishopric Estates*
5. Jennifer Weale, *A History of Bredenbury and its Landed Estate* (1997), 20
6. Phyllis Williams, *Whitbourne: a Bishop's Manor* (1979), 37
7. *Herefordshire Domesday* (1983), 7, 9; 10, 65, 67; 2, 3; 16, 2; 33, 1

Chapter 3 The Church of St Mary, Early Years
1. Finberg (1961), 141, 214
2. *Herefordshire Domesday* (1983), 2, 49; 7, 9
3. S H Martin, 'St Guthlac, Herefordshire's Forgotten Saint', *TWNFC (1953),* 62
4. *St. Guthlac's Charters* f 18, 19, nos 12, 13, 14, 15, 16
5. *The Red Book of the Exchequer*, 279
6. *Royal Commission on Historical Monuments in Herefordshire* (1932), 2-East, 7; *St. Guthlac's Charters* f 18, no 15
7. *Archaeologia on Miscellaneous Tracts relating to Antiquity*, London (1845), vol 31, XII, 26; John Duncumb, *Collections towards the History and Antiquities of the County of Hereford* (1812), 28
8. *Calendar of Patent Rolls 1317-21*, 347; *Registers of Adam of Orleton* (1908), 174-6; Duncumb, 16-29; *Inquisitions Post Mortem* 48 Edward III
9. Colin Platt, *The Parish Churches of Medieval England* (1981), 9; see also Richard Morris, *Churches in the Landscape* (1989)
10. *Register of Bishop Orleton*, 144, 197, 202, 267, 387; ed R Shoesmith and R Richardson, *A Definitive History of Dore Abbey* (1997), 32-33, 100
11. *Register of Bishop Bothe*, 297
12. HRO Diocesan Records BB 71/17 which is a notebook inscribed 'Wm. West 1822' into which several old documents have been transcribed, the earliest 1535-36 and the latest apparently 1704. Many of the documents relate to disputes between the vicars of Avenbury and the impropriators of the rectory
13. D Attwater, *The Penguin Dictionary of Saints* (1983), 32
14. I am grateful to David Annett for this information

Chapter 4 The Domesday Manors: 1066-1600 Avenbury including Brookhouse, the Venn, Little Froome, Hopton Sollers, Noakes and Sawbury Hill

I am grateful to Bruce Coplestone-Crow for so generously providing references and information used in this chapter.
1. Wendy Davies, *Wales in the Early Middle Ages* (1982), 31, 42
2. *Herefordshire Domesday* (1983), 7, 9
3. Ed V H Galbraith and J Tait, *Herefordshire Domesday c1160-1170* (1950), 33-34; *Red Book of the Exchequer*, 279; *Herefordshire Domesday* (1983), 7, 6
4. *Pipe Roll 8 Richard I*, 90; *Red Book of the Exchequer*, 600; *St. Guthlac's Charters* nos 13, 14, 16
5. *St. Guthlac's Charters*, no 15; *Book of Fees*, 806
6. Hereford Cathedral Muniments and Archives, 3598; Francis Havergal, *Fasti Herefordenses and other Antiquarian Memorials of Hereford* (1869), 38, 53; *VCH Worcestershire*, IV, 242, note 13

7. Duncumb (1812), 16-29
8. *Registers of Bishop Swinfield*, 54-55; *Registers of Bishop Cantilupe*, 62; A T Bannister, 'A Lost Cartulary of Hereford Cathedral', *TWNFC* (1914), 268
9. *Feudal Aids*, ii, 378, 384
10. *Patent Rolls 1317-21*, 347; *Register of Bishop Orleton*, 174-6
11. *Feudal Aids*, ii, 394; *Inquisitions Post Mortem*, xiv, no 52; xiii, no 167
12. *Feudal Aids*, ii, 420
13. Hereford Reference Library. Davis Collection LC 942. 44 AB 51, pages 57-68, sale catalogue 15 August 1840; *The Concise Oxford Dictionary* (1964, 1976), 953
14. C J Robinson, *A History of the Mansions and Manors of Herefordshire* (1872), 12, 260
15. *Visitation of Herefordshire 1569,* 8,9; Duncumb (1812), Part I of II, 18-19, 168-170; Robinson (1872), 12, 260
16. HRO 1/4-6 Terrier of Avenbury Parish 1589
17. *Herefordshire Domesday c1160-1170* (1950), 34
18. *Red Book of the Exchequer*, 600; *Book of Fees*, 806, 1482; *Register of Bishop Cantilupe*, 123
19. *Inquisitions Post Mortem*, iii, no 257; *Feudal Aids*, ii, 378; Robinson (1872), 117, 174
20. *Index of Placita de Banco 1327-8,* 201, PRO Lists and Indexes (1909)
21. *Inquisitions Post Mortem*, xiii, no 167; *The Picards or Pychards of the Counties of Brecon, Hereford and Worcester* (1870)
22. *Herefordshire Domesday* (1983), 10, 67
23. Ed J H Round, *Ancient Deeds Prior to 1200* (1888), no 21
24. Ed H Hall, *Red Book of the Exchequer*, 283
25. *Book of Fees,* 806, 1481; *Red Book of the Exchequer,* 275
26. *Feudal Aids*, ii, 379, 384; *Inquisitions Post Mortem*, vi, no 344; xvii, no 1213
27. Amplett (1905), no 355
28. Williams (1987), 32, 39, 50
29. Brome's, *Catalogue of Gentry*
30. *Herefordshire Domesday* (1983), 16, 2
31. *Ibid* 1, l0b; 9, 12; 10, 30-31; 16, 2; 21, 4; Foliot, no 302
32. *Feudal Aids* ii, 379, 384, 394, 415, 420; *Book of Knights' Fees,* 394, 415, 420, 807, 815
33. Amplett (1905), 90; Robinson (1872), 12
34. *Heraldic Visitation of Herefordshire 1569,* 79
35. Duncumb (1812), 20; Robinson (1872), 12
36. T Nash, *Collections for the History of Worcestershire* (1781), I, 364 'Monuments in Eastham Church, Worcestershire'
37. *Herefordshire Domesday* (1983), 2, 3
38. *Ibid* 33, 1
39. Coplestone-Crow (1989), 41
40. *Herefordshire Domesday c1160-1170* (1950), 78, 123-4
41. Duncumb (1812), Pt I, vol 2, 21-22; *Book of Fees* or *Testa de Nevill* (1242-1243), 6, 101, 102, 382, 806, 1274; *Inquisitions Post Mortem* vol I, Henry III, 135, Lawrence d'Abitot 86; iii, 295
42. Duncumb (1812), 21-22
43. *Inquisitions Post Mortem 1303*, 86
44. *Ibid*, iii, no 295; iv, no 135; vi, nos 9, 491, 702; viii, no 502
45. *Herefordshire Domesday* (1983), 2, 3; 10, 65

46. Coplestone-Crow (1989), 41
47. *Herefordshire Domesday* (1950), 77, 79
48. *Red Book of the Exchequer*, 603; *Book of Fees* or *Testa de Neville* (1242-1243), 807, 815

Chapter 5 The Church of St Mary after the Dissolution of the Monasteries

1. Robinson (1872), 1
2. HRO Diocesan Records BB 71/17
3. HRO Terriers of Avenbury Parish 1589, 1619, 1628
4. *Herefordshire Domesday* (1983), 7, 9
5. Frank Barlow, *The English Church 1000-1066* (1979), 194
6. Hereford Cathedral Archives 6 A VI *A Puritan's Survey of the Ministry in the County of Hereford.* 1642; transcribed 1959
7. HRO Diocesan Records BB 71/17
8. Duncumb (1812), 25-27
9. HRO 1/4-6 Terrier of Bromyard Parish 1589
10. Duncumb (1812), 27
11. Title Deeds in the possession of the trustees of the Worcester Consolidated Municipal Charities, to whom I am very grateful for giving me access to their documents
12. Title deeds in the possession of the owners of the Old Vicarage, Avenbury

Peter Corbett kindly provided the wills and other information regarding his Corbett forebears of Avenbury.

Chapter 6 Landowners and Farmers

1. M A Faraday, *Herefordshire Militia Assessments of 1663 (*1972)
2. M A Faraday, 'The Hearth Tax in Herefordshire', *TWNFC* (1973), 77
3. *Heraldic Visitation of Herefordshire 1569,* 9
4. *Heraldic Visitation of Worcestershire 1682-3,* 81
5. *Register of Bishop Swinfield* (1307), 413
6. HRO Avenbury Land Tax Returns
7. HRO Diocesan Records BB 71/17 which is a notebook inscribed 'Wm West 1822' into which several old documents have been transcribed
8. *Ibid*

Chapter 7 The Domesday Manors after 1600

To avoid repetition the following dates refer to:

1663 Militia Assessments also known as Valuation of Estates, HRO Harleian MSS 6766

1665 Hearth Tax Roll HRO Microfilm

It was usually the property owner's name that appeared on the valuation of estates while the occupier was responsible for paying the hearth tax

1812-1831 HRO Land Tax Returns

1835 HRO Electoral Roll, Broxash Hundred

1840 HRO Avenbury Tithe Map and Schedule

1851-1891 10-yearly census returns and enumerators' reports HRO and Hereford Library, Reference Section

Trade Directories for Herefordshire of various dates have also been used extensively

1. *Visitation of Herefordshire 1569,* 8, 9; Duncumb (1812), Part 1 of II, 18-19, 168-170; Robinson (1872), 12, 260, 307
2. Duncumb (1812), 168
3. Williams (1979), 48-49
4. Title deeds in possession of the trustees of the Worcester Consolidated Municipal Charities
5. Duncumb, Part I of II, 18-19, 168-170
6. Ed Hillaby and Pearson, 'Schools and Scholars' *Bromyard a Local History* (1970), 68; Edna Pearson, *Two Churches: Two Communities* (1993), 72
7. Duncumb (1812), 28
8. Title deeds in the hands of the owner of Brookhouse
9. HRO Will of Margaret Pychard 1591
10. Robinson (1872), 114
11. HRO Papers relating to the Freeman family of Gaines, Whitbourne; 12th Feb 1750 Indenture relating to the marriage of Sarah Brome with Thomas Griffiths of Stoke Lacy; also 23rd Jan 1759 Will of Ann Griffiths, widow of Stoke Lacy; 20th July Will of Thomas Griffiths Rector of Stoke Lacy
12. Williams (1987), 97, 131
13. HRO Will of Roger Robinson 1688
14. HRO G87/2/13-17
15. HRO Q/S0/3
16. HRO G87/2/13-17
17. Duncumb (1812), 23
18. Robinson (1872), 12
19. *Reports of the Commissioners for the County of Hereford* (1815-1839), vol 13, 94
20. Duncumb (1812), 23
21. HRO K68/3
22. HRO G87/2/12
23. Weale (1997), 45-48
24. HRO Harleian MSS Silas Taylor, 'Antiquities of Herefordshire' (*c*1655), f27
25. HRO Quarter Sessions Papers Q59/2
26. Abstracted title deed provenance unknown
27. Information from Roy Edwards of Bredenbury
28. HRO Will of Anne Pitt of Noakes 1670
29. Bromyard LHS Archives, A11/9
30. HRO Bredenbury Court Collection F99/23-37; F99/A/23
31. Abstract of the *Original Title of Richard Cope Hopton to an Estate in Bredenbury,* in the possession of David Jones of Batchley, Bredenbury; Weale (1997), 141-144
32. Coplestone-Crow (1989), 42
33. HRO F99/23 -37
34. HRO F99/21
35. HRO F99/21-37
36. HRO F99/33; see also Weale (1997), 70, 143
37. Title deeds to Wiggall in the hands of the owners

Geoff Gillard of New Zealand, who is a descendant of Thomas Payne and his wife Mary (formerly Rogers), has kindly provided more information regarding the Rogers and Payne families of Lower Venn

Chapter 8 Other Farms in Avenbury Parish after 1600

1. James Johnston, *The Finding of St Augustine's Chair* (1898), 5
2. Coplestone-Crow (1989), 29
3. B Brotherton of Bromsgrove, 'Field Names in Munderfield, in the parish of Avenbury, in the County of Hereford', *TWNFC* (1949-51), 264
4. HRO AS 12/3 Particulars and valuation of estates in the counties of Hereford, Gloucester and Worcester belonging to St Katherine's Hospital in Ledbury; see also *The Charities Commissioners' Report Concerning Charities in Herefordshire* (1819-1837), 139 'Mr Fellow's Reports' on Avenbury in Broxash Hundred; there is 'A Descriptive Catalogue of Manuscripts dealing with St Katherine's, Ledbury', *TWNFC* (1921, 22, 23), part III, 231. Walter of Avenbury is recorded on page 250 and he may have been party to the grant of Beggar's Acre although there is no mention of this. There is a local record of a donation by John of Stanford (Court) *c*1273 of 26s 10d annually from 'rents in Hyda' (The Hide, Stanford Bishop). The documents relating to St Catherine's or St Katherine's, Ledbury are in the Dean and Chapter Archives of Hereford Cathedral
5. HRO Will of John Hancox of Munderfield 1598
6. HRO Will of Alice Boyce 1639
7. Title Deeds relating to the Heath in the possession of the owners
8. Robinson (1872), 20
9. Coplestone-Crow (1989), 63
10. Rev W E T Morgan, *Hay and Neighbourhood* (*c*1932), 19. I am grateful to David Annett for drawing my attention to this suggestion
11. Duncumb (1812), 29
12. Avenbury Parish Registers
13. HRO Will of Sarah Charlott 1694
14. Bromyard LHS Archives A58/6
15. Title Deeds for the estate in the hands of the trustees of the Worcester Consolidated Municipal Charities
16. Deeds in the possession of the owners of Down House, near Bromyard
17. *Reports of the Commissioners...* (1815-1839) vol 13, 94
18. Title Deeds in the hands of the trustees of the Worcester Consolidated Municipal Charities
19. P Crosskey 'Ledger Book, 1821-1823, of Mr Delabere Walker, Surgeon and Physician of Bromyard', ed D Waller, *Bromyard Round and About* (1991), 66
20. Title Deeds in the hands of the trustees of the Worcester Consolidated Municipal Charities
21. Title Deeds to 9 and 11 Broad Street, Bromyard
22. Coplestone-Crow (1989), 28
23. Hooke (1985), 129-131
24. *Curia Regis Rolls* (PRO), xiv, no 1701; HRO Quarter Sessions Q /50/2,1674 and 1676
25. Robinson (1872), 230
26. HRO Pencombe Church Terriers abstracted by Stephen Guest
27. Ivor Slocumbe, *Pencombe: Medieval Settlement Pattern* (MS in Bromyard LHS Archives)
28. *Book of Knight's Fees* (1431), 420
29. *Visitation of Herefordshire 1569*, 44; *Visitation of Worcestershire 1682-3*, 81; Deed in Bromyard LHS Archives

30. A H Smith, *English Place-Name Elements* (1970), I, 36
31. HRO G87/2/12-17
32. Abstract of title deeds relating to Keephill, Bromyard
33. Estate map belonging to Keephill
34. Coplestone-Crow (1989), 185
35. Bannister (1914), 274; *Register of Bishop Swinfield* 54-5; Bruce Coplestone-Crow has kindly supplied these two references and other information
36. *Testa de Neville* or *Book of Fees* (1242-1243), 807, 815; ibid (1274), 102, 806
37. Williams (1987), 45
38. Bromyard LHS Archives relating to Goodships
39. Bromyard LHS Archives relating to Northfields

I am grateful to Howard Painter who has very kindly provided much of the information regarding the Cooke family of Munderfield Court.

Chapter 9 Smaller Holdings in the Parish in 1840

1. Hereford Cathedral Archives 6 A iii
2. HRO Will of William Cooke of Munderfield 1738
3. Bromyard LHS Archives Copton Field Farm
4. *Ibid* 1802 indenture for cottage at Munderfield
5. *Ibid* 1779 documents relating to Perns, Munderfield; Smith (1970), II, 62
6. HRO Bishop's Registers
7. PRO E 179/119/492
8. PRO E 179/248/14

Chapter 10 A Fleeting Glimpse of the lives of some 17th-century Avenbury families from wills and inventories

1. HRO Quarter Sessions papers Q/SO/3
2. J W Tonkin, 'The Goods and Chattels of our Forefathers, 1660-1760', *TWNFC* (1985) Part I, 13-35
3. J Bathurst and E J L Cole, 'Leominster Fair, 1556', *TWNFC* (1976), Part I, 72-88, nos 2, 14, 40, 71, 109, 175; see also John West, *Village Records* (1962), 92-131; N W Alcock, *People at Home, Living in a Warwickshire Village,1500-1800* (1993)

Chapter 11 Parochial Care, Duty and Responsibility

Most of this chapter has been based on the Avenbury parish records that were previously kept in the 14th-century oak chest in the chancel of the church, and are now to be found in the Herefordshire Record Office. Valuable assistance in understanding the documents I have gleaned from: W E Tait, *The Parish Chest* (1983)
John West, *Village Records* (1962)
Kate Tiller, *English Local History* (1992)

1. HRO 1/4-6
2. Frederick Sharpe, *The Church Bells of Herefordshire* (1969), 50-52, 763
3. HRO Q/5O/2 F77b
4. HRO Q/5O/2 F44a
5. HRO Avenbury Parish Records
6. I am grateful to Stephen Guest of Pencombe and Allan Roper of Hampton Charles for these two extracts from other parish records

7. HRO Bromyard Poor Law Union Minute Books
8. HRO Q/50/2 F 95b, 105a, 101a, 95b, 135a, 132b
9. HRO Militia Assessments 1663
10. HRO Quarter Sessions Papers Q/59/2 certified 10 July 1676
11. Williams (1979), 150-1
12. An Act for repairing several roads leading from the town of Bromyard, 1751, 25 George II, c.56
13. HRO Bromyard Turnpike Trust accounts; Philip Crosskey, 'Roads and Railways' *Bromyard: a Local History* (1970), 99-105
14. Hereford Cathedral Library chantry certificates; HRO Harleian MSS 6766, Silas Taylor, *Antiquities of Herefordshire* (*c*1655) f27
15. *The Charities Commissioners' Report Concerning Charities in Herefordshire* (1819-1837)
16. *ibid*; HRO papers relating to St Katherine's Hospital, Ledbury
17. HRO Herefordshire Wills 150, 188
18. Hereford Cathedral Archives 6 A VI, *A Puritan's Survey of the Ministry in the County of Hereford.* 1642; transcribed 1959
19. Nikolaus Pevsner, *The Buildings of England, Herefordshire* (1963), 290
20. *Jakeman and Carver Directory & Gazetteer of Herefordshire 1890*
21. HRO Avenbury School Records AL 61/3

Chapter 12 The People, their Occupations and their Homes
Sources and bibliography

HRO Terrier of Avenbury Parish 1/4-6
HRO Quarter Sessions papers Q/S0/2 F44 and F77
HRO Herefordshire Hearth Tax Returns on microfilm
Ed Kevin Schurer and Tom Arkell, *Surveying the People* (1992)
A Whiteman, *The Compton Census of 1676: a critical edition* (1986)
Herefordshire Domesday (1983)
HRO Enumerators' reports Avenbury Parish 1851 and 1871
Hereford Library Reference Section Census Returns
M A Faraday, *Herefordshire Militia Assessments of 1663* (1972)
M A Faraday, 'The Hearth Tax in Herefordshire', *TWNFC* (1973)
Jennifer McCulloch, 'Some aspects of Victorian Bromyard from the 1851 census', *Bromyard: A Local History* (1970), 135-147

Chapter 13 The Church of St Mary, Final Days

1. Duncumb (1812), 28-29
2. *Lascelles & Co Directory and Gazetteer of Herefordshire 1851*
3. *Littlebury's Directory of Herefordshire 1876-77*
4. James Johnston, *The Finding of Saint Augustine's Chair* (1898), 11-12
5. *ibid* 19-20
6. Duncumb (1812), 28-29
7. *Royal Commission* (1932), 7; John Eisel and Marian Holbourn, 'Avenbury Church Bells', *Bromyard: Round and About* (1992)
8. *Royal Commission* (1932), 7
9. George Marshall, 'Fonts in Herefordshire', *TWNFC* (1950), 11, 74
10. *Directory and Gazetteer of Herefordshire 1902,* 84-86

11. HRO Diocesan Records BB 71/17
12. Correspondence and papers in Bromyard Church Vestry
13. *Ibid*

HRO In the final volume of the Avenbury Parish Registers, pages cut from national and local newspapers have been glued in place, presumably the work of the Rev E H Archer-Shepherd. The cuttings describe the proposals to close Avenbury Church and also relate to ghostly events in the parish.

INDEX